INTELLECTUAL PROPERTY RIGHTS

INTELLECTUAL PROPERTY RIGHTS

C.B. Raju, M.A., LL.M., Ph.D.,
Reader, Faculty of Law
University of Mysore
Mysore (India)

SERIALS PUBLICATIONS
NEW DELHI (INDIA)

First Published 2007

ISBN: 81-8387-034-1

Published by

SERIALS PUBLICATIONS
4830/24, Prahlad Street, Ansari Road
Darya Ganj, New Delhi-110002 (India)
Phone : 23245225
Fax : 91-11-23272135
E-mail: serials@satyam.net.in

CONTENTS

University of Mysore

Crawford Hall, Mysore 570 005
INDIA

Tel : Work : +91-821-2419666
Res : +91-821-2419350
Fax : +91-821-2419363

Email : vc@uni-mysore.ac.in

Prof. J. Shashidhara Prasad
Ph.D., CPhys, FInstP
Vice-Chancellor

18th November 2005

FOREWORD

I am happy to know that Department of Studies in Law, University of Mysore is bringing out a book entitled 'Intellectual Property Rights – a public awareness,' comprising research articles. In the present scenario of economic liberalisation and the establishment of World Trade Organisation, intellectual property of an individual has assumed importance which is to be protected by suitable laws. The articles in this book provide basic insight into the issues relating to the intellectual property rights which include copyright, trade mark, patent, and enforcement provisions and remedies for violation. I am confident that this book would be useful to all sections of the society.

PREFACE

In the context of Globalization, Liberalization and Privatisation, the Intellectual Property Rights regime has gained importance everyday. With the emergence of World Trade Organization, there is protection to the authors, writers, producers and inventors for their original works and inventions. The Department of Studies in Law, Manasa Gangotri, University of Mysore, Mysore, had conducted a two-day's National Seminar on 28th and 29th August 2004, which was sponsored by the Ministry of Human Resource Development, New Delhi. Prof. J. Shashidhara Prasad, Honorable Vice Chancellor extended all his support to conduct the above seminar successfully. In the two-day's National Seminar, research paper were presented on Patent, Copyright Trademarks, Designs, Geographical Appellation, Enforcement of IPR and Remedies for Intellectual Property Rights violation. The seminar was attended by many scholars and academicians from various fields. Each presentation of paper was interacted meaningfully by the participants. The inaugural session of the seminar was presided over by the Vice Chancellor of the University of Mysore. Honorable Judge of the High Court of Karnataka, Sri. H.J. Ramesh spoke on the occasion. Prof. C.K.N. Raja delivered the keynote address. There are 20 research articles in this book, which focus on various issues relating to Intellectual Property Rights. The views expressed in these articles are not the views of the editor. I hope this edited book would cater to the needs of the people who really want to know the basic knowledge about Intellectual Property Rights.

—C.B. Raju

1 BIOTECHNOLOGICAL INVENTIONS AND PATENT PROTECTION

*Sreenivasulu N.S.**

Introduction

In the last century we have witnessed the growth of information technology. Information technology is the guiding spirit for many developmental activities. This century is all set to mark the development of biotechnology. Information technology is a milestone in the last century, where as biotechnology is all set to become corner stone of this century. Biotechnology implies the proliferation of human intelligence and knowledge where as information technology provides for the dissemination of the human intelligence and knowledge.

Biotechnology is a study relating to microorganisms and related things. It concerns with the practical application of organisms or their components. Though the concept biotechnology is new, historically speaking biotechnology was an art in the production of wines, beers and cheers. At that time the nomenclature "biotechnology" was not there.[1] A series of advanced technologies spanning biology,

* Guest faulty, Department of Post Graduate Studies and Research in Law, University of Mysore, Manasa Gangotri, Mysore-570006, Karnataka, India.

chemistry, biochemistry, microbiology, protein engineering, process engineering and genetic engineering put together and collectively called as biotechnology.[2]

Biotechnology is having its diverse application in the fields such as agriculture, animal production, production of drugs, production of transgenic organisms, biological fuels, gene therapy, cleaning up pollutants in the environment etc. Biotechnology involves the application of technology to the living organisms such as plant, animal and microorganisms. It is a process of transformation or manipulation of genes to invent novel things such as new varieties of plants, animals or microorganisms. It involves technical interference into biological processes to invent novel things.

Application and Scope of Biotechnology

Biotechnology is a new area of science that compounds life sciences and chemical sciences. Now a day this technology is being used to invent new and developed varieties of plants and animals. It is used to invent new microorganisms, which can be used for different purposes such as to use in the therapeutic and surgical processes, in the production of consumable products, and also in the cleaning up of pollutants in environment. Biotechnology is a modern science less than 30 years old, it is revolutionizing production in certain areas of industry and agriculture.[3] In case of agriculture, biotechnology is used to invent new crops with the qualities such as high yield, resistance to pests and capacity to withstand drought conditions. This technology is used to incorporate different characteristic features of two or more plants into one plant.

Genes in plants, providing for certain special features, would be isolated and put together into one plant with the help of biotechnology. A new and improved variety of plant possessing different characteristic features can be produced through the process called genetic engineering. Genetic engineering involves manipulation of genes or incorporation of foreign genes into a plant so as to make it possess different characteristic features that were not there earlier. This may result in plant producing high yield, improving its capacity to give resistance to pests and ability to withstand drought conditions as such, BT cotton, BT rice and also BT soybean. These are the varieties of plants produced through the process called biotechnology. BT cotton is a cotton variety, which is produced by incorporating foreign genes from different cotton varieties providing for different qualities into the intended plant. This BT cotton is a new variety providing for different features, and available in different varieties.

Here the characteristic features of different varieties are put together into one variety, which is produced through the process of biotechnology. This BT cotton variety provides more yield almost double the yield given by other cotton varieties. Biotechnology has revolutionized the food industry with its innovative genetically modified food. In the year 1996 first genetically modified food was released to the market. Here plants producing consumable food such as vegetables or rice or wheat etc., can be modified and genetically manipulated. Here the intended plant would possess different qualities, which was not their earlier. The genes in plants that are known for such qualities are isolated with an intention to incorporate into the cells of any intended plant. In fact, after genetically engineering the plant and incorporating foreign genes into such plant, the plant would posses the qualities that are possessed by two or more different plants. Here we are getting desired qualities in a single plant through the process of biotechnology by engineering the genes.

Through the process of biotechnology by manipulation of genes, new variety of animals can be invented. These new variety of animals can be used for different purposes, such as; production of medicines, for experimental and testing of medicines and treating methods. Proteins produced inside the animal body are very much relevant in the production of medicines. Through the process of biotechnology proteins produced inside the animal body can be identified and isolated and can be used in the production of medicines. For instance Pig; its body is called as pharmaceuticals factory. Moreover medicines or any curing process will be tested and experimented on animals before it is used for human treatment. One such example is oncomouse invented through the process of biotechnology. Oncomouse is an animal invented to use for cancer testing.

In the medical field, the use of biotechnology is enormous and is producing miracles. Biotechnology is used to invent new drugs, medicines, surgical process, and diagnostic methods. The process of gene therapy has been invented to treat particular gene affected instead of treating the whole body. Biotechnology firms have brought more than 50 new medicines to market, have more than 350 medicines and therapies in various stages of clinical testing and garnered in excess of $ 16 billion in sales in 1998.[4] First gene therapy method to treat deceases has been patented in the year 1995. This gene therapy is a medical treatment invented through biotechnology.

Now a days matters concerning environment are given much importance. Nations are much concerned towards the protection and preservation of environment. Biotechnology helps us in this regard. For cleaning up of pollutants in the environment, microorganisms produced through biotechnology can be used. This has come to limelight when Dr Anandha chakraburthy, a microbiologist in America invented a microorganism which is capable of splitting the oil pollutants in the environment.

Biotechnology is the result of efforts of intellect, the application of human intelligence and knowledge to the biological processes. These human intellectual efforts deserve protection. The new plants, animal varieties, new methods of treatments, new crops producing food articles as such are the inventions of biotechnology. These inventions have to be protected for obtaining the fruits of the biotechnology.

Protection of Biotechnology Inventions through the Grant of Patent

Intellectual property regime protects any new invention having industrial application by the grant of patent. Any invention that is new, not known to the public and which can be applied industrially deserves patent grant under the patent Act[5] The concept of patent protection has now extended to microorganisms, plants, animals, enzymes, viruses and genetic elements such as DNA and RNA etc., produced through biotechnology[6] In the year 1980 for the first time a microorganism is given patent protection. In the year 1985 for the first time a plant is given patent protection, like wise in the year 1988 first animal patent is given[7].

If Biotechnology inventions satisfy all the above requirements then they are entitled for patent protection under the patent law. As biotechnology is an invention under the patent Act, if such invention is novel and not know to the public, if it is industrially applicable then there may be patent grant. As the biotechnology inventions satisfy these requirements for the grant of patent, there would not be any difficulty in granting patent protection to the biotechnogy inventions under the existing patent laws. Patent grant is a "monopoly right to the inventor on his invention for a certain period of time. Once patent is granted after satisfying the above-mentioned conditions, apart from the patent owner, no other person is allowed to use, exploit the patented invention without the owners consent. The owner is rewarded for his efforts of intellect in inventing a new thing, which is useful to the society. This patent protection is available for a period of 20 years.[8]As Intellectual property rights are internationally recognized. Patent protection is available internationally for any new, innovative and industrially applicable invention irrespective of its field of application.

Paris Convention and Protection of Biotechnology Inventions

The convention intends to give protection to industrial property. Here industrial property is understood in the broadest sense and shall apply not only to industry and commerce but also to agriculture and extractive industries and to all manufactured or natural products for example grain, tobacco, leaf, fruit, cattle, minerals, mineral water, beer, flowers, etc.,[9] Biotechnology is having its application in diverse fields such as agriculture, cattle, medicinal and food sector. The understanding of the industrial property in the broadest sense shall comprise the fields such as agriculture, cattle, medicinal, food, and beverages as such. If we want to protect industrial property, it ought to be protected through biotechnology, because this technology comes within the scope of industrial property under the convention. Biotechnology has vast industrial application in different fields.

The rationale behind the protection of industrial property is to provide stimulation to research and development. By stimulating the growth in research and development the convention aims at the proliferation of technology and finally at the economic development. Biotechnology is such a technology having its diverse application in different fields, which would have its impact in the economic and industrial development. So if we intend to protect industrial property under the Paris convention, we should not forget to accord protection to the biotechnology inventions.

Patent Co-operation Treaty and International Patent Protection

The contracting states under this treaty are desirous to make a contribution to the progress of science and technology by extending patent protection to the inventions. The treaty intends to contribute to the progress of science and technology. Science is not static it is dynamic and is coming out with new technologies marking its progress. Biotechnology is one among such technologies that science has invented. In order to contribute towards the progress of science and technology there ought to be protection for the innovations and technologies. Biotechnology is a new wing of science, which can be protected under the patent co-operation treaty as it intends to contribute to the progress of science and technology. The treaty obligates the member states to further the progress in science and technology by their legal endeavors. Member states under the treaty have to give patent protection to the innovations in science to further its progress.

The treaty intends to foster and accelerate the economic development of developing countries by increasing the efficiency of their legal system to protect inventions. Biotechnology is such an invention that has got its role to play with regard to the economic development. With its diverse applications biotechnology has got all the capabilities to mark its impact on the economy of the nations. Inventions involving new plant varieties, animal verities may have its effects on the economic growth. As this new plant and animal verities invented through biotechnology possesses qualities such as high yield, pest resistance capacity, more flesh yield, more woolen, more milk. As such invariably this provides for more production rate. More production in different fields causes economic proliferation.

Moreover the treaty aims to facilitate access to ever expanding volume of modern technology. Access to the modern technology can be provided if we give patent protection for such inventions. Once patent is given for a particular period of time, at the expiry of such period such invention falls into the public domain, so that any one can have access to it. If patent protection is given to any biotechnological invention, at the expiry of the patent duration, such biotechnology falls into the public domain, which can be used by the public.

Further Patent cooperation treaty provides for International patent protection. Once application is made under the treaty and patent is granted then there is no need to apply for patent protection in member states separately and individually. Such patent is valid and enforceable in all the member states. Such being the case, once patent protection is given to biotechnology on an international application under the treaty, and then the invention gets international recognition and is internationally protected.

TRIPS Agreement-A Comprehensive Arrangement for the Patent Protection of Different Inventions

After having a long run of negotiations, finally TRIPS agreement came into being. TRIPS says that patent shall be available for any invention, [10]whether product or process, in all fields of technology, provided that they are new, involve an inventive step and are capable of industrial application. It is important to note that there are three universally recognized criteria of patentability now incorporated into Art: 27 of TRIPS namely novelty, non-obviousness and industrial applicability or utility applies to all inventions including biotechnology inventions.[11] It further provides that patent rights shall be enjoyable without discrimination as to the place of invention, the field of technology.

The TRIPS agreement has become a means to promote a strong and comprehensive standard of patent protection for the increasingly valuable contribution made by science and industry.[12] If patents are made available to all types of inventions in all fields of technology, it ought to include the inventions of biotechnology with in the meaning of inventions under the TRIPS agreement. As biotechnology is a scientific innovation, is a new wing of science and as it is a new face of technological development in life sciences, it ought to include within the meaning of inventions under TRIPS. Moreover the agreement intends to give patent protection for processes as well as products. Biotechnology involves inventing of new products[13]having different qualities through innovative processes. Here, patent protection for innovative process as well for the innovated product can be sought under the TRIPS agreement. (BT cotton, BT rice are examples for patented biotechnological living products) There lies adequate protection for biotechnology invented processes and products under the TRIPS agreement. Now Patents are made available to living things such as new verities of plants, animals and other microorganisms[14]produced through biotechnology.

Utilization of Biological Resources

In the field of biotechnology there is a vast use of biological resources. Infact the biotechnology industry is dependant on the biological resources. Biological resources that exist in the nature are the feedstock for the biotechnology inventions. Here one interesting thing is that the under developed countries have vast biological resources. The developing countries are blessed with vast biological resources and the developed countries have developed adequate technology. Through the biotechnology, the biological pools in the developing countries are exploited for the benefit of few multinational companies or Nations. Biotechnology inventions are based on the biological pools in the developing countries, where as the owners of such inventions are developed countries. These developing countries do not have enough technology to use their vast biological pools for their benefit. The developed countries are exploiting the biological pools of the developing countries by their technology. There is a need for the identification of the biological pools in the developing countries so that these countries may also be benefited with the biotechnological inventions. Here the developing countries which are providing feedstock to the biotechnology inventions are not getting reward for their contributions. Hence there is a need for a mechanism to have equal benefit sharing between the providers of biological resources and the users of such resources in biotechnology inventions. When biological resources are used for the purpose of biotechnology inventions there shall be a reward for the developing countries preserving biological resources. There ought to be a mechanism for sharing of benefits between the Multi National Corporations involved in the biotechnology inventions and the Indigenous people in the developing countries preserving such biological resources.

Convention of biological diversity-1992 (CBD) provides for the conservation and sustainable use of biological resources. At the same time it provides for the equitable sharing of benefits arising from the use of biological resources. This convention insists member states to take all possible measures to conserve biological diversity. Sates are obliged to provide for the sustainable use of biological resources. As developing countries are blessed with great biological resources the interest of these countries have been taken care of in the convention. The convention insists for the equitable benefit sharing on the use of biological resources. It is an obligation to share benefits on using biological resources. Biotechnology has grown in the developed countries compared to developing countries. Most of the biotechnology inventions have taken place in the developed countries after using the biological resources available in the developing countries. Here the developing countries are contributing towards the proliferation of biotechnology through the conservation of biological resources. At this juncture, it is very pertinent to recognize and reward the contributions of the developing world. For this purpose the convention provides for the equitable benefit sharing between the countries using biological resources and the countries conserving such resources.

India has enacted its legislation on the conservation of biological diversity. There are some measures for the conservation and the sustainable use of biological resources. The Act prohibits the transfer of Indian genetic material and biological material outside the country without the Government's approval. Government permission is also necessary before taking any patent or other intellectual property rights over such material. The access to the biological material is also regulated under the Act. The Act has set up bodies at national, state and local level which shall have voice in regulating the transfer, sustainable use and conservation of resources at national, state and local level. The Act provides for the reporting of biological resources and also for the protection of indigenous knowledge.

Biotechnology inventions are based on the use of natural biological resources. But this technology is not equally developed in all regions. At the same time biological resources are also not equally distributed among different regions. Here developed countries are using the biological resources in the developing countries for the biotechnology inventions. So developing countries are also equally contributing for the biotechnology inventions. So the contributions of the developing countries ought to be rewarded through the equal benefit sharing. Convention on biological diversity provides for such benefit sharing on the use of biological resources for the purpose of biotechnology inventions. This convention provides for the conservation and sustainable use of biological resources and for the equal benefit sharing, where as TRIPS agreement provides for the protection of such inventions made by utilizing biological resources. TRIPS agreement intends to give patent protection to new plant, animal varities and microorganisms produced through biotechnology.

Conclusion

Morally speaking, plants and animals as such are not patentable. The argument to support this contention is that plant and animals are products of nature, gifted by god and are not patentable. Living things such as plants, animals, and microorganisms are treated as common heritage or common property. As per the principle of common heritage, living things are not patentable and can't be made private property by granting patent monopoly. In the era of biotechnology now living things are getting patented. As we have already seen Oncomouse, BT cotton, BT rice, BT soybean etc.,

The position in US is such that anything under the sun is patentable provided there is some human intervention. So there is an ample scope for the biotechnology inventions involving living things to get patented there. Countries like Australia, Japan are following almost same way. But, a country like India, traditions are respected, moral standards are followed. The principle such as common heritage or common property is very much relevant. In fact in India, living things such as plants and animals are treated as sacred and god given. People cannot acquire ownership over such natural and living things by way of patents. Indians used to worship few plants and animals as a resemblance of God. At this juncture the patent protection given to living things produced through biotechnology is not fully acceptable to Indians. The amended patents Act is against the principle of common heritage, as it allows for the patenting of microorganisms. India, being a signatory to TRIPS agreement, it has to give patent protection to living things such as microorganisms produced through biotechnology.

Trade related aspects of Intellectual Property rights agreement provides for the patenting of new plant, animal varieties and microorganisms produced through biotechnology. India has amended its patent Act to bring it in conformity with the provisions of TRIPS agreement. India was in transition period till January 2005 to change its laws and to adopt the provisions of TRIPS agreement. This transition period ended by 1st January 2005. Now patent protection for microorganisms is available in India from January 2005 onwards. So it is all set to give patent protection to living things in India. This cleary shows that there is diversion from the traditional principles of the country. India is getting diverged from its traditional, and customary practices to provide patent protection to living things produced through biotechnology. The stage is set and show has begun.

NOTES AND REFERENCES

1. John E. Smith, Biotechnology, Cambridge University press, London, Third Edition, (1996).
2. Forewords to the John E. Smith, Biotechnology, Cambridge University Press, London, Third Edition, (1996).
3. Para No. 1, Page. No. 128, Jayashree Watal, Intellectual property rights, Oxford University press, London, 2002).
4. Pharmaceutical manufacturers Association Annual Report for 1998; *Scot Morrison & Glen Giovannetti, Bridging The Gap;* 13th annual Biotech industry report (Ernst & Young, 1999.
5. Indian patent Act (Amended in 2002.)
6. Page. No. 1.35, Rajiv Jain (1999), Rakhee biswas, Law of patents (Procedure & Practice, Vidhi publishing (P) Ltd, New Delhi, Second Edition.
7. Sahai–suman, "Patenting of life forms; what it implies", Economic and political weekly, April 25, 1992. See also, Intellectual property rights and Biodiversity; Emergence of Biobattles, Pushpam kumar, in Intellectual property rights, By KGR Narir, Ashok Kumar.
8. The Indian patent Act is commensurate with the TRIPS in this regard, Patents amendment Act, 2002.
9. Paris Convention for the protection of industrial property. Article" 1(3), International legal instruments of Intellectual property rights law, Volume: 1, National Law School of India University, Bangalore.

10. Article 27(1) of Trade Ralated aspects of Intellectual Property Rights. 1994.
11. (Para No. 3, Pg No. 132, Jayashree Watal, Intellectual property rights, Oxford University press, London, 2002).
12. Para No. 4, Page. No. 248, Christopher Arup, The new world trade organization agreements, Cambridge University press, New York, 2000.
13. We have already witnessed the invention of BT cotton, BT rice, which are biotechnology-invented products.
14. Article: 27(3) of TRIPS agreement.

2 COMMON LAW REMEDY FOR UNREGISTERED TRADE MARKS

*K. Srividya**

Introduction

Freedom to carry on any business, trade or profession is recognized as a fundamental right under Art 19 (1) (g) of Indian Constitution. In order to carry on any trade and gain recognition in the commercial world, the trader is required to adopt any mark, symbol or other device so as to distinguish his goods from that of the other. Such mark or other symbol or other indicia used by a manufacturer or trader to distinguish his goods from the goods of other concerns is called as "Trade Mark". Trademark adopted by a trader is protected under common law principle of passing off and under TRADEMARKS Act, 1999, which confers him an exclusive right to use the mark in relation to certain categories of goods.

Trade marks Act, 1999 confers protection to trader only if his trademark is registered under the Act. On the other hand well–known trademarks, which are not been registered could still seek protection under common law principle called "Passing off action".

* Lecturer, J.S.S. Law College, Mysore.

This paper briefly looks into various aspects of common law principle for protection of trade mark under Passing off action.

Passing Off and Its Applicability

"Passing off" means passing off one's goods or business as the goods or business of another. Under the Classical formulation, Passing off is explained in the following words, "No man is entitled to represent his goods as being the goods of another man, and no man is permitted to use any mark, sign or symbolic device, or other means, whereby, without making a direct false representation himself to a purchaser who purchases from him, he enables such purchaser to tell a lie or to make a false representation to somebody else who is the ultimate customer"[1].

Passing off is a tortuious remedy. This action is generally taken when the trade mark is not registered under the Trademarks Act. "The gist of the conception of passing off is that the goods are in effect telling a falsehood about themselves which is calculated to mislead. The law on this matter is designed to protect traders against that form of unfair competition which consists in acquiring for oneself, by means of false or misleading devices, the benefit of the reputation already achieved by rival traders"[2].

The applicability of passing off action has undergone a drastic change over a period of time. Initially, this tortuous principle was applied for false representation in goods, subsequently it was extended to business and services and now it is applicable to trade names, domain names, professions and even non-trading activities. Today Passing off is applied to many forms of unfair competition where the activities of one person could cause damage or injury to the reputation and goodwill associated with the activities of another person or group of persons.

Characteristics of Passing Off

Lord Diplock,[3] has identified five characteristics which must be present in order to create a valid cause of action for passing off, they are:

1. Misrepresentation,
2. Made by the trader in the course of trade,
3. To prospective customers of his or ultimate consumers of goods or services supplied by him,
4. Which is calculated to injure the business or goodwill of another trader (in the sense that this is a reasonably foreseeable consequence), and
5. Which causes actual damage to a business or goodwill of the trader by whom the action is brought or (in quia timet actiona) will probably do so.

In *Reckitt and Coloman v/s Borden,*[4] *Lord Oliver of Aylmerton* has identified three elements which has to be proved by the plaintiff in order to succeed in passing off action. The elements are;

(i) He must establish a goodwill or reputation attached to the goods or services which he supplies in the mind of the purchasing public by association with the identifying "Get–Up" (Whether it consists simply of a brand name or a trade description, or the individual features of labeling or packaging) under which his particular goods or services are offered to the public, such that the get up is recognized by the public as distinctive specifically of the plaintiff's goods or services.

(ii) He must demonstrate a misrepresentation by the defendant to the public (whether intentional or not) leading or likely to lead the public to believe that goods or services offered by him are the goods or services of the plaintiff whether the public is aware of the plaintiff's identity as the manufacturer or supplier of the goods or services is immaterial, so long as they are identified with a particular source which is in fact the plaintiff. For ex; if the public is accustomed to rely upon a particular brand name in purchasing goods of a particular description, it matters not at all that there is little or no public awareness of the identity of the proprietor of the brand name.

(iii) He must, demonstrate that he suffers or, in a quia timet action that he is likely to suffer, damage by reason of the erroneous belief engendered by the defendant's misrepresentation that the source of the defendant's goods or services is the same as of the source of those offered by the plaintiff".

(a) Goodwill or Reputation

The Goodwill of a business is an intangible asset, indicating the reputation and connection established with the customers over a period of time.

For an action of passing off, it is necessary to establish, in the first place, the existence of reputation or goodwill in the business, or in the novel features of the goods such as its trade name, mark, or get-up or other indicia.

In most of the instances, goodwill of the business is identified with the distinctiveness of the mark or "Symbol" which has been extensively known by the general public. If substantial number of persons relate a particular mark or symbol with the plaintiff that is sufficient to establish a goodwill in favour of the plaintiff or his business.

In passing off action, the plaintiff has to establish that there is damage to his goodwill in respect of that trade or business.

Shared Goodwill–The Goodwill might be shared with others i.e., the plaintiff need not be the exclusive owner of the goodwill. Thus in the "Champagne" case, the plaintiffs who were Champagne Houses of France established that only wine produced in the Champagne district of France by the Champagne Houses were known as 'Champagne' and that such wine has great reputation and that the use of the term "Spanish–Champagne" would deceive by causing persons to believe that the wine so described was Champagne. Injunction was granted against the use of the term 'Spanish Champagne'[5].

The above case clearly highlights that a name or a symbol may become goodwill of a class of traders. This type of shared goodwill may be acquired as a result of the product having been manufactured from ingredients produced in a particular geographical location or are the result of its having been made from particular ingredients regardless of their provenance.

The plaintiff must prove that, on the date when the alleged passing off was committed by the defendant, he had reputation, goodwill or reputation in his goods or business is concerned.

New technological advancement has provided an opportunity to acquire goodwill in new kind of business in a short period of time.

Trans-Border Reputation–A foreign plaintiff ordinarily acquires reputation and goodwill for his product in India either by selling his products in Indian local market or by establishing manufacturing units in India. Reputation, if not goodwill, can also be created by advertising the product under its brand name through local newspapers and magazines or by advertising their product in foreign newspapers and periodicals which have a circulation in India among the potential customers of the goods. Development of communication and satellite facilities has also encouraged the producers to advertise their products in foreign country through satellite television network. This form of reputation is often called trans-border reputation.

The question arises whether actual use or availability of goods of the foreign plaintiff who has secured a reputation in such trade mark, name has a right to seek passing off action if his trade mark or other indicia has been adopted by the local trader.

This question was answered by the jurists in various case laws. The traditional theory emphasized that the trade mark should be registered or used in the country, where passing off action is claimed. In England principle was adopted in *Alian Benardin v/s Pavilian Properties (Crazy Horse Doctrine)*[6], where relief was refused to a French company on the ground that the said company did not have business in England. In Budweiser case[7], the Court of Appeal held that in order to succeed in passing off action in England the plaintiff has not only to prove that his trade mark has reputation in England but also he has to establish the existence of goodwill and , that goodwill could be proved only by showing the sale of goods in the open market in England.

In India the doctrine of Crazy Horse is not applicable. A foreign plaintiff who has no actual business in India but whose goods or services are well known internationally may file an action for passing off in India, if he can establish the following:[8]

- Its goods or Services has acquired International reputation and goodwill.
- Travelers from India to foreign countries have purchased the goods and brought them to India which is a form of Importation.
- The goods or services have been advertised in International magazines which have circulation in India and many potential customers of the goods or the services have subscribed to such magazines or seen the advertisements.
- The goods have been sold in India on a scale which though not very extensive is not insignificant.
- The defendant could not furnish a satisfactory explanation for the adoption of the mark in question.

The above principles have been applied by the low Courts, in India in various decisions.

In *Caterpillar Inc. v/s Jorange*[9], the plaintiffs were proprietors of the marks 'Cat" and "Caterpillar" registered and used in many countries including India in respect of machine tools, traders and vehicles. They had also used the marks extensively in foreign countries in respect of ready made garments, but not in India, though there was some evidence of advertisement of these readymade garments in India. The defendants used the same marks in India for readymade garments. The single Judge refused to grant interim injunction. An appeal was allowed granting injunction. Madras division Bench considered the transborder reputation in this case.

In another case Plaintiffs were proprietors of Westinn Hotels and Resorts and had established transborder reputation for hospitality services, but they did not have any business activities in India. Defendants used WESTINN as part of its corporate name to provide consultancy services for hotels and resorts reservation. Madras Division Bench granted interim injunction reversing the decision of the lower court. On further appeal to Supreme Court the interim order was modified and the defendant was permitted to use the word WESTINN as part of its corporate name with the condition that in the letter heads of the defendants and advertisements the words "No connection whatsoever with Westinn Hotels and Resorts" shall be added[10].

The above cases establish that in India "Crazy Horse "doctrine is not applicable.

(b) Misrepresentation

The term 'Misrepresentation' means a statement which conveys a false or wrong impression. The following categories of misrepresentation could be adopted for passing off:

- Direct false representation,
- Adoption of trademark which is the same or a colourable imitation of the trademark of a rival trader,
- Adoption of an essential part of a rival trader's name,
- Copying the get-up or colour scheme of the label used by a trader,
- Imitating the design or shape of the goods,
- Adopting the word or name by which the rival traders goods or business is known in the market, and many other ingenious methods.[11]

Direct misrepresentation is the simplest form of passing off. If A says falsely, "These goods I am selling are B's goods", it is a clear case of passing off[12]. Such cases are, however, rare. In Bulmer v/s Bollinger[13], it was observed: "For one producer to compare or contrast his product with the product of another producer cannot constitute passing off, provided that this is done in clear and explicit terms. It would not, for example, constitute passing off if B were to advertise his product as being as good a product as A's , or as an acceptable substitute for A's product, or as a cheaper equivalent to A's product for such comparisons by their nature distinguish B's product from A's".

In *Lever v/s Bedingfield*, it was held that if the defendant has just adopted the idea from the plaintiff's get-up of the goods and that in fact does not deceive the public, then there may be no ground to grant injunction.[14]

It is the court that determines whether there is any likelihood of deception or confusion of the public. The judge in order to ascertain whether the evidence produced by the plaintiff amounts to misrepresentation by the defendant, the court has tc consider the following points:

- The nature and extent of the reputation relied upon;
- The fields of activity in which the plaintiff and defendant carries on the business;

- The similarity of the mark, name, get-up or other distinctive features used by the defendant to that of the plaintiff;
- The manner in which the particular trade is carried on, the class of persons who is likely to be deceived and all other surrounding circumstances.

The burden lies on the plaintiff to prove that there is deception or likelihood of deception. But the plaintiff need not prove that anyone, in fact, has been deceived. It would suffice if he establishes that the defendant's acts are likely to mislead an ordinary purchasers in believing that they are getting the plaintiff's goods when, in fact, they are receiving defendant's goods.

In series of cases it has been observed by the courts that passing off is not restricted to situations involving competing traders dealing in same kind of business; but included also those cases which suggests that the defendants's business is connected with the plaintiff's business in such a manner that it may damage the goodwill of the plaintiff[15].

Motive of the defendant is not relevant in order to obtain protection for the trade mark. A mark even though adopted innocently, would stand on the same footing as that of fraud constituted against the plaintiff.

Imitation of the Get-Up-Get-Up is now-a-days refered to as trade dress[16]. Get-up of the goods comprised in packaging, style of writing, shape and size of the container, its outer wrapper and labels, the colour combination and the manner of arrangement of the other features in the label. Passing off action can be succeeded by the plaintiff if he establishes that the particular get-up has been used exclusively in his goods and that the defendant's goods get-up is similar to that of the plaintiff which is likely to lead confusion in the minds of the public. In *Reckitt and Colmon v/s Borden*[17], the plaintiff had for a number of years marketed their lemon juice in a plastic container resembling that of a lemon. The defendant proposed to launch lemon juice in a lemon shaped plastic container similar to that of the plaintiff's. Injunction was granted.

(c) Damage

Lastly, the plaintiff has to establish that, due to deception or misrepresentation caused by the defendant, the plaintiff has suffered loss or injury to his business or goodwill. Only on the establishment of this the plaintiff would be entittled for remedy against passing off.

Passing Off and Non–Trading Activities

The principle of the law of passing–off has been extended to non-trading business or non-profit making bodies. The necessary thing which has to be established in such a case is that the plaintiff suffers damage or injury. In *Law Society of England and Wales v/s Society of Lawyers*[18], the plaintiff had statutory responsibility for monitoring and regulating the solicitors currently on the Solicitors Roll. The defendant's main object was to provide regulation on a voluntary basis of individuals who are not necessarily solicitors or Barristers, but who provide advice and/ or services such as conveyancing. They used a herald device similar to the plaintiff's crest. The defendant was ordered to change its name.

Passing Off and Domain Names

A name which is used to identify a person's internet service is called a "Domain name". The "Domain name" is similar to that of trademark and as such is entitled to secure adequate protection similar to that of protection conferred to trade mark. Unfortunately in India there are no statutory laws to protect "Domain names". Hence, the courts apply the principles of passing off in the case of domain names. In India the first important case regarding domain names is that of Yahoo[19]. The case involved the use of the domain "Yahooindia.com" by an Indian party. In a suit inititated by Yahoo Inc, Hon'ble Justice M.K.Sharma of the Delhi High Court granted an interim injunction restraining the defendants from operating any business or selling, offering for sale, advertising and/ or in any manner dealing in services or goods on the Internet or otherwide under the trade mark/domain name "Yahooindia.com" or any other trade mark/domain name which is identical with or deceptively similar to the plaintiff's trade mark "Yahoo!". The court also restrained the defendants from using and/or copying the contents of the programs of the plaintiff under the domain name "Yahoo.com".

The court found that considering the vastness of the Internet and its relatively recent availability to the general public, many Internet users are not sophisticated enough to distinguish the subtle difference between the two domain names. Commenting on the Internet and its use the court held that: "In an Internet service, a particular Internet site could be reached by anyone anywhere in the world who proposes to visit the said Internet site. With the advancement and progress in technology, services rendered on the Internet has also come to be recognized and accepted and are being given protection so as to protect such provider of service from passing off the services rendered by other as that of the plaintiff"[20].

In *Rediff Communications ltd v/s Cyber Booth*[21], the Bombay High Court was faced with a case where the defendant had adopted the domain name *www.radiff.com* despite the existence of the well-known website of the plaintiff's *www.rediff.com*. The court found such an adoption by the defendant was completely dishonest and hence injunction was granted.

The Delhi High Court has restrained Lucknow based Networld Infosys from using "Crorepatikaun" and "Kaun Banega Crorepathi as domain names for websites offering online versions of the game based on the format of "Kaun Banega Crorepathi" which was Indian version of the television gameshow "Who wants to be a millionaire" run by US based Celador Productions Ltd. The court restrained Networld Infosys from:

- passing off the name of the gameshow "Kaun Banega Crorepathi";
- Screening shots with the gameshow's circular logo with the distinctive layout and colour scheme; and
- Screening the picture of the gameshow host Amitabh Bachan or photographs of any episode of the gameshow being telecast on cable channel[22].

Recently the disputes relating to domain names are gaining importance. Hence its time that our legislaters look into the matter at the earliest and enact a suitable legislation similar to that of the US Anti Cybersquatting Act so as to confer adequate protection in Cyberspace and Cyberlaws.

Defences Under Passing Off Actions

In an action for passing off the defendant may plead the following defences:

(i) The name, mark or other symbol, which is used by the defendant, is different from that of the plaintiff and as such is not likely to pass off his goods or business as that of the plaintiff.

(ii) The name, mark or other symbol, the use of which is sought to be restrained, is not distinctive of the plaintiff's goods or business.

(iii) Concurrent use of a trade name or mark by the defendant is a good defence. But the defendant has to establish this with satisfactory documentary evidence. In *Edge v / s Gallon*[23], The plaintiffs were using the word "Dolly" in respect of their blue. The defendants were selling blue bearing a trade mark consisting of a washing tub called "Dolly Tub" prior to the plaintiff's use. They proved concurrent use. Injunction was refused. In Manoj Plastics v/s Bhola Plastic[24], the defendants failed to establish concurrent user of mark and design of goods with the help of documentary evidence. Hence, Interim injunction was granted.

(iv) Injunction will not be granted in isolated cases of passing off.

(v) Where the plaintiff is engaged in fraudulent business or indulges in unfair trade practice, then he cannot have any remedy before the law as he has not approached the court with clean hands.

(vi) The defendant may plead that his goods or business is different from that of the plaintiffs. In *Relaxo Rubber ltd v / s Aman Cable Industries*[25], plaintiff had registered RELAXO as trade mark in respect of footwear. Defendant using same mark for cables and PVC pipes. As the goods were totally different interlocutory injunction was refused

(vii) Lastly, the defendant could defend his case by pleading that the plaintiff is not entitled to enjoy the relief on account of delay, estoppel, acquiescence, deceptive use of the mark or symbol, misrepresentation of facts or fraudulent trade.

Delay perse will not bar relief. However, inordinate delay on the part of the plaintiff in claiming relief would deprive him from seeking justice as the plaintiff cannot sleep over his rights and then knock the court's door.

The word 'acquiescence' means a consent inferred from silence, a tacit encouragement under section 33 of the TRADEMARKS Act of 1999 if the proprietor of an earlier trade mark has acquiesced for a continuous period of 5 years in the use of a registered trade mark, being aware of that use, he is not entitled to apply for a declaration that the registration of the later mark is invalid or to oppose the use of the latter trade mark unless the latter trade mark was not applied in good faith. In *Power*

Control v/s Sumeet [26], The Supreme Court observed: "Acquiescence is sitting by when another is invading the rights and spending money on it".

(viii) The defendant could also plead that he was unaware of the Trade mark used by the plaintiff and on gaining knowledge of the existence of plaintiff's trade mark he forthwith ceased to use the trade mark complained of[27].

The above instances are some of the defences that could be pleaded by the defendant and escape from liability in passing off action.

Remedies

The common law remedies such as injunction and damages are now incorporated under Sec 135 of TRADEMARKS Act, 1999. Under sub-section (1) of sec 135 the court may grant in any suit for passing off an:

- Injunction restraining the use of mark or trade name or other indicia.
- At the option of the plaintiffs, either damages or an account of profits.
- An order for the delivery-up of the infringing labels and marks for destruction or erasure.

Injunction–In passing off actions it is advisable for the plaintiff in extremely urgent cases to seek exparte injunction order, and then seek interim injunction at the commencement of the suit. Subsequently if need arises he could proceed to seek permanent injunction. So far as injunctions are concerned their provisions are contained in sections 36 to 42 of the Specific Relief Act,1963 and Order 39 rule 1 & 2 r/w section 151 of the C.P.C.

Object of the injunction is to restrain the defendants from passing off his goods as goods of the plaintiff. Supreme court in *Laxmikant V.Patel v/s Chetan Bhai Shah and another*[28], ruled that in a passing off action establishing likelihood of damage is sufficient for grant of injunction.

Damages and Accounts of Profits

Damages-Damages or compensation may be substantial or nominal. If the plaintiff seeks substantial damage, then the burden shifts on him to establish that the action of the defendant has resulted in damages to him. Where the plaintiff has not suffered any loss, then the court may grant only nominal damages so as to establish his legal right. In *General Electric v/s Pyara Singh*[29] *and Arvind Laboratories v/s Sami Chemical*[30], Punjab and Haryana High Court and Madras High Court respectively granted nominal damages respectively as the plaintiff could not establish that he suffered any loss due to the act of the defendant.

Account of Profits-In *Electrolux and Electrix*[31], it was observed that " the principle upon which the court grants an a/c of profits is that where one party owes a duty to another, the person to whom that duty is owed is entitled to recover from the other party every benefit which that other party has received by virtue of his fiduciary position if in fact he has obtained it without the knowledge or consent of the party to whom he owed the duty". Normally a local Commissioner is appointed for calculating the profits earned by the defendant party. Its left to the discretion of the court ot pass an order for account of profits or damages but not both.

Conclusions and Suggestions

Passing of action comes to the rescue of those traders who have not registered their trade mark, trade name, or other indicia. Yet, it is still disadvantages compared to trade mark registered under TRADEMARKS Act, 1999.

In passing off action the plaintiff has to establish that the defendant's act is likely to injure the reputation of the plaintiff by passing off his goods as the goods of the plaintiff. Under the passing off action the procedure adopted by the court is cumbersome, expensive and also time consuming.

On the other hand, mere registration of the mark confers protection under TRADEMARKS Act, 1999.

Hence, it is advisable for the traders to get their TRADEMARKS registered. So far as protection of domain names is concerned common law remedy plays a vital role. Until the legislators enact a suitable legislation on Cyberspace and Cyber crimes the Cyber squatters are accountable under passing off.

To conclude, the common law remedy of passing off comes to the rescue of traders in absence of registration of their TRADEMARKS. In the present day, domain names conflicts are alarmingly increasing, and common law remedy of passing off plays a vital role in resolving domain names disputes pending before Indian courts.

NOTES

1. Singer v/s Loog (1881) 18th D 395 at 412; P. Narayan, Intellectual Property Law, 3rd Ed., pg. 212, Eastern Law House.
2. Salmond Law of Torts, 17th Ed, at pg. 401; Winfield's Tort, 9th Ed., at pg . 485.
3. Erven Warnick v/s Townend (1980) RPC 31 at 933 (HL).
4. (1990) RPC 341 at pg. 406 (HL); P. Narayan, Law of TRADEMARKS and Passing off, 5th Ed, at pg. 503.
5. Bollinger v/s Costa Brava (1961) RPC 116.
6. (1967) RPC 581
7. (1984) FSR 413, D.P. Mittal-New Law of TRADEMARKS, Passing off and Geographical Indications of Goods, 2000 Ed., Taxmann's.
8. P. Narayan, Law of TRADEMARKS and Passing off, 5th Ed., pg. 532, Eastern Law House.
9. (1998) IPLR 326 (Mad) (PB).
10. Ceasar Park Hotels and Resorts Inc v/s Westinn Hospitality Services Ltd. (1999) PTC 123 (Mad) (DB); (1999) PTC 430 (SC).
11. P. Narayan, Intellectual Property Law, 3rd Ed, Pg. 218.
12. Spalding v/s Gamage (1915) 32 RPC 273 at 284 (HL).
13. (1978) RPC 79 at 104 (CA).

14. (1899) 16 RPC 3 at 11 (CA); Universal Agencies v/s Paul Swolf (1959) RPC 247.
15. Borosil Glass Works v/s O.P Batra (1996) PTC 55 (Del); Apple Computer v/s Apple Leasing 1992 (1) Arb LR 93 (Del); Ciba Geigy Ltd v/s Surinder Singh (1998) PTC 544 (Del).
16. Samsonite Corp v/s Vijay Sales (1998) PTC 372 (Del).
17. (1987) FSR 228 (CA).
18. (1996) FSR 739; P. Narayan-Law of TRADEMARKS and Passing off, 5th Ed at 588.
19. Yahoo, Inc v/s Akash Arora (1999) 19 PTC 201 (Del).
20. Ibid.
21. 2000 PTC 209.
22. Ahuja's-Patent and Trademark News, Vol. 4 No. 6 , Oct, 2001, at 11.
23. (1900) 17 RPC 557(HL); P. Narayan, Law of Trademarks and Passing off.
24. (1983) PTC 368 at 371.
25. (1998) PTC 759 (Del).
26. (1994) IPLR 117 at 127, SC.
27. Sec 135 (3)-TRADEMARKS Act, 1999.
28. S.C Dec, 04, 2001, Ahuja's PTN Vol. 4, No.* at 11.
29. AIR 1974 P & H 14.
30. (1994) PTC 223 (Mad).
31. (1953) 70 RPC 158 at 159.

3 COMPARATIVE ADVERTISING: A CONCERN FOR TRADEMARK

*Padmavathi S.**

Introduction

An advertisement is any information by the manufacturer or service provider to the public, as to a particular product or service. It informs the consumers of the product and promotes sales, thereby helping in increasing their share in market. Thus, an advertisement persuades a consumer in purchasing a product. While using the mode of advertisement a consumer would also opt another method of reaching the top or beating his rival i.e. by comparing his product with that of his rival's. This leads to a change in choice or confusion amongst consumers–be it for an advantage or disadvantage, but definitely a registered or well-known trademark is at stake. Advertisers have always tried to project their goods or service in the best form to the consumers. This is done by highlighting the merits of the advertiser's product or service. But today this has changed its course, and advertisers tend to advertise and highlight their product by comparing their product or service to that of another's and more often the other (rival) brand is named

* B.A.L, LL.M, PGDIPRL, Faculty of Law, Department of Post Graduate Studies and Research in Law, University of Mysore, Mysore.

openly. Now this leads to legal action by the competitors whose products have been compared or criticized by the advertiser. Here opens the legal issue over the comparative advertising techniques. This paper attempts to provide a detailed analysis of trademark infringement in the name of comparative advertising. The paper brings out in part one, the meaning and definition of trademark in the Indian context, in part two analyzes the meaning of comparative advertising and brings out the various ways of comparisons and part three studies the legal systems in India, with the help of case laws, the developments and protection provided for trademarks in the course of comparative advertising.

PART - I

The Concept of Trademark

With globalization and liberalization the commercial market and trade is getting competitive by the day, one product trying to overtake the other, trademarks have assumed the status of important intellectual property rights today. The products are manufactured by different concerns and they acquire wide market across frontiers, and within its boundaries; it is significant to let know the customer of the source or origin of a particular product. This way of identifying a source of product is possible through a mark peculiar to that manufacturer for his product. This purpose is served by a '*trademark*'. Trademark is a symbol that allows a purchaser to identify goods or services that have been satisfactory in the past and reject goods or services that have failed to give satisfaction. It imputes a sense of responsibility on the manufacturer to manufacture quality products. Trademark is a means of advertising i.e. to fix the identity of the article and the name of the producer in the minds of the people.

Definition of Trade Mark

Trademark means a mark capable of being represented graphically and which is capable of distinguishing the goods or services of one person from those of others' and may include shape of goods, their packaging and combinations of colors; and (i) in relation to Chapter XII (other than section 107), a registered trade mark or a mark used in relation to goods or services for the purpose of indicating or so as to indicate a connection in the course of trade between the goods or services, as the case may be, and some person having the right as proprietor to use the mark; and (ii) in relation to other provisions of this Act, a mark used or proposed to be used in relation to goods or services for the purpose of indicating or so to indicate a connection in the course of trade between the goods or services, as the case may be, and some person having the right, either as proprietor or by way of permitted user, to use the mark whether with or without any indication of the identity of that person, and includes a certification trade mark or collective mark[1]. Thus, a trademark is a visual symbol used in relation to any goods or services to indicate some kind of trade connection between the goods or services and the person using the mark.

Mark includes a device, brand, heading, label, ticket, name, signature, word, letter, numeral, shape of goods, packaging or combination of colours or any combination thereof.[2] The Trade Marks Act, 1999 also defines "*well known trademark*" as, in relation to any goods or services which have become so to the substantial segment which uses such goods or service that the use of such mark in relation to other goods or services would be likely to be taken as indicating a connection in the course of trade or at the rendering of service is between those goods or services and a person using the mark in relation to the first mentioned goods or services[3]. A trademark may be registered or unregistered and an unregistered trademark is commonly known as common law mark.

Trademark Infringement

Any person who trespasses the rights conferred by registration of a trademark infringes a registered trademark. In case of trade mark that is not registered then the trademark can be protected under passing off. Passing off is the common law remedy of torts. The basis of passing off is false representation. Section 29 of the Trademarks Act of 1999,in India, says what amounts to infringement of registered trademark.

Infringement and Unfair Competition

Trademark signifies its quality and source of goods, thereby enabling the buyer to make his choice of products. Trademark carriers along itself the reputation and goodwill of the producer. So in this world of business, trade competition is high, this competition shall however be fair competition. Under *common law* trademark infringement is a type of unfair competition and thus trademark infringement is a commercial tort. But in the *Indian context*, there is no tort of unfair competition nor a tort of trademark infringement as both are codified under Monopolies and Restrictive Trade practices Act, 1969 now repealed by Competition Act, 2002 and Trademarks Act, 1999.

PART - II

Comparative Advertising

It is primarily by *advertising* that a product's reputation is created and maintained.[4] Advertising has become a war field trying hard to influence the choice of consumers. Advertising is a means by which the manufacturer informs the consumers of the product and it promotes sales, which in turn helps in increasing their share in market. Thus, an advertisement persuades a consumer in purchasing a product. *Advertising* means "the making of a representation in any form in connection with a trade, business, craft or profession in order to promote the supply of goods or services..."[5]

Comparative advertising is a means for competitors to inform the public that their product is similar to the trademarked product. It is a technique by which a product is compared to a competitive product with the intent of proving the superiority. Indeed the purpose of comparative advertising aims to distinguish one's product from a competitor's product by or through comparison.[6] It aims at beating a leader in the market and increasing sales of the advertiser. *Comparative advertising* in defined as "... any advertising which explicitly or by implication identifies a competitor or goods or services offered by a competitor".[7]

In comparative advertising a new product or existing rival product (competitor), may state that his own product is better than or best, by comparing his own product with a rival's product and thereby cause damage to the goodwill to the rival's product. The comparison could be through a statement, comparative price chart or in the form of mockery etc. However there are varied attitudes towards comparative advertising.[8] Some look at competitive advertising as an effective deterrent against increasing product prices as well as valuable tool to promote competition, product improvement and modernization, others view that it may promote healthy competition on one hand, a few feel it will divest customers from the proprietor.[9] It can also lead to trademark infringement if the use of another's trademark is likely to cause confusion in the mind of the consumer.[10]

Comparative advertising *occurs* where one manufacturer compares the specification, performance and price of his products with a rival's product. If this is done by specifying that in any form the trademark of the rival product, it would amount to trademark infringement. Comparison could be in different *ways*, like: Firstly, comparing could be of the price, the quality or merits etc of the product. Secondly, comparison of similar goods (Cool drinks-Pepsi and Coke, Toothpaste-Colgate and Pepsodent etc). Thirdly, of dissimilar goods or non-competing good (In the case of advertisements used by British Telecom[11] in the UK to stress the low cost of charges for telephone calls by comparing the cost with the low price of every day items such as sausages, a Kit Kat bar etc.). Fourthly, Comparing them could be positive i.e. Associative(if a product is advertised to be as equivalent to its rival). Fifthly, comparison could otherwise be negative i.e. Differentiating (if a product is advertised to be just half the price of that of a rival product).

According to Belinda Isaac,[12] a survey of advertisements reveals that there are three *categories* into which all advertisements fall; First, advertisements that refer only to one brand of product and make no reference to competing products either directly or indirectly–*"non-comparative"* advertisements (NCA); Second, advertisements that refer only to attributes of one brand of product that refer indirectly to the attributes of the rival or competing products-*"indirectly comparative"* advertisements (ICA); and Third, Advertisements that directly compare attributes of one product to attributes of a specifically named or recognizably presented, competing brand–*"directly comparative"* advertisements (DCA). In some countries neither ICAs nor DCAs are allowed, whereas in others one or both are permitted. The UK permits both within limits, whereas Germany & Belgium allow neither.

Trademark Infringement and Comparative Advertising

In comparative advertising, an identical trademark need not necessarily be used, it can be of similar or dissimilar goods but only the quality, and price etc of the goods can be expressed thereby crippling the product of a particular trademark in the market. Comparative advertising could constitute trademark infringement even if the trademark is well known.

Misusing a person's registered trademark in advertising constitutes trademark infringement; also using a well-known trademark in comparative advertising could lead to trademark infringement whether products are similar or dissimilar. To examine if there is a trademark infringement and a likelihood of confusion amongst consumers is a matter of fact and that is to be decided by the language used in the advertisement.

PART - III

Comparative Advertising and Trademark infringement in India

The Pepsi-coke wars, the small cars wars, and surf-tide wars have been quite persistent in the recent past. In India comparative advertising was governed under the Monopolies and Restrictive Trade practices Act, 1969 which is now replaced by the Competition Act, 2002, the Consumer Protection Act, which protects against unfair trade practices and now it is also governed under the Trademarks Act 1999.

The MRTP Commission has resolved many disputes of comparative advertising under the garb of unfair trade practices. The MRTP Act, 1969 was amended in the 1984 to include unfair trade practices. The MRTP Act stated that there would be strict liability to apply a false description, on a total but misleading description, in a course of business, which affects the goods in a material degree.

Trademarks Perspective of Comparative Advertising

The trademarks perspective of comparative advertising was not known until the 1999 Act legislated it into its definition of infringement under section 29. But with reference to trademark infringement in the name of comparative advertising, it is governed under section 29 (8) of the Trademarks Act, 1999. 'Well-known' or unregistered trademarks are also given protection under common law action of passing off, malicious falsehoods or trade libel under the Trade Marks Act.

The way we witness comparative advertising in India are, in print-the price comparison charts of over two brands specially of home appliances, or on television media where the logo of the rival mark is blurred-but which obviously makes the consumer get the point, or where a product is compared with an 'X' brand and states that its own brand is better than the rest or rather the best. Before 1999, Comparative advertisements were challenged on the grounds of disparagement, defamation, copyright, trademark infringement and other general principles of injunction.

In *Reckitt & Colman of India Ltd v Kiwi TTK*[13] the advertisement which appeared on electronic media, shows a bottle of KIWI from which "KIWI" is written on the white surface which does not drip against another bottle described as "OTHERS" which drips. The bottle of "OTHERS" is shown as "Brand X". "Brand X" alleges that this "Brand X" looks similar to the bottle of the liquid shoe polish of the plaintiff for which the plaintiff allegedly had the design registered in its name. There is a red blob on the surface of this bottle which allegedly represents "Cherry", which also appears on the bottle of the product of the plaintiff. S.K. Mahajan J, held that "a manufacturer is entitled to make a statement that his goods are the best and also make some statements for puffing of his goods and the same will not give a cause of actions to the other traders or manufacturers of similar goods to institute proceedings as there is no disparagement or defamation to the goods of the manufacturer in so doing. However, a manufacturer is not entitled to say that his competitor's goods are bad as to puff and promote his goods".

This settled law on the subject appeared to be that a manufacturer is entitled to make a statement that his goods are the best and also make some statements for puffing of his goods and the same will not give a cause of action to other traders or manufacturers of similar goods to institute, proceeding as there is no disparagement or defamation to the goods of the manufacturer so doing. However manufacturer is not entitled to say that his competitor's goods are bad so as to puff and promote his products.

In *Reckitt & Colman of India Ltd v MP Ramachandran & Another*[14] the plaintiff is the manufacture of a whitener sold under the brand name Robin Blue. The defendants are all so manufacturing a whitener and selling their product under the brand name UJALA. It is alleged that for promoting the sale of the defendant's product they are seeking to project as if the goods of the plaintiff are inferior to that of the defendants. Though the name of the brand has not been mentioned in the container in which the product of the plaintiff was sold' in the advertisement yet it has been specially shown and identified as " blue". The same advertisements were also published in newspapers.

The Calcutta High Court laid down *five principles* as a *guiding factor* for granting an injunction:

1. A tradesman is entitled to declare his goods to be the best in the world even though the declaration is untrue.
2. He can also say that his goods are better than his competitors', even though such a statement is untrue.
3. For the purpose of saying that his goods are the best in the world or his goods are better than his competitors' he can even compare the advantages of his goods over the goods of the others.
4. He however, cannot while saying his goods are better than his competitors', say that his competitors' goods are bad. If he says so, he slanders the goods of his competitors. In other words he defames his competitors and their goods, which is not permissible.

5. If there is no defamation to the goods or to the manufacturer of such goods, no action lies, but if there is such defamation, an action lies and if an action lies for recovery of damages for defamation, then the court is also competent to grant an order of injunction restraining repetition of such defamation.

The court held, in the above case, that comparative advertisements were admissible. However, the advertisement should not be in such a manner as to disparage the goods of the competitor. Mere puffing of goods without disparagement is not actionable. The advertisement must be viewed in the light of the above stated tests. But, the courts here were concerned with disparagement of goods and not trademark. But the same test however can be employed for trademark through comparative advertising. It should however be noted that this case dealt with disparagement of goods and not trademarks, yet the same criteria could be applied to trademarks as well, as long as the trademark forms the focal point of the comparative advertisement.

As compared to the above, the case of *Pepsi Co Inc v Hindustan Coca Cola Ltd and Another*[15] was primarily based on copyright and trade mark infringement, the facts state that, Pepsi company incorporation along with Pepsi Co (India) Holdings Limited and Pepsi Foods Limited, the plaintiffs filed suit against Hindustan Coca-Cola and others. They sought for restraint order from infringing upon the registered trademark of the plaintiffs by use of the word "pappi" which according to the appellants is deceptively similar to that of the appellant's product "Pepsi" in the advertisements and commercials. They also sought for a restraint order from infringing upon the copyright of the plaintiffs in the words "Yeh Dil Maange More" in television commercials including copying the roller coaster, commercial of the appellants. They claimed that the commercials infringed the trademark and copyright of the plaintiffs and disparaged the appellant's product resulting in dilution of appellants goodwill and the reputation the court granted an injunction on the copyright claim holding that the advertisement of the respondents had copied that of the appellants. On the trademark claim, the court held that comparative advertising is permissible as long as it does not degrade the other product. It stated that if a trader compares his goods with the goods of a rival without giving the impression that the trade mark is used in relation to his goods, there is *prima facie* no infringement. The court opined that comparison is permissible so long as it does not undervalue the product of the rival. The Cola war in India seems to have settled for now with the Delhi High Court ruling that Comparative Advertisements are admissible in India now[16].

The 1999 Trademarks Act; then widened the scope of the definition of the term 'infringement';

Sec. 29 (8) of the 1999 Act states,

... 8. A registered trademark is infringed by any advertising of that trademark if such advertising;

(a) Takes unfair advantage of and is contrary to *honest practices*[17] in industrial or commercial matters; or

(b) Is detrimental to its distinctive character; or

(c) Is against the reputation of the trademark.

In *Dabur India Ltd v Colgate Palmolive India Ltd,*[18] a TV advertisement for tooth powder, which praised the defendant's product while criticizing its rival, the plaintiff Dabur, with a famous actor endorsing the defendant's product. The advertisement also showed the abrasive characteristics of the plaintiff's tooth powder with an actor explaining its ill-effects. The court granted an injunction and held that visual media has an immediate effect on the viewers' minds, particularly when a well-known actor is endorsing a product.

Conclusion

From the point of Intellectual property rights one needs protection over his trademark, a third person cannot be permitted to take the trademark owner for a ride at the cost of his reputation. The legal regime in this area has though in the recent past, begun to be quite effective. Comparative advertising is not prohibited in any legal system, but subject to regulations under the respective laws. While in India, comparative advertising amounts to trademark infringement if, the advertiser takes unfair advantage of and is contrary to honest practices in industrial or commercial matters; or is detrimental to its distinctive character; or is against the reputation of the trademark. Whether the comparative advertising amounts to trademark infringement depends on the language and the communication used in the advertisement. This is to be judged by looking at the advertisement as a whole. Well, all said and done comparative advertisements can exist if they are true and just i.e. it should be verifiable and based on true facts.

Today regulation of comparative advertising under the trademark law is quite clear. The stands of different countries on comparative advertising are the same i.e., comparative advertising is permitted subject to certain conditions under trademark laws. Further, since an advertisement, influences a human's (consumer's) mind; this area is to be strictly regulated, for otherwise it could have drastic impact on the goodwill of the trademark, by changing the purchase decisions of the consumer. Media is extremely common and developed and should not be to the disadvantage of the trademark owner.

A trademark's goodwill is at stake–it is infringed, it is diluted under the guise of comparative advertising. Infringement of trademark and dilution of trademark should not be permitted in the garb of comparative advertising, for it violates the very purpose of IP protection of Trademarks.

However there should be a real dawn to this and not a disguised one–Comparative advertising should not be permitted at all. Adopting the attitude of countries like Germany in this respect would be fair. For what is *honest practice*–there is no clear demarcation. Absurd & vague regulations will not suffice. The present Act of 1999 does not provide adequate safeguards to protect trademark infringement and dilution that occur through comparative advertising. A manufacturer can be permitted to say his product is the best, which is a tradition of trade, but not by comparing or mocking another manufacturer for, it is unfair a trade practice and of course the time and energy spent by a leader or rival to take position in the customer's mind cannot be dragged down by such means. The trademark law has the duty to protect and preserve the reputation and goodwill of a trademark in stake.

For courts to say that consumers are used to comparative advertising and expect a hyperbole is an escapist attitude of the courts and should not in the name of consumer advantage let comparative advertisement continue at the cost of trademark. The present Act however, does not have adequate safeguards to curb the trademark infringement and dilution that occurs by comparative advertising.

NOTES

1. Sec.2 (1) (zb) of the Trademarks Act, 1999.
2. Sec. 2 (1) (m) of the Trademarks Act, 1999.
3. Sec. 2 (1) (zg) of the Trademarks Act, 1999.
4. Catherine Colston, *Principles of Intellectual Property Law,* (London: Cavendish Publishing Ltd.) 1999, p. 346.
5. Art 2(1) of the Advertising Directive of the EEC.
6. Rutgers L J "*Damages Standards for False Advertising under the Lanham Act: A New Trend Emerges*", 20.125.137 (1988).
7. Art 1 of EC Directive.
8. E. Pompeo , "*To Tell The Truth:Comparative Advertising And Lanham Act Section 43 (A)*", Catholic University Law Review,

1897, p. 565, 566. In 1971 the *Federal Trade Commission* FTC in the US, endorsed comparative advertising, as it was of the view that, through comparison of product attributes, consumers would become more sophisticated and would make more rational purchase decisions. The Federal Trade Commission also viewed that; comparative advertising would lead to product improvement and innovation as well as to decrease in prices. This led to many comparative advertising abuses like false claims, disparagement etc.

9. Supra. no. 4 at p. 391.
10. Keshav S Dhakad and Vaishali Mittal of Anand & Anand, "*India: How To Gain From Comparative Advertising*" at http:/ /www.managingip.com/?Page=17&ISS=14233&SID=495119 (visited on 26.05.05).
11. Belinda Issac, *Brand Protection Matters*, (London: Sweet and Maxwell Publication), 2000, p. 193.
12. Ibid.
13. 1996 PTC 193 T 399.
14. 1999 PTC (19) 741.
15. 2003 (27) PTC 305 (Del).
16. Comments Guarav Choudary, "*High Court Settles Coke-Pepsi Dispute*" Tribune News Service, June 2002,-at http:// www.tribune india.com/2002/20020630/spectrum/book6.htm.
17. Article 10 bis of *The Paris Convention for protection of Industrial property* used the expression "honest practices in industrial or commercial matters", while trying to define an "act of unfair competition" As 'any act of competition contrary to honest practices in industrial or commercial matters constitutes an act of unfair competition'. See, *British Telecommunications plc v AT &T communications (UK) Limited [*1997] 5 E.I.P.R. D-134, see also *British Airways plc v Ryanair Ltd* F.S.R 9 [2001] 541, p. 551. In *O2 Ltd & O2 (UK) Ltd v Hutchison 3G UK Ltd* (2004) WL-Applying the 13 principles laid down in British Telecommunications, but criticizing the "statutory or industry code of conduct" needed to make an honest decision, the court held that unfavorable comparisons made by the defendants between their telephone services and that of the plaintiffs were true and honest, and therefore a defense against infringement.

18. 2004 (29) PTC 401 (Del) The Act states that a tradesman is entitled to make an untrue declaration that his goods are the best, better than his competitors, and can even compare the advantages of his goods over the goods of the others, he cannot say that his competitors' goods are bad.

4 CONFIDENTIAL INFORMATION AND TRADE SECRET

*M.D. Krishna**

Introduction

The term 'Confidential Information' is not clearly defined for legal purpose. It is generally understood to include any information that a company or individual creates, discovers or acquires that is held in confidence and the improper disclosure of which would be harmful to the owner.

Certain steps are advisable to ensure that the confidentiality of this information is maintained. The owner of confidential information must, within its organization, treat the information as confidential securing it from inadvertent disclosure. It may be necessary or practical for the owner of the confidential information to share it with another party.

In a commercial or industrial context certain information must have the necessary quality of confidence. There are 4 elements that should be taken in to account for determining 'Necessary quality of confidence about it'.

* Senior Lecturer, Department of Studies in Law University of Mysore Manasagangothri, Mysore - 570006 (Karnataka)

1. The owner must believe that the release of the information would be injurious to him or advantage to his rivals.
2. The owner must believe that the information is confidential or secret.
3. The first two beliefs must be reasonable.
4. The information must be considered taking into account trade practice.

It is never sufficient to simply mark 'confidential information' and assume that it is protected for all purposes. In many industries and businesses, it is customary that certain key employees, such as sales executives, enter into a non-competition agreement. In addition to other provisions of these agreements, they customarily contains promises by the employee that he or she will not, after employment, disclose any of the 'confidential information' of his or her former employer. In the event that a owner of confidential information seeking redress for improper disclosure, the foregoing practice will assist in convincing the court that the information is normally maintained in privacy and that disclosure is inappropriate.

The information must have been imparted in circumstances importing an obligation of confidence. Here the relationship between the person who gives the information and the person who receives it is very important. The relationship may be based on contract, trust, friendship or even marriage. The obligation of confidence is also a part of the contract of employment.

What is Confidential?

- The mere fact that the two people know a secret does not mean that it is not confidential.
- The information is secret, if it is capable of being kept secret by the imposition of a duty of confidence on any person to whom it is communicated.

- Once the information is available to the public, it ceases to be confidential.
- Just because a secret is disclosed to another person that does not necessarily place it in the public domain.
- The information only ceases to be capable of protection when it is in fact known to a substantial number of people.
- It is clear that if a person is told something as a secret he will be under an obligation of confidence.
- The question is how many people can be told the secret before a 'substantial number' know of it and it ceases to be confidential.
- The court will take the objective view and consider what is reasonable in each case.
- Even if a large number of people have been told .the information, If they have all been bound to an obligation of confidence, the information is clearly not in the public domain.

E.g.: A software company may allow licensees to have access to the computer source code (The human readable coding rather than machine readable code known as object code) for the purpose of error correction and development, subject to obligations of confidentiality. Even if the software is licensed to large number of people, the source code remains confidential information provided the obligations of confidentiality are imposed on and enforced against all the licensees.

Protection of Ideas

Often artists and writers have to submit their original ideas for consideration to another person prior to entering into a contract with that person for the commercial use of those ideas. But in disclosing new ideas and concept to others they often fall prey to the unscrupulous who copy these ideas without permission and without paying the originator of the idea. This information sheet is concerned with the law of confidential information, which is the legal vehicle available for the protection of such ideas.

The law of confidential information is intended to prevent the unconscionable use of author's original ideas, which are communicated in trust and confidence. For the law of confidential information to apply the information must be of a 'confidential' nature i.e., the information must not be public knowledge and there must be an element of secrecy.

In assessing whether information or an idea is of confidential nature a court will examine the following factors;

1. The value of the idea to the artist.
2. The extent to which the idea is known or has been disclosed to others and whether that disclosure was made on a confidential basis.
3. The extent of the measures taken by the artist to keep the idea secret.

The second element, which must be established, is that the information or idea must be communicated in circumstances, which indicate that the person receiving the information, or idea must respect its confidential nature. It is up to the artist or other person asserting confidentiality to establish these elements.

The most effective way of meeting the requirements for protection by the law of confidential information is to have the third parties sign a confidentiality agreement. As a general principle some one who has received information in confidence should not take unfair advantage of it. Employers have the right to protect confidential information, but the law also promotes an employee's individual ability to promote their skills. Necessarily in the course of employment an employee will develop skills, which they are entitled to take with them if they leave.

Confidential information is generally used to describe information conveniently complied throughout the years by an individual or a company such as a clients list, a marketing strategy based on clients preferences. Evidently, not all such information upon which an employee will come across in the course of his work is confidential and even when it is, will not benefit of any protection subsequent to the rupture of the working contract and the absence of an implied duty of confidentiality applied to senior employees or of a restrictive covenant. Document such as list of clients are confidential and an employee is not entitled to copy such a list and take it with him upon leaving his employment. The information and training, which an employer imparts to his employee, become part of the equipment in skill and knowledge of the employee and so are beyond the reach of such a covenant.

Implied Duties

The information collected by an employee during his employment will be more or less confidential depending on the nature of the information itself and the way it should be treated will vary on the circumstances surrounding their use.

There are 3 categories of information accessible to the employee:

1. Trivial things which is within the reach of any interested individual do not require any kind of protection.
2. The confidential information must remain during the entire time which employment exists because there is an implicit loyalty clause in any lease and hire of work. This prohibits an employee to give privileged information to a competitor. However, once the employment is over, the use of skill and knowledge acquired with the former employer is allowed even when in direct competition.

3. The only kind of information's protected even after the termination of work with an enterprise are information's linked to trade secrets which are property of the employer.

Springboard Theory

A person who has obtained information in confidence is not allowed to use it as a springboard for activities detrimental to the person who made the confidential communication and springboard it remain even when all the features have been published as can be ascertained by any member of the public.

The possessor of information must be placed under a special disability in the field of competition to ensure that he does not get an unfair start when the confidential information or trade secrets have leaked to competitor, the application of the springboard theory will protect the "head start" of the owner of this information and trade secret will "set back" those illegally obtained access to the information.

The Canadian court clearly recognized the existence of this theory in civil law. The springboard theory tries to counter a dishonest conduct or to prohibit an action contrary to the proverbial reasonable man behaviour.

In effect the courts have used the spring board theory as an equity measure when the immoral behaviour of the defendant was shocking. In many cases where the theory was applied, the real issue was a breach in the fiduciary duty of a key employee.

Trade Secret

Background

Most businesses have trade secrets. Like other forms of intellectual property, they are valuable commercial assets, which should be protected. However, sometimes the protection is not as stringent as it could be. This is often because the true worth of trade secret, or an appreciation that certain information amounts to a trade secret in the first place, only becomes obvious once the trade secret has been lost to a competitor. But sometimes, however conscious a business is of the value of its secret commercial information and however stringent its security arrangements are, trade secrets will be lost. This is often due to loose talk by employees or effective surveillance or industrial espionage by competitors.

Trade secret misappropriation is not uncommon. All businesses, however large or small, are vulnerable. Cases involving large drug companies for instance, tend to be high profile but for every high profile case there are many more that are not publicized. This is not surprising. Businesses do not want to talk about lapses in internal security or disputes with former employees. It is thus very difficult to assess the cost to industry of the misappropriation of commercial trade secrets. But there are some indicators. American business lost nearly $ 45 billion from misappropriation of proprietary information. The survey also found that the greatest losses were in manufacturing processes, and research and development information.

The concept of trade secrets should also be considered from a global perspective. If a company cannot ensure the protection of its trade secrets in another country, it might decide not to do business in that country. E.g.: Until the beginning of the 90's, Indian law required the transfer of technology (including trade secrets) held by foreign corporation operating in India to Indian controlled entities. A trade secret in simple terms is simply a formulae, device, technique or information that is not known outside of the business and which gives the business an opportunity to obtain an advantage over competitors that do not have it.

A trade secret is an information that derives independent economic values, actual or potential, from not being generally known to and not being readily ascertainable by other persons who can obtain economic value from its disclosure.

Although trade secrets commonly comprise manufacturing processes or customer lists, almost any thing with commercial value can qualify as a trade secret if it is in fact secret. Secrets are an important intellectual resource. They can represent a company's most valuable assets and they can be converted or destroyed even without a physical transfer. As a result, firms are relying increasingly on trade secret law to protect their information and inventions. As a general rule, a competitor is free to use information obtained from or about its competition.

To be considered a trade secret, information must prove two elements:

1. The information is in fact a trade secret.
2. The defendant improperly acquired, used or disclosed the information.

Two proper means of acquiring a trade secret are independent discovery and reverse engineering. Reverse engineering is the process of learning a trade secret by inspecting the product and figuring how it works.

Thus, a person may lose her trade secret by selling or displaying a product, absent a confidentiality agreement, if another person ascertains the secret by examining the product. Trade secrets are usually formulae of manufacturing process unique to its owner and which have been revealed confidentially to an employee. This is not experience acquired by an employee, but more exactly, knowledge belong to the employer and revealed by him for the sole purpose of permitting the employee to produce what the trade secret enables him to do.

The trade secret owner must also take steps to maintain secrecy. Companies often go to great lengths to protect the secrecy of their trade secrets. If the formulae for Coca-Cola was ascertained by 'proper means' some one might be able to lawfully recreate the soft drink and compete in cola sales.

Genuine trade secrets must be closely guarded. Disclose them only to employees who have an absolute need to know them. Make sure that the employees or any one else that sees the trade secrets understand their significance and are contractually obligated not to disclose them.

Unlike patents or copyrights, trade secrets never expire, but can be lost if the secret becomes publicly known. The use of trade secrets is often a less expensive means of intellectual property protection than more formal protection such as patents.

Evaluating Trade Secrets

Important factors a business owner should consider in determining whether information owned and used by his/her business is a trade secret include:

1. The extent to which the information is known outside the owners business.
2. The extent to which it is known by those involved in the owners business.
3. Measures taken to guard the secrecy of the information.
4. The value of the information to the owner or to his/her competitors.
5. The information and
6. The case or difficulty with which the information could be properly acquired or duplicated by.

The principal idea to remember is that a protectable trade secret may not be "within the realm of skills and knowledge" in one's field of business and may not be "readily duplicated without involving considerable time, effort or expense."

Upon examining these factors in comparison to the confidential information of the company it may be prudent to conduct an intellectual property audit to identify the protectable business information and assess the value to the company of that information, i.e., the value of the trade secret.

The Trade Secret Audit

Every company needs to identify its protectable trade secrets and confidential business information on a regular, ongoing basis. Many companies set up a trade secrets programme and then forget about it. Employee manuals contain policies that becomes outdated or are simply not followed. Company definition of "sensitive, proprietary information" may bear no reasonable relationship to the types of information that the company now considers to be "trade secrets". Enforcement of company policies may be lax or nonexistent. The company's trade secrets may be in jeopardy in litigation. The identification and protection of trade secrets and confidential business information is a dynamic process, not a static one. A company's portfolio of trade secrets is constantly changing: some information becomes obsolete and is no longer commercially valuable; new information is created which is extremely valuable but may not be properly protected.

Therefore, the starting point for the development of a trade secrets protection programme is an intellectual property audit to identify the company's protectable trade secrets. If possible, the intellectual property audit should be done in conjunction with counsel so the results of the audit can be protected from discovery through the attorney-client privilege. Moreover this audit should be conducted at least every year, if possible. Once the audit is completed, policies and procedures can then be employed or modified, where necessary, to protect the various items of information identified in the audit as trade secrets.

Trade Secret Protection In U.S.A

The United States of America has passed Uniform Trade Secret Act [UTSA] 1985. Under the UTSA information must not be generally known, not readily ascertainable, have independent economic value due to secrecy, and be the subject of reasonable efforts to protect secrecy. This includes

The following information's are considered as trade secrets

Proprietary Technology information	Proprietary information concerning R&D	Formulas	Processes	Laboratory notebooks
Experiments and experimental data	Analytical data	Calculations	Diagrams	Drawings
Design data manual	Vendor/supplier Information	Research and Development reports	Cost/price data	Proprietary information concerning production/process
Quality control information	Quality control procedures	Quality control manual	Research and Development know-how	Proprietary information concerning sales & Marketing
Sales Forecasts	Marketing and Sales promotion plans	Sales call reports	Competitive Intelligence information	Proprietary information concerning customers
Proprietary customer lists	Customer needs and buying habits	Know-how concerning the Management of Customer confidence	Proprietary Sales and Marketing Studies and Reports	Proprietary Financial Information
Internal Financial documents	Budgets	Forecasts	Computer printouts	Product Margins
Product costs	Operating reports	Profit and Loss statements	ProprietaryAdmini-strativeInformation	Internal Organization
Key decision makers	Strategic business plans	Internal computer software		

essentially any confidential business information. Trade secret law prevents wrongful taking; independent development and reverse engineering are defenses. *How Long A Trade Secret Protectable?* Information is Protectable as long as the information fits the definition of trade secrets. This can be moments or decades.

Protection of Trade Secret

Trade secret protection is a state right. A vast majority of states, including Minnesota have adopted the Uniform Trade Secret Act. Other states have a law or laws similar to the Uniform Act. The rights will seem to be national or international in scope, since registration is not required and since most states and foreign countries protect trade secrets.

Trade secret protection is a must for virtually any business. The Vermont Supreme Court has issued two opinions relating to the protection of trade secrets in the employment context.

In Dicks Vs Jensen (12 VT Week 12 (2001) and Omega Optical Inc. Vs Chroma Technology Corporation (13 VT Law Week 85 (2002). Each case focuses on the requirement that a business make reasonable efforts to maintain the secrecy of its confidential business information. The underlying facts in both the cases related to the appropriation of customer lists and the use of a body of language necessary to produce a technical product. The Vermont Trade Secret Act on the basis of Uniform Trade Secret Act 1985 defines the trade secret as; Information, including formula, pattern, compilation, programme, device, method, technique or process that (A) derives independent economic value, actual or potential from not being generally known to and not being readily ascertainable by proper means by other persons who can obtain economic value from the disclosure or use and (B) is the subject of efforts that are reasonable under the circumstances to maintain its secrecy.

In both cases the court concluded that complaining employers had failed to 'make efforts that are reasonable' to maintain their proprietary information as confidential within the context of employment.

The employer had failed to provide its employees with either explicit or implicit notice as to the confidential nature of its work place information and consequently, the former employees were free to use information such as customer lists and product know-how to compete with the employer once they left employment.

The court specifically noted that without confidentiality or non-compete agreement or other explicit or implicit notice as to confidentiality obligations relating to a customer list, former employees are free to use such lists to compete.

Courts have attempted to define the difference between an employee's skill and an employer's trade secrets. In essence a skill is anything the employee would have learnt regardless for whom he/she worked for in that industry and a trade secret is information that properly belongs to the individual employer and which the employee would not have known but for working for that particular employer.

Trade Secret as Property

The courts indeed describe Trade Secret as property. John Locke's theory of natural law analyses things of intangible as potential "property". Three hundred years ago Locke theorized that a person's labour can form the foundation for property. Although Locke's "Two Treatise of Govt." do not offer an explicit defense of Intellectual property his notion therein of 'labour as property' has been used frequently to justify creators ownership rights in their creations. Locke believed that every person has a property in his body and in the labour of his body. When a person takes things from the common plenitude, as in drawing water from a river or picking fruit from a tree, she joins her labour to the things taken. If a man establishes a business and makes valuable by his skill and attention, the goodwill of that business is recognized by the law as property. The courts and legislature decide whether any particular thing, such as trade secret, will be granted property status in society.

Trade Secret & Criminal Law

The Economic Espionage Act 1996 provides that the theft of trade secrets is now federal criminal offence. This is major development in the law of trade secrets in the U.S. The Department of Justice now has sweeping authority to prosecute trade secret theft in the U.S. via the internet or outside the U.S.

The U.S. under Economic Espionage Act 1996, trade secret can be federal crime. Penalties under EEA are:

$ 2,50,000 Fine and 10 years in Prison for individuals

$ 5 Million for Organizations

If trade secret benefit a foreign Govt. penalties under EEA are stiffer

$ 5,00,000 and 15 yeas in prison for individuals

$ 10 Million for organizations

There have been few prosecutions under the EEA to date, which were approved by U.S. Attorney General.

By passage of this legislation, the United States now recognize that the protection of trade secret is vital to the U.S. economy. Companies are now spending millions of dollars to create and protect trade secret information from competitors. Unless there are strong deterrents to trade secret theft, the competitive advantage of U.S. companies, afforded by trade secrets, will inevitably be stifled. Intangible property assets are often more valuable to the prosperity of U.S. companies than tangible assets. Many manufacturing operations are being moved offshore with the U.S. companies instead producing the intellectual property and "know-how" to produce such products.

The protection of trade secrets is now becoming increasingly important to the competitiveness of American industry and the economic strength of the United States. At the same time that these structural changes have been occurring in the U.S. economy, the world has been undergoing computer revolution. Since at least the beginning of the 1990s, the power of computer technology has grown exponentially resulting in increasingly more powerful means for the theft and transfer of trade secret information.

Aerial Surveillance

Of course not all-industrial espionage takes place in space. Most takes place closer to earth, although not necessarily on the ground. In the case of EI Du Pont de Nemours Vs Christopher (1970) U.S. Court of Appeals for the 5th Circuit) the defendants were retained to take photographs from an aeroplane of a chemical plant under construction and which was owned by Du Pont. The plant was being designed to carry out a new and secret process for producing methanol and it would have been possible to discover the secret process by studying photographs of the plant in a partially completed state. Du Pont noticed the aeroplane and asked its owners for information about their client. They refused to provide it and so Du Pont sued them, arguing that the photography amounted to wrongful obtaining of Du Pont's trade secrets. The defendants argued that they had done nothing wrong; they had not engaged in any fraudulent or illegal behaviour and their activities were carried out in public air space. They also argued that they had not breached any relationship of confidence. The claim was brought under the Restatement of Torts, section 757 (1939) which provides that:

"One who discloses or uses another's trade secret, without a privilege to do so, is liable to the other if;

(a) he discovered the secret by improper means or

(b) his disclosure or use constitutes a breach of confidence reposed in him by the other in disclosing the secret to him.

Circuit Judge Goldberg delivering the Opinion of the court, had this to say: "The question remaining, therefore, is whether aerial photography of a plant construction is an improper means of another's trade secret. We conclude that it is and that the Texas court would so hold."

He went on to say:' In the instant case Du Pont was in the midst of constructing a plant. Although after construction the finished plant would have protected much of the process from view, during the period of construction the trade secret was exposed to view from the air. To require Du Pont to put up a roof over the unfinished plant to guard its secret would impose an enormous expense to prevent nothing more than a school boy's trick. We introduce here no new or radical ethic since our ethos has never given moral sanction to piracy. The market place must not deviate far from our mores. We should not require a person or corporation to take unreasonable precautions to prevent another from doing that which he ought not do in the first place. Reasonable precautions against predatory eyes we may require, but an impenetrable fortress is an unreasonable requirement, and we are not disposed to burden industrial inventors with such a duty in order to protect the fruits of their efforts. "Improper" will always be a word of many nuances, determined by time, place and circumstance. We therefore need not proclaim a catalogue of commercial improprieties. Clearly, however, one its commandments does say "thou shall not appropriate a trade secret through deviousness under circumstances in which countervailing defenses are not reasonably available. However, to cover all information which is given to or acquired by the employee while in his employment, and in particular may not cover information which is only "confidential" in the sense that an unauthorized disclosure of such information to a third party while the employment subsisted would be a clear breach of duty of good faith."

Trade Secrets Protection Under Contract Law

In the case of the classic industrial spy committing an act of industrial espionage, one would not expect to find a contractual relationship, or indeed any relationship at all and a claimant's case will be founded in equity. However, many of the trade secrets cases that come before the courts do involve contracts and, and particularly, contracts of employment.

Quite apart from any express contractual obligations imposed upon an employee during his employment, he will also be bound by implied duties of fidelity or good faith. These duties protect the employer from competition by the employee during the course of employment, and also impose upon the employee a duty to keep confidential and not to disclose his employer's trade secrets and other confidential information. The protection for the employer whilst the employee remains employed is thus fairly extensive. Post employment however, implied protection is more limited.

Conclusion

Currently, trade secret law is primarily a fusion of tort and unjust enrichment law. In establishing that a defendant used improper means in acquiring or using trade secret, courts invoke principles from many other areas of the law, including contract. Because of its unique blend of legal principles, trade secret law warrants and indeed requires the separate legal classification it now holds.

Trade secret remedies reveal much about the societal values inherent in trade secrets and about the rationales behind deterring their wrongful appropriation. These societal values include the trade secret owner's individual security in her resource, her liberty to control her resource, and the requirement that those who would appropriate the trade secret from the owner first obtain her consent.

The old adage "prevention is better than cure" is no more appropriate than in the field of trade secrets. Litigation in this field can be notoriously complicated and expensive, particularly where highly technical trade secrets are involved and the defense alleges that the information the claimant seeks to protect is in fact widely known.

Where a claimant can point to obvious and reprehensible conduct by the defendant in misappropriating confidential information he will no doubt have the wind behind him. Perhaps also in these blatant cases there is an argument that in addition to any civil law remedies open to a claimant, the State itself should uphold some element of commercial morality by the enforcement of a criminal code.

As to the existing civil law, establishing that the information sought to be protected is indeed confidential is central to any dispute. It is always helpful if some form of protection strategy has been put in place. This not only reduces the risk of trade secrets loss in the first place, but will put a claimant in a far more favourable position than otherwise would be the case if despite preventative steps having been taken, a trade secret is nevertheless misappropriated.

The first step in any protection strategy is of course to identify what information is confidential. It is only then that proper strategies can be developed. If business is in a position to impose contractual obligations of confidentiality upon persons to whom such information will be disclosed E.g.: employees, consultant, potential merger partners, then that is what they should consider doing. Thought should also to given to restricting access to information only to those who actually need it. Businesses might consider marking documents with appropriate legends. They might also consider preparing staff manuals explaining the importance of confidentiality and trade secret protection dealing with, for instance, what type of information should or should not go into a newsletter or website, how information is to be transferred from one physical location to another, guidance on disposal, what type of information can and cannot be taken home by employees, etc.

REFERENCES

The Protection of Trade Secrets-Jon Lang, White & Case, www.asisonline.org.

The U.S. Economic Espionage Act of 1996-The Theft of Trade secrets- MHALLIGN @ EXCPC.COM (Trade Secrets Home Page http://execpc.com .

Confidential Information: Solicitors: Confidentiality, Trade Secrets and Non disclosure- Hymphreys & Co.

Protecting your ideas–Google: Venture Solicitor.com.

Protection of Trade Secrets- Paul, Frank & Collins-http://www.pfclaw.com.

Trade secrets, Unjust Enrichment and the Classification of Obligations- By James W. Hill.

Intellectual Property Law-Tine Hard-Linda Fazzani.

Intellectual Property Law-P.Narayanan, Eastern Law House, II Edition, 1997.

5 COPYRIGHT ON INTERNET: ISSUES AND CHALLENGES

*Sudheer**

Introduction

LAW is a response to a challenge; the challenge can be social, economic or technological. Copyright law is no exception to this general rule. Guten Berg's printing technology of 1450,which mothered the publishing industry, also raised the first major challenge to the copyright regime. Then the law came to the rescue of authors/publishers of the literature.

Most significant of the challenges hitherto faced by the copyright law is the emergence of the digital information technology, more particularly the Internet. The present article would have a bird's eye view on the issues related to this.

What is Copyright?

The word "copyright" is derived from the expression 'copier of the words', first used in 1586[1].In the simplest terms, copyright can be defined as an exclusive right to 'copy' certain intellectual works created by a person.

* Guest Faculty, National Law College, Shimoga.

"Copyright" according to Black's Law Dictionary, is the right in literary property as recognized and sanctioned by the positive law[2]. An intangible incorporeal right granted to the author or originator of certain literary or artistic production, whereby he is invested for a specified period with the sole and exclusive privilege of multiplying copies of the same and publishing and selling them.

The statuary definition of copyright is that, it is the exclusive right to do or authorize other/s to do certain acts in relation to;

1. Literary, dramatic or musical works;
2. Artistic works;
3. Cinematograph films; and
4. Sound recording[3].

The term 'copyright' is often referred to as 'bundle of rights' including the exclusive right to reproduce the work in copies, to prepare derivative works based on the copyrighted work, and to perform or display the work publicly[4].

Earlier copyright was given to the authors/publishers of the books (literature)[5]. Later the protection was enormously extended to cover many intellectual creations such as, engravings[6], textile designs[7], sculptures[8], paintings, drawings and photographs[9], dramatic works[10], musical works[11], and so on. The latest addition to its lengthy list is the computer programme[12].

In the case of literary, dramatic, musical and artistic works in order to get copyright protection, they must be "original". This requirement does not apply to the works of cinematographic film and sound recordings. The materials available on the internet, therefore. must pass the test of originality in order to claim copyright over it.

Copyright subsists in India under Copyright Act, 1957 and begins automatically from the moment the work comes into existence (publication) without the need to comply with the requirement of registration[13]. Neither registration nor a claim to copyright in the work requires to be expressly made (eg. Copyright reserved), nor some reasonable notice asserting the claim to copyright in the work (e.g.Ó)[14] need be made. Therefore, copyright subsists in all the materials available on the internet. The copyright protection lasts for the life of the author *plus* sixty years[15].

Internet: Meaning and Functions

Started as a media to exchange the information, Internet has spread its tentacles all over the globe covering most of the activities within its sphere. The credit must go to Tim Berners Le, who created software that allowed other network providers to link on the net and to locate stored information with a single address known as the "world wide web" (www), for both commercial use and private use.

Internet is a network of networks. It is an electronic communication network that connects computer networks and organizational computers and facilitates around the world information exchange[16]. Internet is also a large global network comprised of thousands of smaller networks. The "www" is one element of the net.

The utility of the Internet has reached such a height as many things are capable of being converted into digits by using electronic technology (digitization) and the same can be uploaded, transmitted or obtained through Internet. With the emergence of commerce, commercial activities are done through Internet more conveniently and expeditiously. Now many software, study materials, music, wallpapers, ring tones and many more things are available online and any person can access them from any part of the world.

As the Internet has grown, the problem of on line infringement of IPR has assumed gigantic proportions and developed into an economically significant issue[17]. The net has allowed the content community, comprising of researchers, educators, artists, publishers, music and entertainment industry, to expand their market at an unprecedented rate. The same technology allows any anonymous and invisible pirates to copy and disseminate instantaneously any thing that is available on the Internet[18].

Copyrightable Materials on the Net

Since net is the world's largest repository of information[19], many copyright works are available on the Internet. Foremost and the most significant among them is the 'Computer Software'. Besides this news stories, novels, screenplay, graphics, pictures, Usenet massages, the unique underlying design of web page and its contents including links, original texts, graphics, audio, video, html, urml and unique markup language sequences, list of websites compiled by an individual or organization, even e-mails and all other unique elements that make up the original nature of the material are copyrightable on the Net. Therefore the reality is everything on the Net is protected by copyright law[20].

Copyrighting Infringement on Net

What amounts to copyright infringement? Copyright is infringed when any person reproduces the work of another or publishes, communicates to the public, or performs the work in public, makes adaptations and translation of the work and doing of any of the acts in relation to a substantial part of the work. The requirement is that the reproduction, publication etc., should be done without the consent or license of the owner of such copyright[21].

Materials available on the net are subject to infringement when they are downloaded without the permission of its creator. In software field, it is popularly known as 'online piracy', when software is downloaded from the web and installed but not paid for[22]. Though password system is introduced, those passwords are also decoded by using dubious techniques. As the technology is advancing, newer avenues are being opened for the infringers. The following are some of the new ways of infringement:

- *Catching and Proxy Catching*[23]

Catching is storing of web pages in computers memory at user level or server level. It is the service provided on which the website is stored on automatically. It makes a copy of it and holds it accessible for the users computer where it is stored by the web browser software either in the RAM, the hard drive or any other storage facility. Proxy catching takes place where user's service provider might keep a copy of the site in order to provide fast access to that page for the next time to one of his clients who wishes to access this site. When the author's work, the web site, is reproduced several times there may be infringing acts.

- *Providing links*[24].

HTTP (Hyper Text Transfer Protocol) as such facilitates linking of one web site with another without the knowledge or consent of the owner of the linked website. Linking raises questions whether the link provider is liable for copyright infringement or not? This issue was considered by the English Court in *Shetland Times Ltd. Vs. Dr. Jonathon Wills*[25]. In this case one of the two online newspapers had provided a link (called hyperlink) to the many stories published in the other newspaper, without the consent of the proprietor of the latter newspaper. Therefore it became easy for the online newsreaders to read the stories in other website just by 'clicking' on the mouse. Moreover the headlines and the links created were also the copy of the headlines in the website of another.

It was held that the 'linking' alone does not constitute infringement. Regardless of any provisions of copyright law, there is no barrier to prevent the site owners permitting others to link to their materials. Regardless of whether sites are designed for academic, commercial or personal purposes, it will be a rare site developer who does not wish to receive "visitors"[26].

There is an argument that the materials available on the net are in the public domain since the creator of such work posted that work to the Internet to make it available freely, to anyone without restriction. But this argument cannot be regarded as correct as to download or to reproduce the material, one ought to obtain license (which should be in the written form) from the owner of such copyrighted material[27]. Therefore it can be stated that unregulated copying on the Net amounts to copyright infringement[28].

Fair Use and Abuse

Copyright law tolerates some of the acts which otherwise amount to "abuse" of copyright of the authors. This system is provided to enable the reproduction/use of the copyrighted works for certain public purposes, for the private study and research and promotion of education.

A lengthy list has been provided under S.52 of the Copyright Act, 1957, which enumerates the acts not amounting to copyright infringement. First among them is "fair dealing". The fairness should be decided in the light of the circumstances. If any of the literary[29], dramatic, musical or artistic work is made use of by any person other than the author for the purpose of private use, including research, criticism or review of that work or of any other work, there is no infringement of copyright. The list of exception goes on like, fair dealing for the purpose of reporting of current events, reproduction of the copyrighted material for the judicial proceedings, or for the use of legislature, and so on. The Copyright (Amendment), Act 1999 extended the list of acts amounting to infringement in respect of computer programmes[30] or acts in relation to computer. It has, interalia, provided that making of copies or adaptation of the computer programme from a personally-legally obtained copy for the non-commercial personal use does not result in the infringement.

Further, using of any information relating to software in order to operate newly created software or the observation study or test of function of a computer programme also does not amount to copyright infringement. Many times the 'purpose' for which the copied material is used determines whether there is an infringement or not.

Infringement Liability

Liability for the copyright infringement on the Net can fall upon the infringer himself or upon the Internet Service Provider (ISP)[31]. As we have seen, the person who downloads or catches from the Net copyrighted materials, without the consent of the owner of the copyright, is liable for the copyright infringement. Because of inherent difficulties of enforcing copyright against individual Internet Users world wide, the copyright owners found the answer to this problem in placing legal liability for the copyright infringement on those who allow and enable Internet Pirates to exist namely, the ISPs[32].

ISPs can be brought under the provision of S.51(a)(ii) of the Copyright Act, 1957 for the online copyright infringement. According to this section, if any person 'permits for profit' another person to use 'any place' to communicate any work to the public, when such communication constitutes infringement, or facilitates such infringement under certain conditions, such person may be held liable for such act.

ISPs allow their servers and telecommunication facilities for storing user material and for transmitting such material. The computer servers and other telecommunication facilities are actually located at their business premises and hence they would verily come under expression 'any place', used in the Statue. The provisions relating to the ISPs are specifically enumerated in the Information Technology Act,

2000, where an Internet service provider is referred to as the 'network service provider'. The Act specifically imposes liability on the ISPs, interalia, for the copyright infringement. Accordingly, an ISP may be held liable for any third party information or data made available to him by any other person. He can escape from liability, if he proves the offence or contravention was committed without his knowledge or he had exercised all due diligence to prevent such violation of copyright[33].

However it seems practically difficult for an ISP to filter and police every web page he carries. Hence there is a fear of such provisions of law often remaining a 'dead letter' in the statue books.

The real online copyright infringer is not immune from the liability. Section 43(a) of the IT Act is designed to prevent such persons from infringing acts. According to this Section, if any person accesses or secures access to a computer, computer system or computer network or downloads, copies, extracts any data, database or information from it, including information or data held or stored in any other medium, without the permission of the owner or any other person who is in charge of it, he shall be liable to pay damages by way of compensation not exceeding *one crore* Rupees to the person so affected which is deterrent enough to prevent copyright violation. However while determining the compensation, the amount of gain, and such other things must be taken into consideration.

The liability under Copyright Act falls under two categories; Civil and criminal. As for as the former is concerned, the remedies may be injunction, damages or accounts for profit. In the case of the latter, normally, imprisonment for a term between six months and three years can be imposed. In addition to this the fine amount between fifty thousand and two lakhs shall also be imposed upon the infringer[34].

Challenges

Challenges before the authors of the online copyrighted materials are manifolds. Foremost among them is the policing of the Net. As rightly remarked in the *Religious Technology center* v *Netcom Online communication Services Inc.,*[35] (case), Internet is everywhere yet it is nowhere. Unlike the bookseller's shop, now, through Internet, infringement is more a silent and private act. As Internet has reached the PCs and even Mobile Handsets, it has become very difficult to curb such infringing acts.

Yet another challenge in the field is pertaining to the issue of jurisdiction. As Internet cannot be confined to any geographical boundaries, testing of an act, whether it amounts to infringement and if it does, how to brought him under the clutches of law, i.e., where should he be tried, becomes a tricky debatable question.

The absence of the geographical boundaries may give rise to a situation that the material legal in the country where it is posted will violate the laws of another country where it is received.[36] This process is further made complicated due to the absence of a uniform and harmonized law governing the jurisdictional aspect of the disputes arising out of the use of Internet.

However, this issue of jurisdiction is bravely addressed under the Information Technology Act, 2000. Section 1(2) read with S.75 of the said Act provide for the extra territorial application of its provisions. Thus, if a person (including a foreign national) violates the copy right of a person by means of a computer, computer system located in India, he would be liable under the provisions of the Act.

This long arm jurisdictional provision is not something revolutionary. Many countries of the world are pursuing this type of provision and also this provision is in conformity with the mandate of the United Nations Commission on International Trade Law (UNCITRAL).

Despite of this type of provision, it cannot be said with certainty that the country to which the infringer of copyright belongs fully cooperate with the country where the infringement takes place.

Conclusion

While the technological progress is a boon, it comes with a host of problems. Vulnerability of the copyright law in the Internet media has been provoking the legal fraternity to come out with the sophisticated legal measures to tackle the problems posed by the Internet. However it seems unlikely that the contemporary laws are capable enough to withstand the challenges posed by the Internet. Due to this inability technological problems are addressed through technical measures for e.g. the encription, the use of passwords or special login procedures, anti copying devices, electronic watermarks, etc. Various experiments with the electron copyright management system are underway or have already been completed. Law can also take the assistance of the technology in policing the net.

Jurisdictional problem can also be solved by entering into multilateral agreements and conventions (as the European Union has) involving all the countries of the world. Similarly enacting the uniform laws would also ease the inconsistencies when the infringement is committed. Copyright consciousness should be created in the minds of the website owners and the persons dealing with the Internet. The most appropriate is that one should mind his duty-not to violate the copyright (s) of others.

NOTES

1. B.L. Wadera, "Patent, Copyright, Trademarks, Designs", 2000 Edn. p.
2. Quoted in ibid, p.
3 See, sec.14 of the Copyright Act,1957.

4. Nandan Kamath, "Law Relating To Computers, Internet & E-Commerce-A Guide to Cyber Laws" (Universal Law Publishing Co. Ltd.,: Delhi) 2000, p. 152.
5. First ever legislation to protect the copyright was enacted in the Reign of Anne i.e., Copyright Act of 1970, in England. see W.R. Cornish, "Intellectual Property: Patents, Copyright, Trademark and Allied Rights" (Sweet & Maxwell: London) Fourth Edition, (1999) p. 338.
6. Got statuary protection in 1734 & 1766 (England).
7. In 1787 (England).
8. In 1789 & 1814 (England).
9. In 1862 (England).
10. In 1833 (England).
11. In 1842 (England).
12. "Computer programme" means, a set of instructions expressed in words, codes, schemes or any other form, including a machine-readable medium, capable of causing a computer to perform a particular task or achieve a particular result. Added in 1994 to the Copyright Act, 1957 by way of sec.2 (ffc).
13. However, copyright Act provides for the registration of copyright. It is, however, not a condition precedent to have claim over the copyright. See sec.44-50A.
14. Bushan Tilak Kaul, "Copyright Protection: Some Hassels and Hurdles" *Journal of Indian Law Institute*, Vol. 46: 2 (2004) p. 239.
15. See secs. 22-29.Copyright Act, 1957.
16. Available @ www.skyviewgroup.com/glossary.htm.
17. Raman Mittal "On line Copyright infringement Liablility of ISPs" Journel of Indian Law Institute (2004) Vol. 46:2, p. 288.
18. Ibid.
19. www.nixonpeabody.com/copyright_articles.asp.
20. http://mason.gmu.edu/~montesin/er-internet.htm.
21. See, Sec.51, Copyright Act, 1957 also see S.R.Myneni, 'Law of Intellectual Property' (Asia Law House: Hyderabad) 2001. First Edn. pp.118-120.
22. Ian J. Lloyd, "Information Technology Law" (Butterworth's Landon) 2000, 3rd Edn, p. 39.

23. See, S.M. Bhaskar & R.C.Tripathi. "The Electronic Transactions and Intellectual Property Rights: A leed for Digital time sampling" JILI Vol. 46:2, 2004 p. 208.
24. Ibid.
25. 1997, SLT 669.
26. For an elaborate commentary, see Ian Lloyd, note 22. Supra p. 439-40.
27. Which is contemplated under the Copyright Act, 1957.
28. However a long list of acts, enumerated u/s 52 provide immunity from the 'infringement'. See under the heading "Fair Use & Abuse", *infra.*
29. "Literary work" includes computer programmes, tables & compilations including computer database. Sec.2 (y) Copyright Act.
30. For the definition of the 'computer programme', See, F.N.12, *supra.*
31. An ISP is an entity that connects people to the internet & provides other related services such as web building & hosting .An ISP has the equipment & the communication line access required have a point of presence in the net for the geographic area served.
32. Raman Mittal, supra note.17, p. 288.
33. See sec. 79(1), Information Technology Act, 2000.
34. See sec. 53-A, Copyright Act, 1957.
35. 907, F. Supp. 1361 (1995).
36. Praveen Dalal, "The Long arm Jurisdiction of Courts regarding Copy Right Law in India": Journal of Intellectual Property Rights: Vol.9, Nov. 2004, p. 561.

6 EVOLUTION OF LAW ON INDUSTRIAL DESIGNS

*Chandrakanthi L.**

Introduction

Consumers are often influenced in their choice not only by practical utility and efficiency., but by the appearance of an article. Many people blindly choose an article, which catches their eye by appearance. Some look for artistic merit. some are attracted by a design, which is strange or bizarre. Hence, design of goods increase profits by attracting customers. Producers hunt for an attractive design, which will increase sales. Some intellectuals do hard work by putting much thought, time and expenditure to find a design for a particular article which will increase sales.

Therefore Industrial design as a form of endeavor, and as part and parcel of the business of manufacture, is something which has existed ever since the production of useful article engaged the attention of man from the days of the ancient civilizations, through the middle ages, the eighteenth century and Victorian era, down to the present day thoughts and efforts have continually been devoted to the outline and the ornamentation of the article produced

* Lecturer, Sarada Vilasa Law College, Mysore - 4.

sometimes more consciously, at times less consciously. The designer, who in earlier days was often the craftsmen himself, has sought to blend the efficiency of the article for its purpose with the appeal which is the finished product must make to the eye of its observer. If design of goods is to be encouraged, others of the fruits of their labour must protect those responsible for producing designs against the promiscuous taking. To this end, Industrial designs have been safeguarded by legislation for a great many years. The method chosen has been to confer copyright in their work upon the owner of such designs.

Meaning and Definition of Industrial Design

A Design is something, which is applied to an article, but is not the article itself. An article to which the design is to be applied must be something, which is to be delivered to the purchaser as a finished good. The Buildings and Structures are not articles within the definition of design. But portable structures or models, which are sold as finished articles, may be the subject matter for registration of design. *Section 2(5) of Designs Act 1911 (Indian) Defines Industrial design as follows:*

"Means the exclusive right to apply a design to any article in any class in which the design is registered." It means only the features of shape, configuration, pattern or ornament applied to any article by any industrial process or means whether manual, mechanical or chemical, separate or combined, which in the finished article appeal to and judged solely by the eye, but does include any mode or principle of construction or anything which is in substance a mere mechanical device, and does not include any trade mark defined *in clause (v) of sub section (1) of the Section (2) of the Trade and Merchandise Mark Act. 1958 or property mark as defined in section 479 of the Indian Penal Code.*

From the definition it is clear that the definition is exclusive and only those which have the following characteristics can be brought under the purview of the design namely;

- There should be a definite shape, configuration, pattern or ornament,
- Such shape, configuration, pattern or ornament should be applied to any article,
- Such application to be made by any industrial process or means whether manual, mechanical or chemical, separate or combined,
- And more important such application gives a finished article that appeals to and judged solely by the eye. And Design does not include-
    - Any mode or principle of construction or
    - Mere Mechanical designs and
    - Not a Trade Mark defined under *section 2(1) (v) of the Trade and Merchandise Marks Act 1958 or property mark under section 479 of the Indian penal code.*

Requirements of Registered Industrial Design

Design Must be Applied to Articles

A design is something which is applied to an article and is not the article itself. A piece of paper, on which a pattern is drawn cannot be a subject matter for registration of design. But a paper on which is drawn a three dimensional object with the pattern shown on it may be registered as design because here the design is a representation of the article, on which the pattern is applied. Similarly if the drawing is that of an article like a bottle, vase, chair, table, a motor body it would be registrable as design of it is novel. Here what may be registered is the shape of an article and the drawing on the paper is only convenient representation of the shape of the article. An article to which the design is to be applied must be something which is to be delivered to the purchaser as a finished article, thus in general buildings and structures like a petrol filling station cannot be considered as article within the definition of design. But portable structures which are sold as finished articles may be subject matter for registration of design. The design of a part of an article is not registrable as a design unless the part is sold separately as an article. There are four features relevant to an Industrial design. They are shape, configuration, pattern and ornament. The term shape and configuration refer to the form of an article and is usually three dimensional in nature. Pattern and ornament are decorative features ordinarily applied to the surface of the articles in the case of wallpaper, textile and playing cards. It is two dimensional in nature pictures or devised printed on packages are also considered Industrial Design.

Appeal to the Eye

The definition of design refers to features of shape etc., which in the finished article appeal to and are judged solely by the eye. This shows that not all shapes or configurations or patterns are registrable designs. The features should appeal to the eye and should be judged by the eye and not by any functional considerations. The eye must be the eye of the customer on a visual test. The test involves two steps;

- Whether aesthetic considerations would normally be taken into account to material extent in relation to that type of article and
- Whether aesthetic considerations would be taken into account in relation to the particular article in question.

There must be a special peculiar, distinctive, significant or striking appearance. Something which catches the eye and in this sense appeals to the eye. The customer must be influenced only by the eye and not by the suitability of the article for any particular purpose. It is not necessary that all the features of the design should be visible when it is actually used for the purpose for which the article was brought, For example, an egg shaped chocolate with the exterior and interior having different colours.

Novelty and Originality

A design in order to be registrable must be both new and ori8ginal not previously published in India. Natural objects applied as designs may be novel or original for example the representation of a tree or a building on a spoon may be considered new or original. Here the novelty consists in the application of a drawing or design taken from a material source to an article. The words new or original involve the idea of novelty either in the pattern, shape, or ornament itself or in the way in which an old pattern shape, or ornament is to be applied to same special subject matter. A Paper weight in the shape of an animal may be new and original.. In order to be registrable the design should be substantially different from pre-existing designs applied to the class of article. The novelty or originality of a particular part of the article may be sufficient to import the character of novelty and originality to the whole. A combination of known designs may be considered novel if the appearance of the combination as a whole is new. Colour may form an element in a design, but colour or colouring as such does not constitute a design, unless change of colour create a new pattern or ornament.

No Prior Publication

The design must not be previously published in India though the word publication has not been defined by the *Design Act, 1911* to constitute publication, a design must be available to the public or it has been shown or disclosed to some person who is not bound to keep it secret. For example the display of a design on a skirt of a model in a fashion show constitutes publication of the design. In India, registration of the design in the first instance will be for a period of five years which can be extended twice by five years at time.

Evolution of Industrial Design

In India till 1911 there was no regulation regarding Industrial Design. In the year 1911 an Act called Industrial Design Act, 1911 was passed in India by borrowing all the principles in English Law for the same purpose.

So, the law of designs in India had been controlled by *Designs Act 1911* and Rules made there under in 1933 as the Design rules and now it is controlled by *Design Act, 2000.*

In order to trace the origin of the design we need to focus on the English Law. The Development of statutes with reference to the design is as follows.

Designing and Printing of License, etc., Act, 1787

This is the first Act dealing with copyright in Industrial Designs. It was concerned with designs for certain specified textile materials namely linens, cottons, calicos and muslins. It gave to designers, printers and proprietors of new and original patterns for the materials in question the sole right and liberty of printing and reprinting them for two months from the date of first publication, provided the name of the proprietor was marked on each piece. An infringer was liable to a special action on the case, damages and costs. This Act as a nature of experiment stands in force for one year only.

Designing and Printing of License Act, 1789

It was passed in the year 1789 and was in force till *July 1794.* The provision of this Act were almost similar to those of the *1787 Act* except the period of protection which was extended to *three months* from the date of publication.

Copyright of Designs Act, 1839

The legislature again turned its attention to industrial designs, and during the next 50 years a series of statutes was passed, gradually extending the boundaries of copyright in these works. This Act extended the protection, beyond the confines of the textiles trade and laid foundations for the law of registered designs as it exists today. It gave protection to every new or original design, as follows;

- For the pattern or print, to be either worked into or worked on or printed on or painted on any Article of Manufacture being a Tissue or Textile Fabric, except Lace, and also except Linens, cottons, calicoes, and Muslins...
- For the modeling, or the casting, or the Embossment, or the chasing, or the Engraving, or for any other kind of Impression or ornament on any Article of Manufacture, not being a Tissue or Textile Fabric...
- For the shape or configuration of any Article of Manufacture...
    - This Act includes textiles as well as "any article of Manufacture."
    - It protects ornamentation placed upon an article and also shape in which it was made. It was introduced for the first time as a system of registration.

A new principle was introduced, according to which the proprietor when published his work, copyright in it automatically accrued to him. This principle is still central to one aspect of the protection afforded to industrial designs.

Designs Act, 1842

It repealed the earlier Acts and consolidated and amended the law relating to the copyright of Designs for ornamenting Articles of Manufacture. This Act replaced the legislation which it repealed by a new set of provisions, which, whilst embodying most of what was contained in the earlier Acts, considerably extended their scope. This Act in particular extended the protection to substances also. Any new and original design, "applicable to the ornamenting, of any Article of Manufacture, or any Substance, artificial or natural. Whether applicable for the pattern, or for the shape or configuration, or for the ornament thereof; was now made the subject of copyright.

Designs for sculpture and other things within the provisions of sculpture copyright Acts, which would otherwise have fallen within the provisions of new Act, however , were specifically excluded from its provisions. This Act divided the possible articles of manufacture and substances into classes. and further increased the remedies for infringement, but these were as yet obtainable only if the actual application of the design had taken place within UK.

Copyright of Designs (Amendment) Act, 1843

This Act recited that, whereas by the Act of 1842 the sole right had been given to the proprietor of certain new and original designs to apply them to the "ornamenting" of any Article of Manufacture or any Substance, it was expedient to extend the protection of the Act to designs not of an ornamental character. Therefore copyright should subsist in *"any new original design for any Article of Manufacture having reference to some purpose of utility,"* as far as such design should be for the shape or configuration of the Article.

Copyright of Designs Act, 1850

This Act gave overlapping protection for sculptures that the Act empowered the proprietor of any sculpture, model, copy or cast within the protection of the sculpture copyright Acts" to apply to the Registrar of Designs for registration of his work, for the whole or any part of the term during which copyright might exist under the sculpture Copyright Acts. Sculpture Copyright Acts, 1797 and 1814 provided that any person who should *"make or cause to make any new and original sculpture, or model, or copy, or cast of the Human Figure or Human Figures, or of any Bust or Busts, or of any part or parts of the Human Figure, clothed in drapery or otherwise, or of any animal combined with the Human Figure or otherwise, or of any subject being matter of Invention in Sculpture, or of any Alto or Basso Relieveo representing any of the matters or things hereinbefore mentioned..."* should have the sole right and property therein for 14 years from the date of first publication. This Act remained in force till the passing of the copyright Act 1911 when it was repealed. Two further Acts dealing with industrial designs were passed, in 1858 and 1861, but there were not of major importance.

Fine Arts Copyright Act 1862

This Act had been made to protect ordinary drawings and paintings. This Act provided that the author, being a British subject, or resident within the Dominions of the Crown, of every original painting, drawing and photograph and his assigns should have the sole and exclusive right of, *"copying, engraving, reproducing and multiplying such painting or drawing and the design thereof, or such photograph and the negative thereof by any means and of any size for the term of the natural life of such author and seven years after his death."*

Copyright of Designs Act 1875

This Act gave the powers and duties to the Board of Trade. Under this Act various Designs were transferred to patent office, through the Design Branch for which registration is now carried out.

In 1883 a single consolidating and amending Act was passed embracing both of these subjects, as well as Trade Marks. Hence, copyright in Industrial Designs having become associated with patents for invention and which were directed to be registered at the patent office.

Patents and Designs Act 1907 and Copyright Act 1911

The Copyright Act 1911 was a measure of far-reaching importance. It repealed nearly 18 existing copyrights legislation, most of them substantially in toto, which had been accumulating over a period of two centuries. Now, every branch of subject was brought within the four corners of two statutes i.e., the Copyright Act 1911 and Patents and Designs Acts 1907-1946, regulated the position from 1911 until 1949. In the year 1949 one more registered designs were separated from the patents by Registered Designs Act 1949. This Act amended the definition of a design and the abolition of classification, both of which materially affected the validity as well as the scope of many registered designs. A discussion is made over it in the later part of the article.

Effect of Copyright Act, 1911 on Overlapping Protection

A substantial increase in overlap between industrial designs and other forms of artistic copyright was created in this Act. It was intentional in part and in part it was by oversight. Work of Sculpture acquired copyright as artistic works under this Act, in place of the copyright enjoyed under the Sculpture Copyright Act1814, which was repealed. So, the sculptures ceased to be excluded from registration under the Patents and Designs Act,1907 and sculptures to fall within the scope of both the Copyright Act and the Patents and Designs Act 1907. The Copyright Act, 1911 includes *"works of artistic craftsmanship" and "architectural works of art."* All works of artistic craftsmanship and some architectural works of art, would appear to have been *"designed"* within the meaning of the Patents and Designs Act,1907. Under this Act the scope of artistic copyright was extended to cover reproduction of the copyright work *"in any material from whatsoever"*. After the Act, 1911, reproduction of the drawing in the form of an industrial article would be an infringement not only of industrial design right under the Patents and Designs Acts, but also of artistic copyright under the Copyright Act.

Section 22 of Copyright Act, 1911 limits the extent of the overlap of artistic copyright with Industrial Designs. which it had potentially created by formulating the provisions of the Copyright Act 1911 in wide terms. However this section gave rise to certain problems of interpretation and resulting litigation.

This section interpreted by the rules 89 of the Designs Rules 1920, was that a work was capable of registration as a design, and was reproduced or intended to be reproduced in more than 50 single articles or was to be applied to any of the materials specified in part (b) of the rule, it received no protection under the Act 1911. If however, the intention was to reproduce the design in less than 50 articles, the Act still applied.

The obvious interpretation of the effect of section is that copyright is denied to an artistic work in two circumstances;

- if it is created with the original intention of embodying design to be industrially reproduced;
- if it is not with that original intention, and if the Copyright owner subsequently permits it to be reproduced;

Copyright Act, 1956

This Act was brought to reform the provisions against over lap under *Copy right Act, 1911.* Under this Act, the basic policy remained as the same, but instead of "all or nothing" approach to subsistence of copyright in *section 22,* a new and more subtle approach was adopted by *section 10 of the Copyright Act, 1956.* Hence, the effect of section 10 of the Act,1956 was to make the rights of the owner of the copyright in an artistic work no longer dependent upon the author's intentions at the time he made the work. His rights of exploitation in the industrial field were now made dependent upon his obtaining registration of his work as an industrial design under *Designs the Registered Act,1949.* So that prior publication of a design created as a purely artistic work should not destroy the novelty and originality of the design and thus prevent to its registration, the Registered Designs Act, 1949 was amended to protect a copyright owner against the invalidating effect of previous non-industrial exploitation of his own artistic work.

Designs Copyright Act, 1968

This Act amended *Section 10 of the Act, 1956,* to permit artistic copyright to be enforced without restriction for a period of 15 years from the date when the article concerned was first marketed, whether or not a corresponding design had been registered or whether or not such a design had been industrialized but not registered. For those designs which lack any aesthetic merit, the effective protection will be during the age of *author plus 50years in England and the age of author and 60 years in India.*

Designs Law at Present

There are two forms of design rights recognized by the law. One is the registered designs protected under the provisions of the *Registered Designs Act, 1949* ad the other is the functional designs governed by the provisions of the *Copyright, Designs and Patents Act, 1988.*

Registered Design

The law relating to registered designs was substantially modified in line with a harmonizing *Directive as from 9 December 2001* and numerous changes were made to the Registered Designs Act, 1949 by the Registered Designs Regulations 2001. However in real the designs have always been a substantial complexity, amongst other elements due to the influence of copyright. The Design Law is far from straightforward as there is an overlap between the rights and the extent of it, is not clear.

Under section 1 (1) of the Registered Designs Act, 1949 defines *'design'* as *"features of shape, configuration, pattern or ornament applied to any article by an industrial process, being features which in the finished article appeal to and are judged by the eye and there should be no prior publication means it should be 'new'"*. Registration of novel design with an appeal to eye provides its 25 years monopoly to the proprietor.

Under section 1 (2) of the Registered Designs Act changed the definition of design and it says *"the appearance of the whole or a part of a product resulting from the features of, in particular, the lines contours, colours, shape texture or materials of the product or its ornamentation"*. Appearance and visual significance (over all impression) is important for novelty and individual character test and it should be new means no identical design has been made available to the public. The design must be applied to a product or an article and registration was limited to the article specified. An unregistered design may be applied to part of article, and related only to aspects of an article. There is no requirement of eye appeal. The right lasts for 10 years from the first marketing of articles made to the design (provided this is within five years of the design). In other cases it lasts for a maximum of 15 years from recording.

Design Right

Design Right has been applied to functional designs. But the overlap/ambiguity has continuously crept between the Registered Designs and Designs Right. The Registered designs have a requirement of appearance and individual character, but excluded the components/parts hidden from the normal use such as *"under the bonnet"* part of the vehicles and these may be subject to the Designs Right. There is no valid reason why a new aesthetic or a new design having individual character, when it relates to the shape and configuration of some article, as it can be expected to registered as a design. Such as a design for a drinking tankard which is a new shape or which has a new shape of handle, made industrially or hand-made and which, its makes hopes, people will buy for the visual attractiveness of its shape. This should qualify for both rights. There is no provisions for separate one of these rights in favour of the other. It proved in the presumption of section *224 of CDPA 1988* that an assignment of the registered design automatically carries with it an assignment of the design right where the proprietor of the Registered Design and the owner of the Design Right are one and the same person.

Overlapping of Copyrights and Designs Law

Design law overlap with copyright protection. In case of the drawing if a person copied an article, even he had never seen and no matter how mundane the article was, he would infringe the copyright in the drawing. The design may overlap with sculptures and works of artistic craftsmanship. The design may be recorded in a document in which copyright subsists as a literary work, including computer data, or the design document may be a photograph. CDPA through section *236 and 51(1)* tried to reduce this overlap. Where a work consisting of or including a design is itself protected by copyright, the design right is suppressed in favour of copy right. For example works of artistic craftsmanship like a hand-made wooden to or an item of jewellary. And if an article is made to the design or a copy of such an article is made, does not infringe the copyright in a design document(any record of the design including drawings, written descriptions, photographs and computer data) or model recording or embody but infringe the design right respectively.

International law of Industrial Designs

TRIPS Agreement, Section 4 of the part II of the agreements covers Industrial Design requirements of the protection according to *Article 25* is that members shall independently created Industrial Design that as new or original and it may not be considered as new or original if they do not significantly differ from known designs or combinations of known design features. This protection is not extending to designs dictated essentially by technical or functional considerations. In case of textile designs members are free to secure protection either through Industrial Design law or copyright law. According to *Article 26* duration of protection shall be available atleast for 10 years. Other than the owner, third parties can also be make use of Industrial Design with owners consent.

Paris Convention, 1967

Under this convention along with Patent, Trade marks, Service Marks, Trade

Names protection of Industrial Designs is also considered. For the registration, person has to duly file an application in one of the countries of the union. All members of *WTO* have to follow the provisions of Paris Convention which are related for the protection. Industrial Property as Industrial Design is an Intellectual Property. As Paris Convention is part of the *TRIPS* Agreement India is though not even a member of Paris Convention, she has taken steps for protection of Industrial Design.

Hague Agreement, 1960

The contracting States constitute a separate union for the international deposit for Industrial Designs. Paris Union members are eligible for membership in the Hague Union. The protection requirements are novelty, distinctiveness. For protection along with an application one or more photographs or graphic representation of the design shall be made term of protection is first five years and then renewable for every five years.

Lacarno Agreement, 1968

The International Bureau of WIPO administers this agreement in order to bring uniformity to the classification of Industrial Design to facilitate searchers for novelty and priority.

UK and other Common Wealth Countries over the proceeding twenty years have come to rely upon copyright protection against limitations of the form and appearance of their products. The above are some of the salient features of tortuous history of the subject in Britain. Industrial Design in the earlier periods had been merged with copyright law. But gradually Industrial Designs have been shifted to Paten Act. Though by taking its own course of procedure now Industrial design has got its own independent laws for its protection, if not possible to over come completely from copyright laws. It is also be noted that it is not possible to dispense absolutely from the copyright laws. Any how to it has achieved it independence to a better extent. It has not made a recognizable mark in International field, it has to reach the expectation of the union countries for example community design protection etc,.

REFERENCES

Catherine Colston (1999), "Principles of Intellectual Property Law", Great Britain, Cavendish Publishing Limited.

David I Bainbridge, (2003), "Intellectual property", 5th Edition, Delhi, Pearson Education Pte. Ltd.

Lionel Bently Brad Sherman, (2001), "Intellectual Property Law", Indian Edition, Oxford, University Press.

Raghbir Singh, (2004), "Law Relating to Intellectual Property", Delhi, Universal Publishing Co. Pvt. Ltd.

Salil K. Roy Chowdhury, H.K. Saharay (1999), "Law of Trademarks, Copyright, Patent and Designs", Calcutta, Kalmal Law House.

S.R. Myneni (2001), "Law of intellectual Property" I Edition, Hyderabad, Allahabad Law House.

Vikas Vashishth, (2002), "Law and Practice of Intellectual Property in India", 2nd Edition, New Delhi, Bharat Law House.

W.R. Cornish (2001), "Intellectual Property, Patent, Copyright, Trademark and allied Rights", 3rd Edition, New Delhi, Universal Law Publishing Co. Pvt. Ltd.

http. // www.google.com.

Shttp.// www.lawinfo.com.

7 INTELLECTUAL PROPERTY AND HUMAN RIGHTS: IMPLICATIONS OF TRIPS AGREEMENT

*C.S. Somu**

Introduction

Human rights and intellectual property, two bodies of law that were once strangers, are now becoming increasingly intimate bedfellows. For decades the two subjects developed in virtual isolation from each other. But in the last few years, an explosion of international standard setting activities that beginning to map previously uncharted intersections between intellectual property law on the one hand and human rights law on the other[1].

Human rights concerns have been asserted in a number of contexts as counterweights to the expansion of intellectual property rights. Human rights issues are relevant in a range of issues that intersect with intellectual property protection, including: freedom of expression; public health; education and literacy; privacy; agriculture; technology transfer; rights of indigenous peoples. At the same time, creators of intellectual property are asserting human rights bases for the protection and expansion of intellectual property rights.

The TRIPS (Trade-Related Aspects of Intellectual Property Rights) Agreement was negotiated in the context

* SDM-Institute for Management Development Mysore.

of the Uruguay Round of multilateral trade negotiations under the General Agreement on Tariffs and Trade . TRIPS Agreement is the most comprehensive multilateral agreement that sets detailed minimum standards for the protection and enforcement of intellectual property rights and as a result it is a significant step in harmonizing national intellectual property (IP) systems. The Agreement is one of the agreements annexed to the Final Act Embodying the Results of the Uruguay Round of Multilateral Trade Negotiations which came into force in 1995. This means that all members of WTO are bound by the obligations under the TRIPS Agreement.

The World Trade Organization's, TRIPS Agreement, marks the beginning at which Intellectual Property Protection enters into the global period an represents a significant change in the evolutionary direction of Intellectual Property Protection. However, since the implementation of the TRIPS does not adequately reflect the fundamental nature and indivisibility of all human rights, there are apparent conflicts between the Intellectual Property Rights regime embodied in the TRIPS agreement and International Human Rights Law. The current interpretation and implementation of the TRIPS Agreement raises obvious and very serious human rights issues[2].

On 17 August, 2000, the UN Sub-Commission for the Protection and Promotion of Human Rights, adopted a resolution unanimously on "Intellectual Property Rights and Human Rights" noting, *inter alia,* that: *"There are actual or potential conflicts that exist between the implementation of TRIPS and the realization of economic, social and cultural rights* in relation to, *inter alia,* impediments to the transfer of technology to developing countries, the consequences for the enjoyment of the right to food of plant variety rights and the patenting of genetically modified organisms, "biopiracy" and the reduction of communities' (especially indigenous communities) control over their own genetic and natural resources and cultural values, and restrictions on access to patented pharmaceuticals and the implications for the enjoyment of the right to health."

The resolution "affirms that the right to protection of the moral and material interests resulting from any scientific, literary or artistic production of which one is author is, in accordance with article 27(2) of UDHR and article 15(1)(c) of ICESCR, *a human right, subject to limitations in the public interest.*"

It further "declares, however, that since *the implementation of the TRIPS Agreement does not adequately reflect the fundamental nature and indivisibility of all human rights,* including the right of everyone to enjoy the benefits of scientific progress and its applications, the right to health, the right to food and the right to self-determination, *there are apparent conflicts between the intellectual property rights regime embodied in the TRIPS Agreement, on the one hand, and international human rights law,* on the other."

International Bill of Human Rights

Following international instruments constitute the body of international human rights law;

- Universal Declaration of Human Rights, 1948.
- International Covenant on Economic, Social and Cultural Rights, 1966.
- International Covenant on Civil and Political Rights, 1966.
- Optional Protocol to the International Covenant on Civil and Political Rights.
- Second Optional Protocol to the International Covenant on Civil and Political Rights, aiming at the abolition of the death penalty

The Universal Declaration of Human Rights (UDHR) is the most general embodiment of today's international human rights norms. Its provisions have been incorporated into national constitutions, regional conventions, and international covenants—the most important of which are the International Covenant on Civil and Political Rights (ICCPR) and the International Covenant on Economic, Social and Cultural Rights (ICESCR). Intellectual property occupies an ambiguous status in terms of these rights categories, insofar as the right to property is protected under the ICCPR, whereas "the [author's] right to benefit from the protection of the moral and material interests resulting from any scientific, literary or artistic production," is one of the cultural rights enshrined in the ICESCR. Moreover, intellectual properties of cultural significance to minority groups may be seen as aspects of the right to cultural identity under the ICCPR, which further complicates their status. Nonetheless, such categorical ambiguities should not be great cause for concern; the United Nations has repeatedly stated that the two sets of rights are interdependent and indivisible, and most contemporary commentators agree that the distinctions between the categories have been overstated. Although economic, social, and cultural rights have been juridically marginalized in comparison to civil and political rights, both in terms of the institutional frameworks developed for their implementation and in terms of their judicial interpretation, failure to monitor the violation of economic, social, and cultural rights has less to do with the legal obligations established by the ICESCR than with political problems of resolve[3].

Key Human Rights at threat under the TRIPS Regime

Adoption and implementation of TRIPS Agreement has posed threat to the following human rights;

1. Right to Health;
2. Right to Food and Food Security; and

3. Rights of Indigenous and Tribal communities;

Right to Health

Preamble of World Health Organization (WHO) declares that the enjoyment of the highest attainable standard of health is one of the fundamental rights of every human being.

Health is defined in WHO's Constitution as a state of complete physical, mental and social well-being and not merely the absence of disease or infirmity.

Article 25 of the Universal Declaration of Human Rights (UDHR) provides, in paragraph one that:

"Everyone has the right to a standard of living adequate for the health and well-being of himself and of his family, including food , clothing , housing and medical care and necessary social services, and the right to security in the event of employment , sickness, disability , widowhood , old age or other lack of livelihood in circumstances beyond his control...".

Right to Health' actually does not mean 'Right to be healthy' but rather 'the Right to a variety of facilities and conditions necessary for the realisation of the highest attainable standard of health[4] (ICESCR, General Comment 14). Another similar view of 'Right to Health' may be 'The right to the highest attainable standard of health in international human rights law is a claim to a set of social arrangements-norms, institutions, laws, an enabling environment-that can best secure the enjoyment of this right. (WHO).

Art.12 of the ICESCR reads as follows;

1. The State parties to the present covenant recognize the right of everyone to the enjoyment of highest attainable standard of physical and mental health.
2. The steps to be taken by the State Parties to the present covenant to achieve the full realization of this right shall include those necessary:

(a) The provision for the reduction of the still-birth rate and of infant mortality and for the healthy development of child;

(b) The improvement of all aspects of environmental and industrial hygiene;

(c) The prevention, treatment and control of epidemic, endemic, occupational and other diseases;

(d) The creation of conditions which would assure to all medical service and medical attention in the event of sickness.

UN Declaration on Social Progress and Development under Art.19 imposes an obligation on State Parties to make provision for free health services to the whole population and of adequate and curative facilities and welfare and welfare medical services accessible to all.

Content of Right to Health

The UN Committee on International Economic, Social and Cultural Rights–the treaty body responsible for implementing and monitoring ICESCR–has published a General Comment 14 to ICESCR that outlines the content of the international right to health. This General Comment is extensive and quite specific and intended to apply to nations that have ratified the ICESCR. It addresses the content of the right to health and the implementation and enforcement of the right to health. It also provides remedies for individual parties who have been denied the human right to health[5].

General Comment 14 begins with some observations about the normative content of the right to health. Specifically, it states that;

- "the right to health is not to be understood as a right to be *healthy*" and that
- "the right to health contains both freedoms and entitlements."

The General Comment 14 specifies the freedoms and entitlements as follows:

The freedoms include the right to control one's health and body, including sexual and reproductive freedom, and the right to be free from interference, such as the right to be free from torture, non-consensual medical treatment and experimentation. By contrast, the entitlements include the right to a system of health protection which provides equality of opportunity for people to enjoy the highest attainable level of health[6].

General Comment 14, then observes that the right to health extends not only to timely and appropriate health care but also to the underlying determinants of health, such as access to safe and potable water and adequate sanitation, an adequate supply of safe food, nutrition and housing, healthy occupational and environmental conditions, and access to health-related education and information, including on sexual and reproductive health.

These provisions of General Comment 14 indeed prescribe a broad and inclusive conception of the content of the human right to health[7].

Further, General Comment 14 , provides that the health care system of a states party must have certain institutional characteristics to realize the right to health. These include the availability, accessibility, acceptability and quality of needed health care services and facilities. "Availability" means that the states party has sufficient facilities and services for the population given the country's state of development. Services include those that affect the underlying determinants of health, such as safe and potable drinking water. "Accessibility" to health care facilities and services include the four dimensions: non-discrimination, physical accessibility, economic accessibility (affordability), and information accessibility. "Acceptability" means that services and facilities must be respectful of medical ethics and culturally appropriate as well as being designed to respect confidentiality and improve the health status of those served. "Quality" means that services must also be scientifically and medically appropriate and of good quality[8].

TRIPS Agreement and Public Health

Implementation of the TRIPS Agreement gives rise to concerns regarding access to affordable medicines. It is feared that patent protection for pharmaceutical products and processes will have the effect of reducing or eliminating competition from generic production of medicines. The Agreement obliges WTO Members to adopt and enforce high standards of intellectual property rights protection, which are derived from the standards used in developed countries. Implementation of the TRIPS Agreement-by recognizing and strengthening protection of intellectual property rights over pharmaceutical products and processes-may lead to high prices, low access to medicines and a weakening of the mostly generic pharmaceutical industries in the developing countries[9].

Art. 27 (1) of the TRIPS declares that patents shall be available for any invention, whether products or process , in all fields of technology, provided that they are new, involve an inventive step and capable of industrial applications. Granting products patents will have an adverse effect on drug industries which manufacture life saving drugs which are essential for maintaining the health of the public especially in cases like HIV/AIDS patients.

The issue of access to essential medicines replays the original debate between developing and developed countries regarding the TRIPS Agreement. Developed countries continue to maintain that high levels of intellectual property protection provide the necessary incentive for investment in research and development, which is the best guarantee of access to essential medicines for all countries. In contrast, developing countries maintain that strict constructions of the TRIPS Agreement fail to recognize the legitimate interests of intellectual property rights users, especially in the context of crises such as HIV/AIDS[10].

A Declaration on TRIPS and Public Health was issued by a consensus of all WTO members at the Doha Ministerial meeting in Qatar in November 2001. The Declaration provides in part:

"We agree that the TRIPS Agreement does not and should not prevent members from taking measures to protect public health. Accordingly, while reiterating our commitment to the TRIPS Agreement, we affirm that the Agreement can and should be interpreted and implemented in a manner supportive of WTO Members' right to protect public health and, in particular, to promote access to medicines for all."[11]

The Declaration acknowledges that HIV/AIDS, tuberculosis, malaria, and other epidemics are grave public health problems afflicting developing countries. It also reaffirms "the right of the WTO Members to use, to the full, the provisions in the TRIPS Agreement, which provide flexibility for this purpose."

India as a party to ICESCR has an international obligation to protect peoples' right to health. Article 15 (1) (b) of the ICESCR recognizes "right of everyone to enjoy the benefits of scientific progress and its applications". From the international covenants on human rights it is clear that accessibility and availability of drugs are recognized as important components of right to health. The Supreme Court of India recognized the enforceability of right to health within the scope of Art. 21 of the Indian Constitution in Vincent Painkurlangara V Union of India[12]. The Supreme Court often interpreted fundamental rights in consonance with international treaties. Hence, the implementation of product patent should not result in the denial of rights guaranteed under the Constitution of India and the ICESCR. According to Sec.2 (d) and Sec. 2 (f) of Protection of Human Rights Act, 1993 rights under the ICESCR are the rights that the National Human Rights Commission (NHRC) is required to protect[13].

Health is a reflection of a society's commitment to equity and justice. Health and human rights should prevail over economic and political concerns.

Right to Food and Food Security

Food security and the capability of the developing nations to feed its population has been a matter of concern and has remained as a great concern to developing countries even today. Right to food is a human right, protected under international human rights and humanitarian law. Article 25 of UDHR and article 11 of ICESCR[14] are the more authoritative international human rights provisions on the right to food. The right to food is a basic human right as well as a basic human need. It is a component of the right to an adequate standard of living. It is also closely linked to the right to life.

Right to Food has been authoritatively defined in general comment No. 12 of the Committee on Economic, Social and Cultural Rights as follows: "The right to adequate food is realized when every man, woman and child, alone or in community with others, has physical and economic access at all times to adequate food or means for its procurement".

According to the *General Comment No.12,* the right to food also implies three types of obligations-the obligations to respect, protect and to fulfil. The obligations to respect existing access to adequate food requires States parties not to take any measure that result in preventing such access. The obligation to protect requires measures by the State to ensure that enterprises or individuals do not deprive individuals of their access to adequate food. The obligation to fulfil (facilitate) means that States must pro-actively engage in activities intended to strengthen people´s access to and utilization of resources and means to ensure their livelihood, including food security. Finally, whenever an individual or group is unable to enjoy the right to adequate food by the means at their disposal, States have the obligation to fulfil (provide) that right directly[15].

Intellectual Property Rights (IPRs) may by itself not have been a problem as a concept. What has become a contentious issue is the nature of the meaning and interpretation it has taken on in recent times, its contemporary application and its extrapolation beyond mechanical and literary inventions to the biological science and agriculture. This apparent imposition has tended to marginalize weak developing countries as well as impact negatively on their agriculture and food security[16].

Since their independence, many developing countries have experimented with different policy options of agricultural development to achieve food security. In the sixties, the international/national agriculture policy was predicted on the research achievements of the green resolution and the development of high yielding varieties (HYV). The strategy was the adoption and use of improved crop varieties (Mono-culture) complimented with organic fertilizer, water management and crop protection chemicals to endure increased yields and food self-sufficiency. The strategy was underpinned by the establishment of internationally funded agricultural research institutes and a virile foreign aid programme by friendly developed countries[17].

The controversy with the extension of the concept of intellectual property rights to agriculture is highlighted by the simplistic economic importance and interpretation that is sometimes assigned to it. The contradiction is accentuated by the globalization of the concept and the problematic assertion of the TRIPS Agreement suggesting that "Intellectual Property Rights are individual rights". In the African or any other developing nation context, this mere assertion does not make it so. In most parts of the continent, improved varieties (land races) of foods crops cultural stories and practice, traditional knowledge etc are considered as community owned rather than individual property. For example, a bio-resource prospector may collect, identify and create nomenclature for a series of Africa food and medicinal plants and through compilation and authorship of the resultant publication claim exclusive intellectual property rights which excludes the originators from its use. This scenario can be cited for several instances where resource flow from Africa are transferred by external entrepreneurs, authors and inventors through IPR regimes resulting in products priced beyond the reach of those from whom the knowledge originated. There could be worse problems associated with the distributive effect of harmonized IPR regimes. Multionationals are creating new plant varieties using germplasm[18] obtained from developing countries and these new plant varieties may be sold back to these countries resulting in royalty (revenue) out flow from the south to the north in relation to products that would not have been possible without the contribution of the south. In this case, globally harmonized IPR regimes have major implications for access and equitable sharing of benefit. As globalized intellectual property regimes set minimum standards of protection, traditional territorial notions of sovereignty are eroded contrary to the basic tenets of the convention on Biological Diversity (CBD). This is because those who hold large blocks of intellectual property are not sovereign nations but multi-national corporations. With Africa holding less than 1% of the worlds intellectual property rights, it may well be true to infer that the development path of African States will be determined by those IPR owners who together have exclusive right to the worlds stock of knowledge and the technologies associated with it[19]. What is true for African countries in relation to exploitation of intellectual property is also true for almost all the developing countries.

Rights of Indigenous and Tribal Communities

The Working Group on indigenous populations set up in 1972 by the sub-commission on Human Rights Commission of UN has defined 'indigenous people' as follows;

"Indigenous populations are composed of the existing descendants of the peoples who inhibited the present territory of a country wholly or partially at the time when persons of a different culture or ethnic origin arrived there from other parts of the world, overcame them to a non-dominant or colonial situation; who today live more in conformity with their particular social, economic and cultural customs and traditions than with the institutions of the country of which they now form a part, under a state structure which incorporates mainly the national, social and cultural characteristics of their segments of the population which are predominant."

Some of the traits of indigenous and tribal communities are;

(a) descent from population groups present in a given area, most often before modern states or territories were created and before modern borders were defined, and

(b) maintenance of cultural and social identities, and social, economic, cultural, and political institutions separate from mainstream or dominant societies and cultures.

(c) self-identification and identification by others as being part of a distinct indigenous cultural group, and the display of desire to preserve that cultural identity,

(d) a linguistic identity different from that of the dominant society,

(e) social, cultural, economic, and political traditions and institutions distinct from the dominant culture,

(f) economic systems oriented more toward traditional systems of production than mainstream systems, and

(g) unique ties and attachments to traditional habitats and ancestral territories and natural resources in these habitats and territories.

Indigenous peoples also are described with reference to their ways of life. In many cases, indigenous peoples live in separated communities or cultural or ethnic groupings. Such communities and groupings often are located in areas geographically distant from urban centers and often function at the periphery of the political, social, cultural, and economic systems of the dominant or mainstream society. At the same time, however, it is not unusual to find indigenous peoples communities on the fringes of urban areas, comprising indigenous peoples who have migrated but remain distinct from the mainstream. Indigenous peoples communities in a given country can reflect varying degrees of acculturation and integration into the dominant or mainstream society.

Paragraph 29 of the Draft Declaration on the Rights of Indigenous Peoples[20] recognizes that 'Indigenous peoples are entitled to the recognition of the full ownership, control and protection of their cultural and intellectual property. They have right to special measures to control, develop and protect their sciences, technologies and cultural manifestations, including human and other genetic resources, seeds, medicines, knowledge of the properties of fauna and flora, oral tradition, literatures, designs and visual and performing arts.'

The harmonization of intellectual property rights laws to ensure that these are consistent with TRIPS could be disastrous for indigenous peoples. It is similar to how national laws and policies on land, forests, governance, etc. were imposed on indigenous peoples without any consideration whatsoever on customary laws in these same areas. In this case, however, it is an international body, the WTO, which is acting like national governments. In this case diverse laws and policies regarding IPR protection have to be recast in the mold of TRIPS[21].

The key impact that TRIPS has on indigenous peoples is that it denigrates, undermines, and discriminates against indigenous ways of thinking and behaving. Intellectual property rights are monopoly rights given to individuals or legal persons (such as transnational corporations) who can prove that the inventions or innovations they made are novel, involved an innovative step and are capable of industrial application. Indigenous knowledge and cultural heritage are usually collectively evolved and owned. If indigenous peoples have to use western IPRs to protect their own knowledge and innovations, they will have to identify individual inventors. This will push scrupulous indigenous individuals to claim ownership over potentially profitable indigenous knowledge which will cause the further disintegration of communal values and practices. It can also cause infighting between indigenous communities over who has ownership over a particular knowledge or innovation[22].

The concept of exclusive ownership and alienability which is inherent in TRIPs will have to be internalized and imbibed by indigenous peoples even if it goes against their usual practice of making available such knowledge for the common good. The identity and survival of indigenous peoples as distinct peoples depends to a large extent on the age-old practice of common sharing of some resources, knowledge and skills which are not alienable. With TRIPS, indigenous peoples will now have to think of how their knowledge will be protected against so-called "biopirates." Sharing of knowledge becomes a dangerous proposition because it might be appropriated by those who have the capacity to use the system to claim exclusive ownership over such knowledge and commercialize it[23].

In reviewing the genesis of intellectual property protection and the main purpose of this special kind of legislation, it is clear that the current intellectual property law model is the product of Western traditions rooted in individualism, specifically, ownership by private individuals. This differs from the concept of ownership that pertains to the creative works of indigenous cultures, which are the result of collective efforts. As a result of viewing all works of art from an accidental perspective, the focus given to intellectual property legislation is necessary narrow and limited in scope[24].

Conclusion

Unless human rights advocates provide an effective intellectual and organizational counterweight to economic interests, the intellectual property landscape will be reshaped in the years ahead without adequate consideration of the impact on human rights. The development of a global economy in which intellectual property plays a central role underscores the need for the human rights community to claim the rights of the author, creator and inventor, whether an individual, a group or a community, as a human right. It is equally important for human rights advocates to protect the moral interests and rights of the community to secure access to this knowledge. Yet another human rights consideration is whether relevant laws identifying rights to creative works and scientific knowledge and determining the nature of the subject-matter which can be claimed as intellectual property are consistent with respect for human dignity and the realization of other human rights[25].

The resolution passed by the UN Sub-Commission for the Protection and Promotion of Human Rights, reminds all governments of the primacy of human-rights obligations over the economic policies and agreements. Furthermore, it makes a number of recommendations, among them that the WTO and particularly its Council on TRIPS take existing state obligations under international human rights instruments fully into account during its ongoing review of the TRIPS agreement. The resolution also requests governments to protect the social function when shaping national and local legislation.

It is pertinent to note here that the remark made by the US Supreme Court Justice Louis Brandeis in International News Service V Associated Press: the general rule of law is, that noblest of human productions–knowledge, truth ascertained, conceptions and ideas-become, after voluntary communication to others, free as air to common use[26].

In its 1970 advisory opinion in the Namibia Case, the International Court of Justice has ruled that States which deny fundamental human rights are in "flagrant violation" of the UN Charter. The combination of the supremacy of the UN Charter in international law, plus the elaboration of the human rights referenced in the Charter in an instrument such as the UDHR that has achieved the status of customary international law, provides a solid basis for the proposition that basic human rights norms enjoy primacy over States' obligations under trade treaties[27].

Article 103 of the UN Charter expressly states that in the event of a conflict between States' obligations under the UN Charter and their obligations under "any other international agreement," their obligations under the UN Charter shall prevail. Furthermore, the International Court of Justice has confirmed this hierarchy in international law in its 1992 ruling in the Aerial Incident over Lockerbie Case[28]. TRIPS being a trade agreement, States' obligations under the international law of human rights take precedence over other obligations under international law, including trade agreements.

NOTES

1. *Professor Laurence Helfer,* Human Rights and Intellectual Property: Conflict or Coexistence's Research Paper No. 2003-

27 and Program in Law and Public Affairs Princeton University. http://ssrn.com/abstract = 459120.

2. Forum on Science and Technology for sustainability , http://ksgnotes1.harvard.edu/BCSIA/forum.nsf/proj/iprs_humanrights visited on 13/3/2005.
3. Coobe J Roosemary, 6 Ind. J. Global Leg. Stud. 59, Fall, 1998.
4. http://www.unhchr.ch/html/menu2/6/cescr.htm.
5. *The Right to the Highest Attainable Standard of Health*, U.N. Doc. E/C, Dec. 4, 2000, ICESR General Comment 14 (2000).
6. Ibid.
7. Ibid.
8. Ibid
9. Manual On Good Parctices In Public-helath-sensitive Policy Measures And Patent Laws, http://www.twnside.org.sg/title2/manual.htm.
10. Gathii Thuo James, The Legal Status of The Doha Declaration on Trips And Public Health Under The Vienna Convention on The Law of Treaties, *Harvard Journal of Law & Technology,* Volume 15, Number 2 Spring 2002.
11. Declaration on the TRIPS Agreement and Public Health, WT/MIN(01)/Dec/2 4 (Nov. 14, 2001) [*vailable at* http://www.wto.org/english/thewto_e/minist_e/min01_e/mindecl_trips_e.pdf.
12. 1987 (2) SCC 165.
13. Letter from the Affordable Medicines Treatment Campaign to India's National Human Rights Commission, available at http://hrw.org/english/docs/2004/10/22/india9556_txt.htm.
14. Art. 11 of ICESCR imposes an obligation on state parties to recognize the right of everyone to an adequate standard of living for himself and his family, including adequate food, clothing and housing, and to the continuous improvement of living conditions. Also To improve methods of production, conservation and distribution of food by making full use of technical and scientific knowledge, by disseminating knowledge of the principles of nutrition and by developing or reforming agrarian systems in such a way as to achieve the most efficient development and utilization of natural resources.
15. http://www.righttofood.org.

16 Prof. J. A. Ekpere Intellectual property Rights and Food Security: Implications for Africa's Agriculture, http://www.infoagrar.ch/ipr-symposium/documents/paper_ekpere.pdf.

17. Ibid.

18. The genetic material, especially its specific molecular and chemical constitution, that comprises the physical basis of the inherited qualities of an organism.

19. Ibid.

20. Draft Declaration on the Rights of Indigenous Peoples, as agreed upon by the members of the Working Group on Indigenous Populations at its Eleventh Session,23 August 1993, UN Document E/CN.4/Sub.2/1993/29.

21. *Victoria Tauli-Corpuz,* International Forum on Globalization, http://www.ifg.org/pdf/cancun/issues-TRIPSindigenous.pdf.

22. Ibid.

23. Ibid.

24. http://www.undp.org/csopp/CSO/Newfiles/ipaboutfaqs.html.

25. Champan R Audrey, Approaching Intellectual Property as a human right : Obligations related to article 15(1)(c), Published by American Association for the Advancement of Science.

26. Stokes, Simon, Digital Copyright: Law & Practice, Butterworths, 2002.

27. Elliot, Richard, TRIPS and Rights: International Human Rights Law, Access to Medicines, and the Interpretation of the WTO Agreement on Trade-Related Aspects of Intellectual Property Rights , available at http://www.aidslaw.ca/Maincontent/issues/cts/briefs/TRIPS-human-rights-briefPDF.pdf.

28. Ibid.

8 INTELLECTUAL PROPERTY RIGHTS–AN ANALYSIS

*Shruthee M.G.**

Introduction

Man is the only creator in this earth who is endowed with creative and inventive mind. His power of imagination and creativity has led him to invent new things and making his life more comfortable and luxurious. In this present period any new things man creates through the application of his mind is held to be his property. Such properties are termed as intellectual property. Intellectual property is in the nature of intangible (incorporeal) property, which means, a property which has no physical appearance but exists only in the eye of law, such as patents, copyrights, trademarks etc. Intellectual property is a result of human creativity, involving mental and creative labor. Its subject matter is formed by new ideas generated by man and their application to human needs and desires resulting in benefits to the mankind.[1]

Intellectual property law regulates the creation, use and exploitation of mental or creative labor[2] Intellectual property law is that area of law, which concerns legal rights

* Lecturer, Vidyavardhaka Law College, University of Mysore, Mysore-570006, Karnataka.

associated with creative efforts or commercial reputation or good will.[3] Intellectual property rights are created by incorporating information in tangible object capable of multiplying in an unlimited number of times at different location any where in the world. The property is basically in the concept, idea, and thought and thereafter in the actual product, work and process etc.[4]

The term "Intellectual property" has come to be internationally recognized as covering Patents, Industrial designs & Trademarks used to be considered as different kinds of Industrial property. But when copyrights, confidential information were included the phrase Intellectual property gives more appropriate description. Although the creation of a trade mark has very little to do with intellectual creativity it cannot be doubted that patents, designs and copy rights are the products of intellectual effects and creative activities in the field of applied arts or technology and fine arts.[5]

The law relating to Intellectual property in India is undergoing changes so as to bring them to harmonize with the corresponding laws in the developing countries. This has become necessary after India signing the GATT & TRIPS and becoming a member of WTO[6]. In the beginning, intellectual property was of little importance, but after industrial revolution the awareness increased, gaining importance and the necessity for its protection was felt. Initially a number of intellectual property rights were known collectively as 'industrial property', which includes patent, trademarks and designs. But later under the leadership of WIPO (Worlds Intellectual Property Organization) copyright and many other rights were brought under one umbrella and industrial property was renamed as 'intellectual property'.

Difeerent Forms of Intellectual Property Rights

Traditionally, a number of Intellectual property rights such as patent, trademarks and designs were known collectively as industrial property rights. But later other rights such as copyrights and confidential information added to industrial property, and the phrase used to described the entirely of right is 'Intellectual property' and this has become the phrase normally used to describe these undivided & sometimes disparate, right collectively[7]. Now industrial property, copyright and confidential information was brought together and named as 'Intellectual property'. Following are the different forms of Intellectual property rights.

1. Patents
2. Trademarks
3. Copyright
4. Geographical indication
5. Industrial designs
6. Integrated circuits and
7. Confidential information.

Patents

Patent is a monopoly right granted to a person who has invented a new & useful product or an improvement of an existing product or a new process of producing a product. Under the Indian patent Act as amended in March 2005, patents may be granted to any new inventions; such as a new machine, apparatus, equipment, or even to a novel and genetically modified life form[8]. Patents are made available for all inventions in any field of technology whether product or process irrespective of their origin or nationality.[9]

Trade Related aspects of Intellectual Property rights agreement postulates for patents grants for any new invention irrespective of its nature. Having signed[10] TRIPS, India brought changes in its patent law in order to fulfill its obligations under TRIPS. Now in India patents are made available to any new invention irrespective of its nature, field, technology or place of origin including patents on life.[11]

Further Indian patent law has been amended to its entirety to bring it in conformity with the TRIPS. Earlier to TRIPS there evolved important conventions on industrial property law including patents under the Paris Convention on Industrial Property.[12] TRIPS respects Paris convention and marks significant progress over it.[13] Any person who has endeavored to invent any new product or process can apply for a patent grant. Patent consists of an exclusive right to manufacture the new product invented or manufacture a product according to the invented process for a limited period. After the expiry of the duration of patent the invention falls into public domain then anybody can work or make use of the inventions.[14]

The object behind granting patent monopoly on invention is to encourage research & invention, so that it would lead to the development of new technology to stimulate progress in industry. Grant of patent monopoly induces the inventors to disclose his invention, instead of keeping it secret. It induces the manufacturer to invest capital in new lines of production, which might not appear profitable if many competing producers embarked on them simultaneously[15] However in order to grant patent any invention has to satisfy few requirements i.e., the invention;

(a) Must be New

(b) Must involve inventive step or non-obvious

(c) Must be industrially applicable [utility/usefulness]

Patents are given to product invention as well as process inventions. An invention that consists of a new alloy is an example of a product invention. A machine, apparatus or other articles. An invention that consist of a new method or process of making or new alloy is a process invention. Patents are also granted for secondary innovations such as improvements on existing products or processes.[16]

Patent grants the exclusive right to exploit the invention, to make, to use, sell and distribute the patented product or article or substance or to use or exercise the method or process if the patent is for a process. Patent owner shall have right to assign, license, surround, prevent or refrain other or third parties from doing any of the above acts without his consent subject to certain exception under the patent law. Patents are generally granted for a term of twenty years. Till the expiry of the term of twenty years, except the patent owner, no other person can exploit or use the invention. Patent holder is given right to exclude others from using or exploiting the invention.

The owner of the patent has got some obligations to be performed along with right to exclude others. The patentee (patent holder) is under an obligation to work on the invention. The patentee should exploit the invention, in order to satisfy the needs of the society with regard to the invention. At the failure of the patentee to exploit the invention for the above purpose there may be granted a compulsory license to any interested person. Any person who is interested to work on the invention can apply for compulsory license in case of the patentees' failure to exploit the invention. However no such application shall be made till the expiry of three years from the date of the grant of patent.

Patents are enforced against infringement. Any person who uses or exploits a patented invention without the consent or authorization from the patent owner does violate the rights of the patent owner. In such circumstances patent owner can sue such person for infringement of his patent. There available legal remedies against infringement in the form of injunction i.e. restraining the infringer from using the invention or damage or accounts of profit to undo or to compensate the loss suffered by the patentee. However Government can use or exploit any patented invention without the consent of the owner in the interest of public purpose. In such circumstances the patent owner cannot sue the Government for infringement. Ultimately the objective behind patent law is to stimulate, promote, protect and enforce the patents. It encourages further innovations in all fields of technology by guaranteeing certain rights to the patent holder and also by protecting such rights against unauthorized use or infringement.

Trade Marks

A trade mark is a visual symbol in the form of a word, a device or a label applied to articles of commerce with a view to indicate to the purchasing public that they are goods manufactured or otherwise dealt in by a particular person or a particular organization as distinguished from similar goods manufactured or dealt in by others. In other words a trademark is a visual representation attached to goods for the purpose of indicating their trade origin. It gives a limited exclusive right to use the mark in relation to goods or articles. For example Coca Cola, Bata, LG are the trademarks of certain products. These marks represent the goods or products on which they are used. Coca Cola represents a particular soft drink, Bata represents products of a particular shoe company and LG represents products of a particular electronics company. These trademarks are names or visual symbols used on specific products to represent such products. When trademark is used in connection with service, it's called as service marks. The holder of the Trade mark gets limited exclusive right to use the mark in relation to those goods.[17]

Trademark is a mark capable of being represented graphically & which is capable of distinguishing the goods or services of one person from those of other & may include shape of goods, their package & combination of colures. [18]Trademark helps the customer or purchaser to identify the products & its origin; it generates its unchanged quality. It ensures to the product, to identify the goods as his from other it advertises the products. It helps in creating an image for the products in the minds of the purchasers. Here the protection could be extended for an indefinite duration subject to periodical renewal.

Characteristics of a Trademark

Trademark has a distinctiveness or capable of distinguish between good of one from other (distinct in itself). It should not be deceptively similar to other marks. A good trademark must possess following characteristics. In order to be registered and also in order to be protected a trademark should possess following characteristic features.

1. Distinctiveness
2. Appeal to the eye as well as ear
3. Capable of being applied to an article of commerce
4. It Must not be deceptively similar to other marks
5. Easy to spell and write
6. It Must be descriptive and suggestive of the product on which it is applied
7. It Must be short
8. It must not belong to class of marks, which are prohibited for registration.[19]

Any mark possessing all the above characteristics is eligible for registration and protection under the Trademark law. Paris convention on industrial property as well as Madrid convention provide for the law on trademarks. However recent TRIPS agreement[20] provides for clear and comprehensive law on trademarks. TRIPS agreement respects both the above conventions on trademarks and marks significant progress over them in providing better legal regime over trademarks. TRIPS have expanded the scope and purview of trademarks by including service marks. Service marks are marks representing a particular service such as medical service, courier services, and airline services. Service providers can register any mark suitable for their service to represent their service. India has brought a new trademarks Act in the year 1999, to bring its trademarks law in conformity with TRIPS[21]. Under the auspices of TRIPS now in India, there available protection for service mark which was not there earlier. Further the trademarks Act, 1999 provides for collective marks representing products or services of a group of people. A group of people may register a mark as their collective mark representing their products or services. Collective marks are useful in order to bring different products under one mark. Here different products could be represented by a single mark. Collective trademark implies goods originated or manufactured from a particular source or a particular set of people.

Registration of a trademark gives the proprietor the right to its exclusive use. Proprietor of the trademark has a right to assign or allow other person to use the trademark, as a registered user or permitted user. Apart from the proprietor if anybody uses the marks or applies the mark on other goods than the goods for which it is registered does infringe the trademark. In such circumstances the holder of the trademark can file a suit for infringement of his right over his registered trademark. He may also file a suit against passing off i.e., against passing such goods by using his trademark for undue advantage In case of infringement there available remedies in different forms.

Civil Remedies: Here remedies are in the nature of injunction, damages of account of profit or order for delivery up of infringing labels & for destruction or erasers.

Criminal Remedies: Any unauthorized dealings with the trademarks can be punished with either imprisonment or fine.[22]

Apart from these two ways, proprietor may seek remedy from Intellectual Property Appellate Board[23] constituted under the Act. As the commerce and industry progress the need for representing one's products or services grows in order to expose or advertise products and services. As the trademark serves the purpose of representing a particular product or service, its significance in the commerce and industry has grown tremendously. In the era of globalization usage of marks to represent products or services could give competitive advantage to the respective trader or businessman.

Copy Right

Copyright is another form of Intellectual property right. This right is also a statutory right. Copyright means the exclusive right to do or authorize to do certain acts in relation to:

1. Literary, dramatic, musical & artistic work,
2. Cinematography films & sounds recordings.

There are many acts which fall under copyright (specific right). In short, copyright is the right to copy, reproduce or publish the work in which copyright subsist, for commercial exploitation. Under copy right Act as amended in the year 1999[24] the holder of the copyright has an exclusive right for a limited period to exploit for economic gain, which in terms encourage the creator of the work (copy right holder) to create more and more new work. There are few international conventions on copyright, namely:

1. Beans convention for the protection of literary &artistic works 1896,
2. Rome convention 1961,
3. Universal copy right convention and protocol 1971,
4. WIPO copy right treaty 1996,
5. WIPO performance & phonograms treaty 1996 and
6. TRIPS.

Trade Related Aspects of Intellectual Property rights agreement[25] respects all the earlier copyrights conventions. India brought amendment to its copyrights Act 1957 in order to bring the Indian law in conformity with the above international conventions. Here copyright protection is given to the original work. A work, which is copy or duplication of earlier work, is not protected. The work must be new and original in order to be protected under the copyright law. Here the important thing is that an idea is not protected but the new way of expressing the idea is protected. Further the work should originate from the author himself.

Copyright is a negative right, in the sense it prevents others from copying or reproducing the work.[26] Copyright is a bundle of rights. It consists of right to reproduce, right to publish, right to convert the work into cinematographic versions, right for translation into different languages, right to adaptation, and also neighboring rights such as right to public performance, right to broadcasting, right to recording etc., Copyright could be assigned or licensed or sold. Copyright subsists for a period of 60 yrs from the death of author with certain exceptions. After the expiry of the period the work become public property.

The new creation of works is protected irrespective of quality of work. Copyrights are protected through registration. Copyright rights Act as amended in the year 1999 provides for the registration of original works. The Act specifies the subject matter in which copyright subsists. In other words, the Act specifies the works, which are eligible for copyright protection.[27] Any original work may be registered under the Act in order to get protection. Registered copyrights are protected against unauthorized use or infringement. Unauthorized use or infringement of copyright violates the rights of the copyright owner. In case of violation of copyright i.e. infringement, remedies are available in the form of injunction or damages or accounts of profit or delivery of infringing copies to the copyright owner. Where as under penal remedy convicted is punished with imprisonment or fine or with both.[28]

Copyright law intends to protect rights of the author or the original work. Any author of an original work could get his rights over his work protected by registering his work.

From the commercial point of view copyrights are very important because it involves a bundle of rights. The owner of a copyright on a particular literary or dramatic work not only gets rights to reproduce and publish his rights but also right to translation, adaptation conversion of the work into cinematographic work, recording, etc., Therefore once the work is registered he can commercially use the invention for the above purposes. The owner can himself use the work for the above purposes or he can sell his rights, which may be in turn used for the above mentioned different purposes. Such being the case copyright is a significant right having enormous commercial value.

Geographical Indications

A geographical indication is defined[29] as an indication used to identify the goods, whether natural or manufactured goods emanating from a particular area or country or region or territory known for particular quality or characteristics of the goods [30] Basmati rice, Banaras silk, Swiss chocolates are some of the well know geographical indications. Basmati rice is grown in the geographical regions of India and Pakistan. Its characteristics features or its quality is attributable exclusively to the conditions of geographical regions of India and Pakistan. Basmati rice could be grown in other geographical regions other than Indian and Pakistan. But it does not possess the quality and characteristics that possessed by the basmati rice grown in India and Pakistan. On the same lines Banaras silk, its quality and characteristics are attributable exclusively to the geographical regions of Banaras or Varanasi. A silk produced in other places could not be called Banaras silk and at the same time it does not possess the quality and reputation that the Banaras does possess. The same is with the Swiss chocolate, a chocolate exclusively produced in the region of Switzerland. On the same lines we can take Dharwad Peda, Mysore Silk.

Geographical indications are protected through the Geographical indications Act, 1999. TRIPS agreement provides for the blue print on the protection of geographical indications.[31] Earlier to TRIPS there is Lisbon convention governing the field of geographical indications. However TRIPS provides for the precise legal norm on geographical indications. Geographical indications are protected through registration. The registrar under the Act, who supervises registration and provides protection to geographical indications. The controller general of patents, designs and trademarks under the trademarks Act, 1999 shall be the registrar of geographical indications. There is a registry under the Act, which provides for the registration of geographical indications.

Any association[32] of persons or producer's of any organization or authority established under the law representing the interest of the producers of the concerned goods may apply to the registrar for the registration of geographical indication. Application shall be advertised in order to invite opposition. In case of no opposition, geographical indication shall be registered and protected for a period of ten years. [33]There is Register[34] under the Act where all the registered geographical indications are entered. Registration is with reference to particular goods and area from where the goods are originated or manufactured. In other words, geographical indications Act protects goods originated or manufactured in a particular geographical region ensuring certain quality. However there are few prohibited geographical indications from protection[35] Following geographical indications are prohibited from registration and as well as protection;

1. A geographical indication, which would be likely to deceive or cause confusion.
2. The use of which would be contrary to any law.
3. An indication, which contains scandalous or obscene matter.

4. An indication that is likely to hurt religious feelings.
5. An indication, which is disentitled from protection in a court.
6. An indication, which involves the use of generic names.
7. An indication, which falsely represents particular goods to be originated from a false geographical regions.

Registration confers on the owner an exclusive right to use the geographical indications on the products for which it is registered. Geographical indications could not be assigned or transferred as the same is prohibited under the Act.[36] Others cannot use the invention Assignment or transmission of a registered geographical indication is prohibited.[37] If anybody uses a registered geographical indication on goods other than the goods for which it is registered it does amount to false application of geographical indication. On the same lines if a registered indication is used on goods originated in a region other than the one for which it is registered it does amount to false application of the indication.[38] Therefore an indication shall be used or applied to a particular set of goods originating from a particular geographical area.

Any registered owner of a geographical indication has a right to sue an unauthorized user of geographical indication for infringement or under unfair competition or for passing off also.[39] Relief may be granted in the form of injunctions, accounts of profits or damages.[40] The person applying false geographical indication or falsely representing goods shall be prosecuted under the Act.[41] There lies a penalty for applying false geographical indications in the form of imprisonment, which may extend to three years and with fine, which may extend to rupees two Lacks.[42] Further selling of goods to which false geographical indication is applied does also attract same punishment as above[43] and in such circumstances falsely represented goods may be forfeited.[44] Geographical indications denote specialty of a particular region in producing certain goods. Goods, which are not produced in other areas apart from a particular geographical location, shall be recognized and protected through registration. Where the quality of certain goods is attributable to the geographical conditions of a specific region such specialty of such particular geographical region shall be recognized through protection of geographical indications. Application of geographical indications indicates for specific goods with certain qualities in contrast with other goods.

Industrial Designs

Generally speaking, an industrial design is the ornamental or aesthetic aspects of a useful article. The ornamental aspect may consist of the shape and/or patterns and /or color of the article. The ornamental or aesthetic aspect must appeal to the sense of sight. Industrial design is a "shape or configuration or pattern or ornamentation or composition of lines or colors" applied to an article. The article must be reproducible by industrial means, therefore the design is called industrial.[45] Paris convention provides for international law on industrial designs. The TRIPS agreement[46] provides for a blue print on industrial designs with reference to designs. In India we had Industrial designs Act 1911, now we have Industrial designs Act of 2000. As per the above conventions and the Act an industrial design must possess certain characteristics in order to be protected. That is it must be,

1. New [novelty]
2. Appeal to eye
3. Applied to articles (industrial application)
4. Not previously published.

An industrial design must be new in the sense hitherto unknown, it must appeal to the eye; in the sense it must be visible. Hidden shapes or pattern, which does not appeal to the eye, are not protected. At the same time an industrial design must be capable of industrial application. The design must be capable of applying to any product; in the sense goods could be produced in the shape or pattern of the design intended for protection. Further the design must not be previously published in India. Any design satisfying the above requirements could be protected. Industrial designs Act 2000 offers protection through registration. There is Controller of industrial design under the Act who registers new industrial designs.

Any person claiming to be the proprietor of any new or original design not previously published in any country can apply for registration of his design. Further to be registered a design must not be contrary to public order and morality. The application for registration of a design shall be accompanied by specified fee. The controller shall advertise the application in order to invite any objections. If any objection is raised, the applicant shall be given an opportunity to clear objection. Decisions shall be made after hearing the parties. After the objections are removed or when there are no objections, design may be registered and the same shall be entered in the register of design under the Act.

On registration, there conferred exclusive rights on the owner to use or apply the registered design. The holder can also assign the design or issue license to third person. It confers on the holder the right to exclude unauthorized person from applying it to other articles.[47] These rights are called copyright in design. Industrial designs are protected for a term of ten years.[48] If any person without the authorization from the owner used or applies the registered design he does infringe the monopoly of the proprietor of the registered design and is guilty of piracy for which he is liable to a fine of a sum not exceeding twenty five thousand rupees. In case of any infringement, the holder is entitled for both civil & criminal remedies in the form of injunction, damages, accounts of profits, delivery up of infringement articles, imprisonment, fine or both.[49]

Integrated Circuits/Layout Designs

'Layout design' means a layout of transistors & other circuitry elements & includes lead wires connecting such elements and expressed in any manner in a semiconductor integrated circuit. Semiconductor integrated' circuit means a product having transistor & other circuit elements which are inseparable formed on a semiconductor material or an insulating material of inside the semiconductor materiel and designed to perform an electronic circuitry function.[50] The Treaty of intellectual property in respect of integrated circuits governs the law relating to integrated circuits.[51] The treaty provides for the protection of integrated circuits.[52] The recent TRIPS agreement by respecting the above treaty does provide for the registration and protection of integrated circuits. Having ratified TRIPS in order to fulfill its obligations in India brought integrated circuits and layout designs Act in the 2000. As per the act, a layout design or an integrated circuit must fulfill certain requirements. They are;

1. It must be original & new
2. It must be inherently distinctive
3. It must not be commercially exploited any where in India or in conventional countries before the date of application for registration except few exception.
4. It must not come within the scope of any of the design prohibited.

Here protection is given for a period of ten years and there is no provision for renewal. It confers an exclusive right to use, sell & distribute for commercial purposes the layout design for a limited period. He can use the layout design in an integrated circuit and can produce any article incorporating such integrated circuit. It confers right to assign or can also allow other to use as registered user. It also confers right to sue in case of infringement. Any person without the authorization of the registered owner uses the layout designs in any integrated circuit or produces any article by incorporating such integrated circuit he does infringe the right of the registered owner of such layout design. The infringer shall be liable to pay to the right holder a sum equivalent to reasonable royalty such as would be payable under a freely negotiated license in respect of such a layout design.

Protection of layout designs and integrated circuit has gained significance in the light of the electronics revolution spread of information technology. Modern day life is associated with integrated circuits. Television we watch, radio we listen the telephone or mobile we use, vehicles we travel, computer we use and many such electronic goods are made of layout designs and integrated circuit. Such being the case protection of layout designs and integrated circuits is very much needed.

Confidential Information

After the industrial revolution, the concept of property has undergone drastic changes. Protection of property has been applied to new area like geographical indication, integrated circuits and confidential information. Confidential information means any information that requires to be kept in secrecy. The essence of the law of confidential information is that a person, who has obtained information in confidence due to his position, requires keeping it confidential. It depends on the broad principle of equity that he who has received information in confidence shall not take unfair advantages of it. He must not make use of it to the prejudice of the person from whom he derived it. Further he should not use it or disclose it to any body without obtaining consent from the person from whom it was derived.

Law extends protection against unauthorized use of confidential information or law restrains the use of it in breach of good faith. Here the information may be a trade secret. For example, a method of production not protected by patent, or a business secret, such as the financial arrangement of the undertaking or a piece of domestic information like the salary of clerks or the efficiency of the firms filing system. Some of these informations would be of a highly confidential nature, as being potentially damaging if a competitor could obtain it. Paris convention for the protection of industrial property provides for the protection of confidential information. Further the TRIPS have extended its area of protection to confidential information also.[53] In India we do not have any specific law on the protection of confidential information or trade secret. The law of contracts and the concept of fiduciary duty and concept of breach of trust do govern the field. As per the contract, breach of confidentiality could be enforced and as per the concept of fiduciary duty an employee has got a duty to keep the employer's trade secret confidential. However to constitute confidential information an information should fulfill following requirements.

1. The owner must believe that the release of such Confidential information would be injurious to him or would be beneficial to his rivals or others
2. The owner must believe that the information is Confidential or secret & it must not be already in public domain.
3. The information must be judged in the light of the usage & practices of the particular industrial or trade concerned.

The owner of such confidential information has the right to sue the person who has disclosed such information having an obligation to keep it secret. The remedy is in the nature of injunction, damages, compensation or account of profit or delivery up of such materials. The owner of confidential information can sue the infringer against breach of trust or fiduciary duty. Confidential information or trade secret plays an important role in the development of any company or association.

The information is confidential only when it is kept secret. If the secrecy is revealed or disclosed the information is no more confidential. Only in formations, which are confidential are kept secret is protected under the law of confidential information. Companies do require keeping their internal affairs secrets. They also require to keep their trade secrets confidential. Secret may be with regard to the method of manufacturing of any product or business strategies or future plans. Coca Cola Company does keep the method of manufacturing cola secret since decades. The method of manufacturing cola is their trade secret which they able to keep secret, hence it is confidential. If any employee of Cola Company does reveal the method of manufacturing the cola to anybody he infringes the trade secret of that company which is protected and enforced. After the industrial revolution trade secrets have become an important issue as every industry or company intends to keep their trade secrets confidential in order to have a better edge over the competitors. It is nothing but just keeping the secrets secret, in order to protect the confidentiality of secrets.

Conclusion

In this modern era intellectual properties have gained a lot of importance. Right from morning till night we come across different intellectual properties. Since morning coffee, sanitary equipments, taking bath, break fast, dressing, mid day meals vehicle, veining chats, dinner in the night, sleep on the bed we come across and use different products which are intellectual properties of some intellectual. Someone may be having patent over the coffee that we drink in the morning. Some one may be the patent owner of sanitary equipments that we use. Some one might have registered the rice that we use for preparing break fast or meals under geographical indications. The vehicle that we use may exhibit some trademark or design. Mobile phone that we use or television that we watch consists of layout designs and integrated circuits. Drinks that we take may carry some trade secrets. Every day the music that we listen or literature or newspaper that we read may consist of copyright owned by some author.

Such being the case it is necessary for an ordinary man to have knowledge about the intellectual property rights. Common men come across intellectual properties from dawn to dusk. The goods having a very wide spectrum and associated with food, shelter and clothes; the things of necessity, comfort and luxury do come under intellectual property. From waking up from a Gautier bed, using a comfortable Sleepwell mattress and pillows, having a cup of Taj Mahal Tea, then wearing a Nike track suite and shoes for a morning walk, he deals with these properties. A Modern Bread or Mother Dairy Milk or a cup of Nescafe at the breakfast, going in a Zen car to the office, using a Compaq computer and coming back in a car. In the evening, watching Sony Television and fixing alarm in his/ her Swatch watch to wake-up in the morning, using the products, which are intellectual properties of some one.

These properties have been covered under a patent or a copyright or a trademark. Common man's life is very closely linked with articles and products, which are protected by law under intellectual property rights. The copying, imitation, adaptation, and un-authorized reproduction of these things, without the permission of the owner, may amount to a serious offence. Therefore, the knowledge about intellectual property right is must for a common man. Paris convention of industrial property is convention, which covers patents trademarks designs and confidential information. For copyrights we have Berne and Rome conventions and other conventions. For trademarks we have Madrid convention. For integrated circuits we have treaty on intellectual property in respect of integrated circuits. For geographical indications we have Lisbon agreement.

However, by compiling all the above conventions and agreement there evolved one comprehensive agreement known as the magnakarta of all intellectual property rights in the form of Trade Related aspects of Intellectual Property rights (TRIPS). TRIPS mandate its member states to ensure the protection of all forms of intellectual properties through registration. India being a signatory to the TRIPS agreement guarantees protection to different forms of intellectual property rights by amending the existing laws and also by enacting new laws. However on confidential information and trade secrets India is still lagging behind since we do not have any law on it.

NOTES

1. Catherine Colston–principles of Intellectual property Law.
2. Lionel Bentley Brand Sherman pg. 1.
3. David Bain Bridge's 'Intellectual property' persom education (Singapore) Pvt. Ltd. Delhi .1st edition reprint, 2003, pg. 2.
4. Satyawrat ponkshe's–The management of Intellectual property, hate & ponkshe, patent attorneys, New Delhi, 1st edition–1991, pg. 4.
5. P. Narayanan's 'Intellectual property' Eastern Law House Pvt. Ltd., New Delhi, 3rd edition–2004, pg.
6. Ibid. Pg. No.
7. David Bain Bridge's 'Intellectual property' person education (Singapore) Pvt. Ltd. Delhi.1st edition reprint, 2003 pg. 5.
8. As per the amended patent Act 2005, now patents are made available to life such as new and genetically modified microorganisms, plants, animals or genetic materials of human being.
9. See: TRIPS: article 27.
10. India signed TRIPS agreement on April 15th 1994; The then commerce minister Pranab Mukarjee signed the agreement.

The agreement came into being on 1-1-1995. However India was given time to bring changes in its intellectual property laws. India did bring changes in its intellectual property laws in order to comply with the TRIPS. This process of bringing changes in the intellectual property laws got completed in March 2005 with the latest amendment brought to the Patent Act. Till 2005 India was under transition, since 1-1-1995 till 1-1-2005. This period is known as transition period was granted under the TRIPS. At the expiry of this transition period that is on 1-1-2005 TRIPS came into being for India.

11. There was and still there is vehement opposition in India against providing for patents on life. However life has become patentable subject matter through out the world including India under the auspices of TRIPS.
12. See: Paris Convention on Industrial Property; a well-known convention on patents.
13. See: TRIPS art: 27 to 34.
14. P. Narayanan's 'Intellectual property' Eastern Law House Pvt. Ltd., New Delhi, 3rd edition–2004, pg.11.
15. Ibid. No. 12.
16. See P. Narayanan's 'Intellectual property' Eastern Law House PVT LTD, New Delhi, 3rd edition–2004 Pg. No. 23.
17. See P. Narayanan's 'Intellectual property' Eastern Law House Pvt. Ltd., New Delhi, 3rd edition–2004, Pg. No.146.
18. See: Trade Marks Act 1999 sec2 (1) (2) (b).
19. See: The emblems and names (prevention of improper use) Act 1950, for prohibited marks.
20. See; TRIPS art: 15 to 21.
21. See: Indian Patents Act 1999.
22. See: The trade marks Act 1999 for the term of imprisonment and amount of fine.
23. Intellectual property appellate board established under the trade marks Act 1999.
24. See: Indian Copyright Act, 1957, as amended in 1999.
25. See; TRIPS art: 9 to 14.
26. See: Dr. Wadhera, Law relating to patents, trademarks, copyright, designs and geographical indications, Second edition, Universal law publishihng Co. Pvt. Ltd, Delhi, 2003.

27. See: Sec:13 and 14 of the Copyright Act, as amended in 1999.
28. See: The copyright Act, as amended in 1999. for the term of imprisonment and amount of fine.
29. See: The geographical indications of goods act 1999.
30. P. Narayanan's 'Intellectual property' Eastern Law House Pvt. Ltd., New Delhi, 3rd edition–2004, Pg. No. 381.
31. See: TRIPS Art-22-24.
32. See: Sec: 11 of the Act.
33. See; Sections: 13,14,16, and 18 of the Act.
34. See: Sec: 6 of the Geographical indications Act, 1999.
35. See: Sec: 9 of the Geographical indications Act, 1999.
36. Saee; Sec: 24 of the Act.
37 Ibid.
38. See: Sec: 38 of the Act.
39. See: Sec: 66 of the Act.
40. See; Sec: 67 of the Act.
41. See; Sec: 38 of the Act.
42. See: Sec:39 of the Act.
43. See: Sec:
44. See; Sec: 46 of the Act.
45. Dr. G. B. Reddy's, Intellectual property rights and the law, 4th edition, 2004-05,Gogia law publication, Hyderabad, pg. 23.
46. See: TRIPS art: 25 and 26.
47. See; TRIPS art: 26.
48. See; Sec: 11 of the design Act 2000.
49. See; Sec; 22 of the Designs Act, 2000.
50. Section (h) & (r) of the semiconductor integrated circuits layout Act, 2000.
51. See the Treaty of intellectual property in respect of integrated circuits.
52. See; art: 2-7,12 and 16 of the Treaty of intellectual property in respect of integrated circuits.
53. See: TRIPS Art: 39.

9 INTELLECTUAL PROPERTY RIGHTS & AVAILABLE REMEDIES–AN INDIAN EXPERIENCE

*Srikumar**

Introduction

Intellectual property as the world knows, is a merge of knowledge and property. The importance of both these concepts are known to all and thus the significance of the concept of intellectual property needs no much elucidation. Intellectual property is that area of law which concerns legal rights associated with creative efforts or commercial reputation and good will.[1] In other words, this is a branch of law which protects some of the finer manifestations of human achievement. Even though this field of law can be categorized as 'young', a thorough analysis of this law reveals that, the scope and ambit of this law has been widening by leaps and bounds. This century is described as an era of intellectual property rights due to the exponential growth in the regime of this field. Revolutionary changes have been brought about in the fundamental concept of property today, wherein individual rights are given the upper grade. So today, where the doors of every national market has been opened for world wide competition in the

* B.A., L.L.M., Advocate, Trivandrum.

wake of globalization, liberalization and privatization, to put in a more precise manner internationalization (as some economists regard globalization as a mere mirage)[2], the concept as well as protection of intellectual property has acquired considerable significance.

Intellectual property is a creation of intellect and thus this branch of law recognizes the creative skill and accords protection to them from unfair competition and infringements. Thus it is the mental or creative labour that is protected here. While considering the genuiness of this law, the basic question that arises is, why should we grant intellectual property rights? At the very periphery, this is a class of property; quite distinct form other forms of property, which gives rise to different issues and situations due to its strategic, rampant and innovative exploitations. The inherent uncertainties regarding its value and use add to its peril and moreover it is not something that can be kept in a safe-deposit vault or be deposited in a bank or locked up in a house, it is in whichever form, is easily and readily available to the general public and is therefore more easy to steal. [3] Thus protection becomes inevitable. Further, the justifications attributed as an answer to the question posed in the opinion of Bentley and Sherman tend to fall in two general categories.[4]

1. The instrumental justification focuses on the fact that intellectual property induces or encourages desirable behaviour.
2. The ethical and moral agreements like the recognition of creator's natural or human rights over the product of their labour.

The legitimacy of the right can be further asserted on a jurisprudential basis also, as according to Sir. Brainbridge, by comparing to the Hohfeldian principles. Intellectual property gives rise to rights as well as duties which are legal co-relatives according to Hohfeld. Here the right is to do certain things while the duty is as owed by other not to infringe that right, devoid of intention. Further comparing with the Hohfeld's system, there exist privileges and no rights, here the creator has the privilege to exploit the work and the co-relative is that, persons other than the owner has no right to do this, however with exceptions[5]. So, the yearn of the society to disseminate knowledge, the need of such knowledge for the propagation and upliftment of society, the economic support, the urge for innovation and novelty all justify intellectual property. Adhering to the principle that knowledge begets knowledge and it tends to expand infinitely, the assertion of intellectual property as a right is fully legitimized. Thus, the right is asserted. It is here the maxim; '*Ubi jus ibi remedium*' becomes meaningful and assertive. So, where there is a right, there is to be a remedy and there is a remedy.

Race Towards Enforcement

The unprecedented growth, the immense need coupled with rampant as well as innovative exploitation and infringement has turned the coins of intellectual property rights. Today, so widespread is the concept that place matters less. A need was felt to frame conventions and multilateral agreements to tackle the scenario and back up the state laws. As the private international laws of nations vary an international guideline was regarded as a solution. Starting with the Paris, Berne and Madrid agreements culminating in the TRIPs agreement [6] were all efforts put on for the above need. Conferring adequate protection became the need of the society more than the need of the creator. The existence of both conflicting interests and socio-economic environment within the nation states burnt the fire for most of the above prescribed efforts. However, in 1994 an Agreement, which was termed as the most comprehensive, the Trade Related Aspects of Intellectual property Rights or TRIPs came into force, which dealt with the various angles of intellectual property rights.

Confining ourselves to the elected topic, we can, as a starting point have a small discussion on TRIPs and enforcement of intellectual property rights before stepping into the various remedies available, under the various Indian statutes.

Trips and Enforcement

A very natural question that may crop up in the minds of people is that, why a mention to TRIPs, while dealing with remedies in the Indian scenario, especially when we have independent statues to provide insight into the matter. The idea is very clear, as it is TRIPs which provide for the basic minimum standards to be followed by all these statutes.

This agreement formed under the auspices of WTO, is the blue print. The state parties have to follow these minimum standards as the basis, along with which they have been conferred absolute freedom to adopt steps in giving effect to such provisions.[7]

Part III of the TRIPs containing a total of about 21 articles[8] deals with 'Enforcement of Intellectual Property Rights'. These provisions are aimed at:

1. Measures adoptable by intellectual property holders from the judicial, administrative and customs authorities against as well as threatened infringements of their rights.
2. The civil as well as criminal in nature procedures, by which such measures may be obtained.[9]

Thus the agreement makes a distinction between infringing activity in general in respect of which civil procedures and remedies must be made available and counterfeiting and piracy-the more blatant and egregious form of infringing activity in respect of which additional procedures and remedies must also be provided namely criminal procedure and such other measures.[10] Further the agreement also requires that the enforcement procedure must be such as to permit effective action against any act of infringement of intellectual property rights and the remedies expeditious and in certain cases deterrent.[11] The aspects of due process[12] , merits of case[13] and other factors of natural justice are served as the guidelines to enact effective enforcement mechanisms. Thus it is these minimum standards that weave the threads for a stable enforcement mechanism. The state parties can however utilize their freedom to modify and effectualise the mechanism by incorporating new mode, but with the instructions of TRIPs forming the foundation. So, having such an international agreement is a boon. But, the only factor is to follow it up with the race in time and see to it that, if not a mile ahead, at least it travels with time and adopts timely changes so as to enable it to serve the forth coming human generations also. The Indian system also like many others attributes its acknowledgement to TRIPs guidelines, as it serves as the fundamental basis of Indian statues with regard to intellectual property. So the remedies available are also in consonance with the TRIPs agenda.

Remedies Against Infringements: Indian Purview

As mentioned earlier, where there exists a right there is remedy. The only difference is in the form of its availability. In the intellectual property scenario, the aspect of remedy becomes very important as violations or infringements are at its peak. Further, one will have interest and attitude to invest his labour in something only if it acquires some gain for him coupled with adequate protection. In stricto senso, a person will have interest in creativity only if two pre conditions are satisfied.

(a) his labour should bear returns

(b) his creation is guaranteed protection from infringers.

It is here remedies play a major part. It is this area that values the legal prominence of a state, Sir Cornish has very rightly remarked, that 'Intellectual property rights are of course the basis of many contractual dealings. But their fundamental characteristic is their power to constrain those who have no relationship with the right owner. They are rights that depend for their effectiveness to a peculiar degree, upon the speed and cheapness with which they can be enforced. This explains why, so often in the modern law, it is cases in this field that test the procedures and remedies provided by courts'.[14] We are fortunate to have one of the finest legal system in the world having codified laws and established procedures. The Indian parliament and the judiciary are striving hard to grant effective protection against this black sheep nomenclatured as infringement. Though there lie miles and miles to go before achieving the end, the start and progress is truly encouraging.

Intellectual Property Laws of India

India has codified and enacted statues on all subjects relating to intellectual property: The Patents Act 1970, The Copyright Act 1957, The Trademarks Act 1999, The Designs Act 2000, The Geographical Indications of Goods (Registration and Protection) Act, 1999 and the Semi-conductor, Integrated Circuits Lay-out Designs Act 2000, thus covering the whole of the concept.

Being a signatory to the World Trade Organization (WTO), by 2005, India is compelled to implement the WTO standard intellectual property protection [15]. Bearing in mind this and the alarming development in this field coupled with even more risks of infringement, India too powered its legislations. The Patent Act 1970 was amended by Patent (Amendment) Act 2003, The Copyright Act 1957 was strengthened in 1994 and then as amended up to 1999, The Trade Marks Act 1999 replaced the 1958 Act, The Designs Act 2000 superseded the 1911 Act and other new statutes on various novel fields took the center stage.

All these Acts contemplate and provide for remedies. The remedies provided there under can be categorized as follows.

1. Civil remedies and Administrative Reliefs
2. Criminal remedies

Thus whenever need arises these remedies can be unfolded under these Acts. Compared to their infancy, the provisions of these acts have been gaining maturity and becoming more stringent with the passage of time. Each of these Acts has specific provisions in this regard also. Although there are variations between these specific fields, their similar contents and other common grounds justify in treating these matters at one place. So let's trace out the various remedies available under these Acts.

Civil Remedies

Civil remedies are the most sought after remedies. This is mainly because the right owner will not have much interest in putting the infringer behind bars, while his interest will to be prohibit such act, acquire damages and place himself in such a situation as if the infringement had never occurred. Further it has been found that civil remedies are easier than criminal remedies, though the time factor goes against civil remedies, the remedy of injunction to a great extent helps to cross over the time tide.

The civil remedies enumerated in the Acts are of the following nature:

(a) Anton Pillar Order
(b) Injunctions (including Mareva injunction)
(c) Damages
(d) Accounts for profits
(e) Delivery of infringing materials

Chapter XII (Sections 54-62) of the Copyright Act, 1957 (amended up to 1999), Chapter XVIII (Section 104-115) of Patents Act 1970, Sec 22 of the Designs Act 2000, Sec 134-135 of Trade Marks Act 1999, all point fingers to the above mentioned remedies.

Generalizing the provisions, a suit may be instituted in any court of original jurisdiction, subject to their pecuniary and territorial jurisdiction, But the designation of the lowest court is 'District and Sessions' judge, further if a High Court is having original jurisdiction, then the case can be filed in High Court directly also[16]. These provisions along with the provisions of other general laws, like the Code of Civil Procedure 1908[17], and the Specific Relief Act 1963[18] provide the scope for a proper civil enforcement.

(a) Anton Pillar Order

Prior to dealing with injunctions, a small insight is to be given into a relief called Anton Pillar order. This order cannot be literally called as an injunction, but being an interlocutory relief this can also be included under this heading if needed.

It is an order passed in the interim stage, known after the name of the plaintiff in the case where it was introduced. In *Anton Pillar KG Vs. Manufacturing process Ltd,*[19] the court of appeal in England held that, in exceptional circumstances, where the plaintiff constituted strong prima-facie case with very serious potential damage and when there exists clear proof that the defendants possessed vital material which they might destroy, then the court has inherent jurisdiction to order the defendants to permit the plaintiffs' representatives to enter the defendants premises to inspect and remove such material. In some cases such an order can be passed on the plaintiff's exparte application also. Thus this is a very strong interim remedy to see that the ends of justice are not salvaged.

(b) Injunctions

Injunctions are very effective modes of temporary redressal. Upon reasons beyond the control of the legal system, an action for breach of an intellectual property rights may take considerable time before it is finally concluded. That is why so much of importance is attributed to injunctions as it provides a sudden temporary remedy. An injunction is a judicial process whereby a party is ordered to refrain from doing or to do a particular act or thing[20]. The main object of granting an injunction as an interim relief is for the preservation of property in dispute and to maintain status quo till the rights and claims of the parties are adjudicated.

There exist mainly two types of injunction.

1. Temporary or interlocutory injunction
2. Permanent or perpetual injunction

An interlocutory injunction secures immediate protection from an existent infringement or from the continuance of infringement or an anticipated infringement[21]. O XXXIX R1 & 2 of the Code of Civil Procedure deals with the requisites and procedures to seek temporary injunctions. Under this, to obtain an interlocutory injunction one has to establish:

(a) *A prima facie case:* The applicant must make out a prima-facie case for the claims raised by him in such a manner as to satisfy the Court that there exists a bonafide dispute, a strong case and a probability of the applicant being entitled to the relief claimed by him.

(b) *Balance of convenience in his favour:* Another pre-requisite is the existence of balance of convenience in favour of the applicant i.e. the Court must be satisfied that the hardships most likely to be caused to the applicant by refusing the injunction is more than that which is likely to be caused to the opposite party by granting it.

(c) *That refusal to grant would cause irreparable injury:* Further the applicant must satisfy that he will be put to irreparable loss and injury if the injunction is not granted and there exists no other remedy open to him which can shield him from the consequences.

Even though these conditions are satisfied there may arise other circumstances leading to refusal to grant such a relief as it is the complete discretion of the Court to entertain such remedies or not. The injunction granted is in the form that the defendant be restrained from infringing the plaintiff's right. This will also cover variations of what the defendant has been doing if they too would amount to infringement[22]. Thus this gives a certain amount of protection to the right holder and thus a very effective and widely used remedy. Temporary injunctions may be granted at any stage of a suit and they continue for a specified time or until a further order of the Court. Permanent injunction is a final injunction granted after full trial according complete protection. The relevant provisions of the Specific Relief Act 1963 (Sec. 38-42) governs this aspect, here there is complete prohibition. This can only be granted by the decree made at the hearing and upon the merits of the suit; the defendant is thereby perpetually enjoined from the assertion of a right.[23]

Another form of injunction that is granted in certain fields like trademark is an order for Mareva Injunction. Where by the court has power to freeze the defendants' assets, where there exists a probability of the assets being dissipated or cancelled so as to make a judgement against him worthless or unenforceable. [24]

(c) Damages

The word damage literally means any loss or harm caused as a result of an injury to a person or property. As according to law, compensation in money is realizable for this injury and this is damages. Here, when a party infringes on the intellectual property of another, he suffers a loss or injury as against his intellectual labour. So, for this compensation can be asserted.

According to Halsbury's Laws of England damages is a pecuniary compensation which the law awards to a person for the injury he has sustained by reason of the act or default of another.[25] In short it is a recompense that law grants for the wrong that another has done. Damages generally seek to put the plaintiff in a position that he would have occupied had the infringement not occurred. So it is an award to compensate the plaintiff for the harm caused to him. This remedy is a boon to the right holder which fills him with life once again. However, damages are properly assessed before awarding them. Here the courts deal with recurrent circumstances that act as guidelines. So here Courts must find out whether the payment ordered is in truth liquidated damages or penalty. The assessment procedure thus differs with case. In contrast to ordinary damages, exemplary damages may also be awarded in rare circumstances to cause a deterrent effect. However this is done only in extreme cases of profit making.

(d) Accounts for profits

As a corollary of injunction, a defendant might be ordered to account to a plaintiff for profits made from the wrong doing and this is not a notional computation as with damages, but an investigation of actual accounts[26]. Here, this remedy an alternative to damages, calculates the profit emanated by the infringer through infringement rather than the loss caused to the plaintiff. Sometimes, the account will give a better recompense than damages when the defendant has been making profits that the plaintiff would not himself have made. However the plaintiff can ask for either damages or accounts of profits as he should not be entitled to be both reimbursed and compensated.

(e) Delivery of Infringing Materials

In order to back either injunction or the final order the court may seize the infringing materials and may order the delivery up of such infringing articles or order their destruction thus restraining the further scope of infringement. These are the remedies in civil nature available to a right holder in cases of infringement. The civil remedy field is quite well versed in itself, granting proper redressal to the aggrieved. The only lacunae can be the time factor and in turn the cost, which can be worked to a great extent by proper planning and inducing sincerity into the work that one, is performing.

Criminal Remedies

Earlier Civil Law was the only recourse to accord protection for infringements. This was effectuated by common law remedies. Soon, the density and quantity of intellectual property violations started inflating. This inflation coupled with the immense growth in the field made things truly burning and uncontrollable. The Civil remedies were felt inadequate and this opened the avenues for criminal action. The foremost platform for this was set up in the field of Copyright, by way of the Statute of Anne 1709, which provided for remedies in the way of penalties for infringement, confiscation of infringed copies and compensation.[27] This small step taken has been slowly transforming itself into a giant leap with time. Thus criminal remedy is the next alternative available to the right holder. The TRIPs agreement also provides for criminal remedies. Today piracy has become rampant, and as a response the criminal procedures have undergone some drastic changes also. The present state of affairs in the intellectual property field has compelled this change and truly one has to admit that this change has been gradual but magnanimous. It is now a well accepted fact that items covered under the intellectual property legislations in India are identified and protected because of the public interest involved and it is in this public interest coupled with the interest of the right owner that criminal law is commanded to aid enforcement authorities in the protection of intellectual property[28]. As in the civil law scenario, every Act has separate provision on the enforcement of criminal procedures.

The remedy mainly involve

(a) fine,

(b) imprisonment,

(c) search and seizure and

(d) such other penalties as the court deems fit.

The main leap in this regard is that now piracy has been made a cognizable offence and thus an FIR can be framed hereunder for proceeding with the case. The remedy here lies in filing of criminal complaint before the Chief Judicial Magistrate or Chief Metropolitan Magistrate, of the concerned jurisdiction. The specific intellectual property statutes along with the Indian Penal Code, Criminal Procedure Code and other relevant provision of the Acts in question make sure that the criminal procedure lives up to the expectation. Even though minimum punishment has been prescribed, the Courts have been conferred the power to award a lesser punishment after stating special reasons.

The Patent law is a field where criminal law is not found with its vigour so as to afford protection against infringement of patent rights. Here from the very beginning civil law alone has been used. Though a separate chapter (Chapter XX),has been included in the Patents Act 1970, enumerating penalties for certain acts (like falsification of entries, wrongful use of word patent office, failure to supply information etc...) there is no express provision making infringement of patent rights an offence[29]. In the opinion of Prof. N.S. Gopalakrishnan, history itself adduces reason for this and the concept was originated and developed with the idea of helping the development of industry rather than affording protection to the proprietary right of the individual and this was the position till recently[30]. But today, when violations are increasing, the protection of this right is slowly getting recognized. It is also felt for protecting the larger interests of society, one of the main aims of patents.

The copyright and trademark fields are the areas where criminal procedures have expanded. Under the Copyrights Act, Chapter XIII (Sections 63-70) deals with criminal procedures and remedies. Hereunder, a police officer not below the rank of Sub Inspector is given the power to seize without warrant all infringing copies of the work and accessories for making infringing copies wherever found and produce them before a Magistrate. This makes the Copyright Act more effective as the delay in obtaining warrants before conducting raids can be eliminated. This power to the police officer can be exercised even at the preparation stage. The effect of this provision is that even a threatened infringement of the copyright can be nipped in the bud, possibly even before the commission of an offence[31]. Under the Copyright Act, knowingly infringing as well as an abetment for the same is punishable by imprisonment for a term of not less than 6 months which may extend to 3 years and with a fine of at least Rs. 50,000/- to Rs. 2,00,000/-. In the case of computer software, use of pirated programmes is now an offence, punishable with the same penalty. Thus there has been substantial strengthening of the copyright law. There exists no statutory presumption of copyright ownership.

Enforcement of trade mark owner right had been weak in the past, but is steadily improving as the courts and police respond to domestic concerns about the high cost of piracy to Indian right holders[32]. The trademark provisions are also stringent Section 103-125, are the provisions in this regard under the Act, Sections 103-105 are very important. The punishment for offences relating to trademarks has been enhanced so as to prevent counterfeiting in any manner whatsoever. The penalty for false trademarks or trade description and for selling the same is now for a term ranging between 6 months to 3 years with from Rs. 50,000 to Rs. 2,00,000. The Act also empowers a police officer not below the rank of Superintendent of Police, to search and seize the goods. Both Copyright and Trademark Acts enumerate provisions for enhanced penalty on second or subsequent conviction. The Designs Act 2000 (Section 22). The Geographical Indications Act and the Semi conductors–Integrated Circuits–Layout Designs Act also provides for imprisonment (6 months–3 years) and fine (Rs. 50,000/- Rs. 2,00,000/-).

Further along with these specific statutes the requisite provisions of IPC (say as under Section 483 counterfeiting is made an offence), Criminal Procedure Code (like Section 93-94 for issue of search and seizure warrants, Section 154 & 156 for lodging an FIR and search and seizure) and other relevant Acts can be cited to corroborate the proceedings.

Thus, there has been considerable improvement in this field of law. But, one has to accept the fact that, the criminal law has not been properly explored, and where explored it looks frustrated and the results are not that encouraging[33]. The fact is that in India there is no serious threat of being caught and punished when found involved in piracy. Say, copyright piracy is a theft and therefore is a crime. But because of its white colour nature many a time copyright piracy is not perceived as a crime at all or at least not as serious as thefts are ordinarily considered.[34] But however, one has to acknowledge the development of the criminal procedure in this field of law. Further development is possible only when the public and other public interest organizations rise to the occasion and project the lacunae and the suggestions needed for development.

Administrative remedies are the next form of relief's. They are relief's ensured by the various authorities and institutions formed under each of the specific Acts. They mainly deal with rectification, transfer cancellation and such other remedies. If the requirements of the Act are not complied with an application showing the same to the designated authority can bring in certain reliefs. Such authorities in certain cases can suo moto also take up proceedings. This is also another form of remedy that can be obtained well within the ambit of the Acts.

Influence of Digital Era

This article will not achieve completeness if no mention is made with regard to the digital revolution in the sphere of intellectual property. In the middle ages, Francis Bacon, was able to write that, 'Knowledge, of itself, is power'; but today it has become a truism to assert that, 'information is power' and to state that we live in an information society[35]. The internet medium, aptly the Supreme World Controller today, has adjudicated the concept of geography as meaningless.

It mainly poses two challenges, namely;

(a) if a person is online, he is both every where and no where at once and

(b) no single entity or country owns or controls the internet.

This change however did not skip the world of intellectual property also. Copyright was the field primarily affected. But today with the growth in trade and companies owning intellectual property rights changing their business models and seeking new opportunities, the patent, trademark and other related systems are also coming to limelight. Given the world-wide reach of the internet, the millions of websites on the world wide web, the ease of access to and copying of others intellectual property and the famed anonymity of this new medium, perhaps the most difficult task for intellectual property owners is detecting infringement and identifying the infringer[36].

Dealing in detail with respect to the impact of digital era becomes quite difficult in the present context. So lets evaluate in brief, an aspect of the internet most closely connected with intellectual property-its concepts, infringement and remedies available-that of Domain Names.

Domain Name Disputes-Their Resolution and Remedies

Lets now throw a glance as to what a domain name is, how disputes arise, here and how they are resolved and what are the remedies available.

Domain Name?

Today internet is no more a technical magnum opus. It has evolved itself from that position to that of a necessity to the whole mankind. One aspect of internet is their use by commercial organizations and individual to promote themselves, their products and in some cases to buy and sell. This is mainly capitalized on the notion of Domain Names. This is needed for identification. A simple example can enumerate this concept. Which to ordinary eyes may seem as complicated. 'Pfizer' is a very famous pharmaceutical company carrying business throughout the world. They may have the domain name *www.pfizer.com.* Any person who types this in his computer will be welcomed by the site of the company. So through browsing, one can come to know all about Pfizer company, their latest products and also one can place orders. Thus it is clear as to how close a domain name brings customers and products. Technically speaking a domain name comprises of groups of alphanumeric characters separated by dots wherein a first group comprises of the name of the enterprise or a brand name or trading name followed by a 'top level' name identifying the nature and sometimes the location of the organization.[37] Thus internet domain names are of importance and are valuable corporate assets. So it is very similar to a trademark in the physical field and thus is entitled to equal protection.

In India, the information technology field is regulated by the Information Technology Act 2000. But this Act does not address issues concerning intellectual property especially those related to trademarks. Intellectual property infringements even though committed on internet attracts the ambit of physical laws which till now have not become competent enough to tackle internet issues. It is here that we find fingers pointed towards new legislations in this field to tackle this menace. Domain Name disputes due to its characteristic distinctivity and other related attributes has given rise to a parallel set of administrative reliefs in accordance with the judicial panorama.

Domain Name Disputes

In this virtual world of cyber space the easiest and most practiced manner for the consumers to satisfy their need is to type in a domain name of the brand or company they are looking for. So this natural connection between trademarks and domain name has been exploited by some who have registered the trademark of others or have assumed confusing or identical names as domain names and then tried to sell those domain names back to the trademark owners or third parties at a high profit.[38]. This method of infringement in this field is called as cyber squatting. Squatting itself mean occupying or dwelling illegally and here it denotes some one sitting on the property of another. An illusory example can make the position even clearer. We are all familiar with the electronic giants 'SONY' who will definitely want their domain name to be *www.sony.com*. But any squatter devoid of any legitimate reason might have already registered this name and then will start bargaining with the home company for the same for whom this name is their trademark. The intention of a squatter is made easy by the domain name registration mechanism which is on a 'first come first serve basis'. Moreover its universal character speedy and easy registration all make it easy for the cyber squatters. Blurring of trademarks, meta tag litigations etc... are some other forms of infringements in this field.

Domain Name Dispute Resolution & Remedies

The process of resolution and remedy, naturally lies in the judicial proceedings. But as mentioned before the characteristics of domain names (ie, easy and speedy registration, universality, interests of the aggrieved etc...) has transformed the judicial proceedings far from satisfactory. This gave rise to a parallel administrative system formulated by Internet Corporation for Assigned Names and Numbers (ICANN) under the auspices of WIPO, which was adopted in 1999 and called as the Uniform Domain Name Dispute Resolution Policy. It employs a mandatory process to resolve issues, which are enforced through contracts imposed by ICANN on all domain name registrants mainly through domain name registrars. However this administrative process in no way excludes the jurisdiction of domestic courts. If the decisions are contradictory then the court rule prevails. Also either party may appeal to a court of competent jurisdiction before the mandatory administrative proceeding has commenced or after such proceeding has concluded, also, 'ICANN policy provides for a ten business day period in which the domain name registrant may bring a law suit in an appropriate court to prevent the implementation of the ICANN policy decision[39]. ICANN advocates for a fast settlement of disputes by setting up a panel and hearing them and then passing the requisite orders.

The remedies available are mainly.

(a) transfer of domain names

(b) cancellation of domain names

(c) in very rare cases-costs.

However the case has to be proved beyond doubt, that the name in question was identical or confusingly similar, the alleged squatter had no legitimate interest and lastly that the squatter acted in bad faith. This dispute resolution mechanism has achieved quite a lot of success and many cases (including Indian) has been resolved under the policy.

Before concluding, a word of appreciation is to be paved for the Indian judicial action in this field. The *"YAHOO!"* case (Yahoo Inc. Vs Akash Arora)[40] is the best example. The facts here was that the defendant created a website 'Yahooindia.com', a very nearly identical one to that of the plaintiffs renowned 'yahoo.com'and provided similar services. The court here observed that.........*as a matter of fact in a matter where services are rendered through the domain name in the internet, a very alert vigil is necessary and a strict view is to be taken, for its easy access and reach by anyone from any corner of the globe,* and granted the plaintiffs injunction. The same was the decision even in the case where the word in the name was a dictionary word[41]. There have arisen number of cases since then in this field. The 'Yahoo!' case decision has been treated as a bible in this field.

Thus Indian judiciary has acted with good reflex in the present situation. But the question that rises is whether the method of resolution is keeping pace with development in this field. The answer is quite disappointing. The drastic developments in this field has stunned the field of law, but it is to be admitted that the duty of law is to protect and preserve and no development can be an excuse in achieving this aim. As the ICANN policy is still in its infancy, one can truly hope that these policies coupled with the judicial system would embark a new era of dispute resolution in the near future.

Conclusion

As the main intention of this article is to create public awareness, it becomes inevitable to understand what is needed along with what we have. Now as we have come to know what is there for us, it becomes necessary to evaluate whether they are sufficient and whether they are properly enforced.

Considering the day-by-day rapid development of intellectual property rights, the remedies available will not reach a degree of sufficiency in the near future. Further the thought process is to be invoked in order to mould the laws, so as to make them capable to assimilate the changes in the future also. This becomes important as intellectual property is a field prone to uncertainties. So a highly futuristic outlook with flexible laws is what we need and that is where we are still lagging. Further the laxity in the country's enforcement machinery is mainly due to its slackness viz. the police on one hand and the passive attitudes on the part of right holders on the other add to the misery[42]. So a legal and administrative system, learned in this field of law has become very necessary to explore more into the fields of civil and criminal remedies, which is still unexplored completely and strengthen the enforcement mechanism. The system is not alone to be blamed. The 'not so serious' attitude of the right holder is also a reason for the situation. So let's arise and awake, let's be conscious of our rights and pledge not to sleep over it. It is high time that we realize that, we the people are the heart of our system and for putting life into it, we have to beat with all vigor, energy and dedication. This is the medication for a new sunrise over the horizon, for a prosperous enlightening and justice oriented judicial system.

NOTES

1. David Brainbridge, *'Intellectual Property'* (Delhi, Pearson Education, Fifth Edition, Indian Reprint 2003) p. 3.
2. John. N. Adams, 'Industrial Property in a Globalised Environment : Issue of Jurisdiction and Choice of Law, *International Intellectual Property and the Common Law World* (Ed.) Charles Rickett and Graeme W. Austin (Oregon, Hart Publishing, 2000) p. 251.
3. A.S. Aanand, *Intellectual Property Right–An Indian Experience*, (1997) 6 SCC (Jour) p. 1.
4. Lionel Bentley & Brad Sherman, *Intellectual Property Law* (New Delhi, Oxford University Press, First Indian Edition 2003) p. 4.

5. Supra nt. 1. p. 11.
6. This was followed by Brussels Convention, Lugano Convention, Brussels I. Regulation, 1971–Hague Convention, 2001& 2004 Hague Drafts and Dreyfuss–Ginsberg Proposal.
7. S.K. Verma, 'Enforcement of Intellectual Property Rights: TRIPs Procedure & India'. 46 JILI (2004) p. 184.
8. Articles 41-61: Article 41–General Obligations, Article 42-49–Civil and Administrative Procedure and Remedies; Article 50–Professional Measures; Articles 51-60–Special requirements related to border measures and Article 61 Criminal Procedures.
9. Supra nt. 7, p. 184.
10. Overview: The TRIPs Agreement, available at http://www.wto.org/ english/ tratop_e/trips_e/intel 2_e.htm as viewed on 24.09.05.
11. Art. 41, Para 1 of TRIPs.
12. Art. 41, Para 2 of TRIPs.
13. Art. 41, Para 3 of TRIPs.
14. W.R.Cornish, *Intellectual Property* (Delhi, Universal Law Publishing Company, Third Edition, Second Indian Reprint 2003) p. 41.
15. Devan Ramachandran, 'Intellectual Property Rights–An Overview' 2003 (3) KLT (Jour) p. 57.
16. Vijay Pal Dalmia & Neelam Dalmia, 'Legal Opinion on Intellectual Property Rights, Trade Mark, Copyright, Infringement and Violation of Trade Marks, Civil and Criminal Remedies' available at http://www.i-n-d-i-a.info/indian legalguide/ as viewed on 26.09.2005.
17. Sections 15-18, CPC dealing with place of suing and Order XXXIX R 1 & 2 dealing with temporary injunction.
18. Sec. 38-42 of Specific Relief Act 1963 dealing with Permanent Injunctions.
19. (1976) 1 All ER 779; (1976)2 WLR 162, CA; also see Suprant. 3 p.3; see also Suprant. 14 p. 66.
20. *Halsbury's Laws of England* (Third Edition, Vol. I) p. 243.
21. B.L. Wadhera, *Law Relating to Patents, Trade Marks, Copyright, Designs and Geographical Indications* (Delhi, Universal Law Publishing Company, Second Edition, 2002) p. 378.

22. Supra nt. 14, p. 56.
23. *Mitra's Legal and Commercial Dictionary* (Calcutta, Eastern Law House, Fourth Edition, 1985) pp. 436–437.
24. Supra nt. 21, p. 207.
25. Supra nt. 20, p. 216.
26. Supra nt. 14, p. 63.
27. For interpretation see *Millar Vs. Taylor* (1969) 4 Burr.2303; also see N.S. Gopalakrishnan, *Intellectual Property and Criminal Law* (Bangalore, National Law School of India University, 1994) p. 234.
28. N.S. Gopalakrishnan, *Intellectual Property and Criminal Law* (Bangalore, National Law School of India University, 1994) p. 233.
29. Sec. 118-132, Indian Patents Act, 1970.
30. Supra nt. 28, pp. 245-246.
31. Supra nt. 3, p. 6.
32. Supra nt. 15, p. 58.
33. Supra nt. 28, p. 263.
34. Supra nt. 15, p. 62.
35. Ian.J.Lloyd, *Information Technology Law*,(London, Butterworths, Third Edition, 2000) p. 7.
36. Rodney. D.Ryder, *Guide to Cyber Laws* (Nagpur, Wadhwa Publication, First Edition, 2001) p.149.
37. Ibid p. 151.
38. Ibid p. 150.
39. Ibid p. 155.
40. 78 (1999) Delhi Law Times 285; also see Suprant. 36 p. 154.
41. Held in N.R Dongre Vs Whirlpool Corp. 1996 PTC (16) Whirlpool; also see Suprant. 36 p. 155.
42. Supra nt. 15, p. 62.

10 INTELLECTUAL PROPERTY RIGHTS IN OUTER SPACE

*T.R. Maruti**

Introduction

In recent times, intellectual property rights have turned out to be a topic of immense shrunk in the realm of international trade. With the rapid technological growth and contemporary geopolitical development[1], the objectives of the laws governing IPR have taken firm roots in the arena of trade and commerce. Outer Space, which is a Common Heritage of Mankind where the concept of national sovereignty is benign, has become a potential playground for technological applications for services deriving profit, thus attaining many global players. The significance of IPR in the context of the activities in the space throw open many vistas of intellectual competence and business oriented investments by super powers.[2] Outer space was declared as a *res communis which* is not subject to the sovereignty of any state, and where states are bound to refrain themselves from any acts that can adversely effect the use of an outer space by the other states.[3] The issues relating to the ownership of inventions made in space as individual notion

* Lecturer, Department of Studies and Research in Law, University of Mysore, Manasa Gangotri, Mysore, 570006

or under a joint program in a common platform is still a subject of debate in International forum. The spirit of IPR thus originally devised to protect the investment of the inventor to promote the creativity and to serve the society at large has taken new dimensions in due course, in the realm of globalization of trade, geopolitical realities, alignment and compulsion.[4]

Contentious issues in the field of the invention made in outer space arise on account of the dual nature of intellectual property rights i.e. national and international nature of patent laws and the dissimilarity in the patent laws exiting in various countries. The issue of place and time of invention itself could cause problems when the Space Treaty concepts are extended. A part of international law, space law has imparted new look to this discipline, space exploration has integrated global society. It has become an open minded and liberal society. The global economic liberalization is largely due to the impact space exploration. Global communication, education and economic benefits through remote sensing, micro gravity have produced a new inter development world society of 21st century. At the beginning of space age, space activities were predominantly public activities or governmental space programs mainly devoted to exploratory and experimental as well as military space operations, but they were not commercial. The global policy for the free goods and services trade as well as fair competition have expanded and thus create new patterns of relative investments in space activities. They range from government-government, government-private sector, to business enterprises themselves. This lies in the areas of exploration usage and commercial exploration of outer space.

Space activities are, like all human activities, subject to international and national law and regulations. In space activities for profitable commercial ventures bring about the motives for international co-operation and competition which create new legal problems, emerging from other activities i.e. space communication, space industries, and launching of the services, etc. Space law is no longer the sole prerogative of states. Space activities will in the future be conducted on three frontiers by states, international organization and the private sector. Thus intellectual property has attracted a significant amount of interest in an international scale since the end of last century.[5] Moreover, in regards to an applicability of national patent laws to outer space activities, the problem of territorial limitation creates some interesting problems, for instance, how can one deal with infringements of IPR in an outer space or how can an inventive activity actually take place on board a space station, etc. Therefore, problems will occur when an invention is used or infringed in an outer space. Since there is no provision of the patent law applicable to the extra-territorial area of an Outer Space. Some provision of the Outer Space Treaty can be defined as the main concept exercising extraterritorial jurisdiction over space objects. It is also for the patentability of invention in space, as the international patent treaties namely, the Paris Convention, the Patent Co-operation Treaty and TRIP's Agreement, etc., mainly address non-jurisdictional aspects of national patent systems similar to the validity and entitlement of a patent. Thus in order to secure specifically exclusive rights of inventions, it seems to be tolerable in an Outer Space. The number of human endeavor in space has grown by leaps and bounds and space has now become an arena for intense commercial competition, especially among the developed nations.

Further, the developments in space technology also led to the emergence of new areas of science like space medicine or space biology etc. The space technology also facilitated the use of outer space for military missions like reconnaissance early warning, navigation and global positioning systems. Apart from this, various spin off benefits are derived from space activities in the field of new materials, process and products. The law to fill the gap evolved rapidly impelled by technological innovation.[6]

Manufacturing of special materials, large crystals, exotic pharmaceuticals preparations, using of the unique environmentalist of micro gravity and high vacuum are now thought to be a possibility. Permanent space station with or without human presence is a reality of the day for industrial realization of space products. Mining and excavation of asteroids and generation of power from outer space are the possible trends in the days ahead. With ever increasing applications of space technology in various fields, the concept of outer space has gained greater prominence, though no clear definition of outer space exists. In view of this, space law is rapidly changing aspects of international law.[7] Space law is the newest main field of international law and it depends more than other fields on probe and fast technical progress. The study is intended to touch on a number of the factors that influences the identification of the legal regime governing intellectual property rights associated with reach and innovation in outer space. Intellectual property law has evolved for centuries in an earth bond context, [10] that has left a vacuum [11] as concerns its applications in outer space. Patent law is fundamentally national in its origin[12] and in scope of application, [13] notwithstanding efforts towards international harmonization,[14] the general rule is that patent will be owned by the inventor.[15]

States are free to determine all aspects of their participation in international co-operation in the exploration and use of outer space in an equitable and mutually acceptable basis. Contractual terms in such co-operative ventures should be fair and reasonable and they should be in full compliance with the legitimate rights and interests.[16] At present, when taking into consideration the importance of protection for an invention made in an outer space, we may pose many questions, such as can invention made in space be protected on earth? Do the existing patent law systems adequately cover human activities carried out in an outer space? Does the phenomenon of a legal vacuum occur in the area of conception as well as the use of invention in outer space? The growing number of states appears to be taking an active interest[17] in the more advanced process of space exploration.[18] The dichotomy between the common-law traditional property rights, and civil law natural law theory of property rights create reasons. These property rights would derive from the jurisdiction conferred by article VIII[19] and could be conferred and recognized by any country in the absence of territorial sovereignty. The rights conferred include:

1. The right to exclude others from space facilities and safety zones
2. The right to be free of interference from others
3. The right to control the activities of all natural persons and legal entities within the owner's space facility and safety zone.
4. The right directs the activities of space vehicles and persons inside those vehicles while the vehicles are in the space facility and safety zones.
5. The exclusive right to appropriate resources within the space facility and its related safety zone.
6. The right to sell property rights.

In accordance with the terms of the Outer Space Treaty, the property rights are subject to following limitations:

1. If the owner of the space facility or safety zones stops using his property for peaceful purposes, the property rights shall immediately terminate.
2. If the owner of the space facility or safety zones abandons, the property for 2 years or more, the rights shall terminate.

3. If the owner of an orbital facility deviates from the registered orbital parameters by more than for a period of one month or more, the rights shall immediately terminate.
4. Owners may not establish property rights, which would prevent other from having free access to outer space and celestial bodies.

A property right is a right to exclude someone from doing something. In view of this the place of the invention is not very important as we can learn from TRIPs Agreement.[20] This implies that an invention made in the outer space can be patented on earth without any special problem. Invention is a human activity, which can be performed in every part of the world including outer space.[21] Without the property rights, there will not be adequate investment and space resources will be under utilized. Establishing property rights on space will cost millions not billions, and can be done decades ahead of commercialization or colonization. Existing national and international law provide a rudimentary framework for commercial activities and settlement in outer space and on celestial bodies. There is much that national governments can do to encourage private activities through international agreements and national legislation.

Remote Sensing

When the Romans evolved the maxim *Cujus est solum est usque ad coelum,*[22] they were not aware of the possibility that photographs of the earth might be taken from orbiting satellites. The current law is that the right of a land owner to claim trespass above his land upto the skies is not to be interpreted literally. Nevertheless, an international convention, which harmonizes the principles relating to remote sensing by privately owned enterprises would be welcome. Intellectual property rights depend for their very existence an international co-operation, both in establishing minimum standards and also on their enforceability. In relation to copyright, trademarks and patents provide an overview of international schemes, which lay down international minimum standards of protection and enforceability.

The objectives of protecting intellectual property are to encourage invention, investment in innovation and disclosure of new technology and to recognize and reward the innovator. This sophisticated technology has reached a highly developed stage and it has given rise to legal issues, including ownership and protection of the copyright in the images, data base rights, data protection, breach of privacy and the law of trespass.

For example, if a British commercial entity were to take photographs of the earth from satellites it owns, copyright in those photographs would belong to the owner of the satellite, as the authors of the photograph i.e. the creator thereof. In English Law, the creator of a photograph has certain moral rights, i.e. the right to be identified as the creator of photograph, the right not to have the photograph subject to "derogatory" treatment and the right not to have any photograph falsely attributed to it as creator. Commercial satellite companies will publish in their websites, reproduction of photographs taken from their satellite for the commercial exploitation thereof. Website reproductions are deliberately of lower resolution, but any authorized copying thereof without license, will nevertheless amount to an infringement of copyright.

Given the very high costs of these activities and the risks involved, the private sector will only be interested in investing in the use of these international space stations for research, development and eventually production, if it can be assumed that the results of the efforts can be safeguarded from misappropriation, unauthorized use and copying. IPR will have to be protected, patients, copyrights etc, must be available and infringements must be prosecuted. Legal certainty and clarity is also needed to assess potential liability. From the industry point of view, IPR should give the investor a competitive advantage by excluding others from the use of an innovation, and by related commercial and marketing advantages as well as an improvement of the overall image of the holder of these rights.

Trade Secretes in the Outer Space Exploration

Trade secrets or know-how include any transferable, technical information which is not generally known and not patented. It can encompass ideas, concepts, inventions, manufacturing process and other confidential information. Technical information does not have to be novel or attain any levels of inventiveness. It is fundamental to the maintenance of a trade secret that it is protected and not disclosed to third parties except under circumstances that ensure the preservation of the holder's rights. Trade secret protection may be critical in certain circumstances to protect invention stemming from outer space research or other un paten table manufacturing process employed in outer space. The outer space exploration industry is heavily permitted by information technology. For most among the areas which use computer software, is the specific manufacturing industry and marketing division of aerospace equipment producers.[23]

There is no doubt that among the software used in space, some may be considered by the owners of such information as trade secrets. This being the case owners of information technology cannot avoid their employees, particularly those who are employed in the technological and scientific aspects of such information, acquiring intimate knowledge and know-how of the technology involved in such instances. It is only possible; therefore that such information may be leaked in certain circumstances by the employers concerned or any other person who may acquire knowledge of the technology through partnerships and other collaborative relationships with the owner of the employer. Employees in particular, may become dangerous competitors of their employer once their employment ceases, thus becoming a potential threat to the latter in his endeavor to safeguard his information. A trade secret is information that is secret or not generally known in the relevant industry and that gives its owner an advantage over competitors. Trade secret protection exists as long as the information is kept secret or confidential by its owner and is not lawfully and independently obtained by others. Examples of trade secrets include formulas, patterns, methods, programs, techniques, processes or compilations of information that provide ones business with a competitive advantage. The owner of a trade secret may recover damages resulting from the improper disclosure or use of its trade secret by another. Its factual secrecy cannot be presumed. Trade secrets can be protected by criminal law, e.g., through rules against theft, through provisions against criminal conspiracy in law of delict or tort unjustified enrichment, and unfair competition. Furthermore, contract arrangements may be chosen to preserve the secrecy of valuable discoveries or process. However, if nothing is agreed, the common or civil law or criminal law of the state, which governs the module, shall apply. An obligation to maintain confidentiality also might arise as a fiduciary duty or be based on good faith.

Problems and Importance of Invention

The area of intellectual property and its enforcement is wisely brought into the realms of international economic and political bargaining. Although the traditional conventions went some way to dealing with the problems, they did have serious shortcomings. The economic potential for trademark, copyright and patents alike has for a long time exceeded national parameters. Without international co-operations that potential would either become exploited or redundant, this issue has assumed modern significance as evidenced by TRIPs agreement. The pre-trips framework reflected the long-standing recognition that intellectual property rights are legitimate subject of international legal discipline. The GATT initiatives has vindicated this wholly such protection is essential for the collective, i.e., global, welfare. The international intellectual property law is a patchwork area of intersecting multilateral and bilateral agreements and their resulting harmonization of national laws. It has become an increasingly important and frequently litigated area, particularly in the patent, copyright and trade marks arenas. In all national legal systems, an invention is protected through a grant of patents, for instance, an exclusive right to exploit the invention. The main reason for the grant of a patent, in general, is to encourage inventive activities in order to benefit the general public. In an exchange to this exclusive exploration right, the patent holder is obliged to publish the invention. Patent systems have developed as a check and balance between the interests of the inventor and of the general public.

Micro Gravity

Which laws protect the research process conducted in space and the results of such research conducted in space? Can an infringement occurring in outer space give to liability under patent law?[24] These issues have at this movement, still a somewhat "exotic" character.[25] This because micro gravity activities, which take place in the near zero gravity of outer space have not developed as quickly and did not yet mature and create a commercial dimension as other space applications, such as for instance, satellite remote sensing and satellite telecommunications. Further more, the private sector activities active in the field of space activities are not necessarily very interested in micro gravity research at this stage.[26] Although pharmaceutical and biological aspects may have a potential interest in micro gravity activities.[27] This is a far cry from a market of commercial production in outer space. Apart from the technical and financial barriers for micro gravity research, a clear legal, structure is also needed[28] in order to encourage private sector participation.

Conclusion

The field of IPR and space activities is only beginning to take on its economic and ethical importance. The protection and enforcement of IPR should contribute to the promotion of technological innovation and to the transfer and dissemination of technology, to the mutual advantage of producer and user of technological knowledge and in a manner conducive to social and economic welfare, and to a balance of rights and obligation. It is important that as soon as regulatory actions will be taken to ensure applicability of IP on activities in outer space. In this way the regulation of space activities will have to be placed in a proper perspective, namely as a part of international law having its own special characteristics. With the large reservoir of intellectuals, technological base and ambitions to utilize the hi-tech applications to meet the needs of common man, cannot afford to ignore the implication of IPR related issues not only from the perspective of trade and commerce also from the point of technological development, industrialization and social justice. In view of this or in a similar vein there ought be mutual co-existence, reciprocity, comity, good order and harmonization between the various states. With this background there is a need for new framework for universal justice in face of existing geopolitical disparities and economic future of mankind. Moreover, an integrated, global system must be implemented. It is also necessary to improve co-ordination to eliminate duplication and identity gaps and increase the availability and affordability of activities in the outer space.

NOTES AND REFERENCES

1. Masson Tanj, L zwaw Poblo, M J Menders De Leon, *Air and Space Law* De Larg Ferenda. Wassenberhg Published by Martinas Nijhoff publisher. Boston /London International Institute of *Air and Space Law* Leiden University.
2. Gabriel Lafferranderif *"Out look on Space Law"* the Thirty Years.
3. Abeyrayantne Ruwantish, *"Air Frountiers of Aerospace Law"* (Aghaste Publishing Ltd. Gower House Crofi Road Aleshot Hunts Gu 2nd 3.H.R. England).
4. Supra note *Air and Space Law.*
5. William's. Slomansion, Fundamental *Perspective On International Law* (4th Edition) 2003.
6. Sir Robert Jennings DC and Sir Arthur Watts, *Oppenheam's International Law* 9th Edition Vol. 1 Peace Part 2-4.
7. John O' Brien *International Law*, (Covendish publishing Ltd. U.K).
8. Supra Note *frontiers of Aerospace Law.*
9. By V.S. Mani, S. Bhatt, and Bal Krishna Reddy, Recent *Trends In International Space Law and Policy* New Dehli, Laners Books 1997.
10. http//www.oasa.unvina.org/space law.
11. http//www.oasa.unvina.org/html.
12. http//www.space future.com/egil glosary egi ?
13. http//www.inescap.org/bullitin/bal 21 April 28.
14. see International Patent conventions as European Convention, the Patent Co-Operation Treaty, the Paris Convention, the Bern Convention, the Rome Convention and the TRIP'S.
15. James T. Fawcett and Poul Torremans "Intellectual Property Rights and Private International Law, Published by Cluvender Press Oxford 1998.
16. Article 1 of the Outer Space Treaty 1967.
17. Stanford Law Review Volume, 50 April 1998 Number 4.
18. Myre S. Mac Douglas, Herald D. Lasswell,and Inan A. Vlasie *Law and Public Order In Space* New Haven and London Yale University Press 1962.

19. Outer Space Treaty.
20. Article 27 of the TRIPs Agreement.
21. Said Mostashar 'Research and Innovation in Outer Space' Liability and Intellectual Property Rights.
22. Jenks C. Wilfred, *Space Law* Stevens and Sons, London. And also see *Law of Air* by McNair.
23. Debroy Bibek *Intellectual Property Rights,* BR Publishing Corporation,1998.
24. Micro gravity.nasa.gov/mgnews/spring /97.
25. http//www. Esrin.esait/export/esacp/pr26.
26. http//wwwesapb.esrin.esa/it/bulliten/ballet82/hiero82html.
27. http//www131.176.49/space flight-/map/ac intern-html.
28. http//www.estec esa sn/space flight/ace html.

11 PRODUCTION PATENT REGIME: CHALLENGES AND OPPORTUNITIES

*M. Suresh Benjamin**

Introduction

With the passing of the Patent Amendment Act of 2005, India has complied with the international obligation under the TRIPS Agreement of the WTO. TRIPS requires member states to make available patents in all fields of technology for both products as well as processes. Until January 1, 2005, the Indian Patents Act 1970 provided patents only for processes. The power of the Government not to grant product patent in the field of medicines, foods, and agro-chemicals is no longer available. While drug companies are wooing (Novartis AG, Merk & Co., and Astrageneca Pharmaceuticals) drug scientists with attractive salary packages, India will have to consider MAILBOX applications for patents filed from abroad since 1995. Understandably, there are 7000 applications in the Mailbox out of which 250 applications relate to 'new chemical entities'. As a result, it is apprehended that with the effect of the Patent (Amendment) Act 2005, it would be a threat to domestic industry and there would be price rise in the products

* Lecturer, Saradavilas Law College, Mysore - 570 006.

especially in drugs and medicine . The challenge before India is that how she is going to eliminate this apprehension by offering protection to the IPR? Why is India crying hoarse? The purpose of the article is to examine the pros and cons of the TRIPS in term of the health care, impact of the third set of amendments to the Patent Acts 2005 and focus the flexibilities available within the framework of the TRIPS to face the challenges.

Patent System in India

The history of intellectual property system in India can be traced back to 1856. The first legislation on the subject was brought into force in the form of an Act on protection inventions based on the British Patent Law of 1852. As per this legislation, a system was introduced in India in the form of granting of certain privileges to an investor of new manufacture for a period of 14 years. This Act was enacted with some modifications in 1859, in which patent monopolies were called Exclusive Privileges. According to this legislation, an inventor of a new manufacture, by filing a specification disclosing the invention could obtain the exclusive privilege of making, selling, and using the invention in India and authorizing others to do so for the term of 14 years from the date of filing of such specification. In 1872 the Patents and Designs Protection Act was passed which was subsequently replaced by the Protection of Inventions Act 1883. These Acts were consolidated as Inventions and Designs Act 1888. Subsequently the Act of 1888 was replaced by the Indian Patents and Designs Act 1911[1].

Since then due to substantial changes in the political and economic conditions of the country, it was found desirable to enact comprehensive law on the subject. The Patents Bill, 1953 was introduced in the Lok Sabha but it lapsed on the dissolution of the first Lok Sabha. In 1965 the Patents Bill 1965 was moved in the Parliament but could not be proceeded with for want of time and eventually lapsed with the dissolution of the third Lok Sabha in 1967[2]. The Parliament passed the Bill in 1970 after a long debate. The Patent Act 1970 came into force on the 20th April, 1972.

Patentable Invention

Although no general rule can be laid down as to what constitutes invention, yet invention is being defined as follows-"invention" means any new and useful art, process, method or manner of manufacture; machine, apparatus or other article; substance produced by manufacture and includes any new and useful improvement of any of them.[3] Whether invention is patentable or not, depends upon the fulfillment of three requisite conditions namely (a) novelty (b) Non-obviousness and (c) industrial application. The Patent Act enumerates inventions, which are not patentable for e.g.; invention relating to drugs, medicines, foods, method of agriculture or horticulture; process for the treatment of human beings, contrary to law or morality etc.,[4]

WTO & TRIPS

Following World War II , it was found necessary to revitalize world trade. Trade was intended to be as free as possible, promising greater progress of the participating countries than by adherence to protectionist self-sufficiency[5]. With the objects of free trade and tariff, the GATT (General Agreement on Tariffs and Trade) came into force in January 1, 1948 initially among 23 states. Traditionally GATT has been regarded as a forum for establishing international trade rules confining only to the goods sector[6]. Domestic issues such as policies and matters outside the goods sector were regarded as outside the jurisdiction of GATT[7]. The earlier seven rounds of negotiations confined themselves to trade issues with a view to liberalizing the global trade in goods.

Seven rounds of negotiations which were undertaken under the auspicious of the GATT contribute towards the liberalization of world trade. The eighth round of negotiations which was commenced in Punta del Esta, Uruguay in 1986 and concluded in 1993 included new areas for negotiations such as agriculture, textiles and intellectual property rights. Issues relating to IPR were incorporated in the agreement by way of appellation of the term "Trade Related Aspects of Intellectual property Rights which is now popularly known as TRIPS. The agreement establishing the WTO was concluded at Marakkesh on April 15th 1994 and came into force on January 1, 1995[8].

There are 73 articles with 7 parts in the TRIPS. TRIPS recognizes two important principles namely National Treatment and Most Favoured Nation Treatment. (Part II provides for Standards concerning the availability, scope and use of IPR). TRIPS covers 7 categories of IPR:

(a) Copyrights

(b) Patents

(c) Trade Mark

(d) Geographical indications

(e) Industrial Designs

(f) Integrated Circuits and

(g) Trade secrets.

The principal object of TRIPS is to provide certain norms and standards to be followed by the member countries in respect of IPR especially in the area of patents. TRIPS agreement relating to patent provides the following provisions;

(a) to extend the protection to the product patent in all the fields of science and technology without any exceptions.

(b) to increase the duration of the patent to 20 years from the date of filing;

(c) to grant the compulsory license on the individual merits of the case with the consent of the patent holders;

(d) the burden of proof (BOP) lies on the dependant;

(e) the patent rights are equally available irrespective of whether the product are locally manufacture or imported;

(f) protection for micro organisms and

(g) enactment of effective system for new plant varieties.

Now, let us look at the system under the existing Patent Act 1970. Any inventions relating to the medicinal, surgical, curative, prophylactic or other treatment of human beings[9] and any method of agriculture or horticulture are not Patentable[10].The term of every patent granted under the act shall in respect of an invention claiming the method or process of manufacture of a substance, where the substance is intended for use, or is capable of being used as food or as a medicine or drug, be five years from the date of sealing of the patent, or seven years from the date of the patent whichever period is shorter ; and in respect of any other invention, be fourteen years from the date of the patent[11]. In respect of grant of compulsory license, the Patent Act 1970 provides that after expiration of three years from the date of the sealing of a patent, any person interested may make an application to the controller alleging that reasonable requirements of the public with respect to the patented invention have not been satisfied or that the patented invention is not available to the public at a reasonable price and praying for the grant of a compulsory license, to work the patented invention. The controller if satisfied that the reasonable requirements of the public with respect to the patent invention have not been satisfied or that the patented invention is not available to the public at a reasonable price, may order the patentee to grant a license upon such terms as he may deem fit[12]. Beside this, the Central Government may also make an application to the controller for an order that the patent may be endorsed with the words "Licenses of Right" on the ground that the reasonable requirements of the public with respect to the patented invention have not been satisfied or that the patented invention is not available to the public at a reasonable price[13]. The burden of proof lies on the plaintiff who alleges the infringement of his patent right. There is no protection of patent for micro organisms and new plant varieties of plant.

The implication of the TRIPS

The Indian concerns about the TRIPS Agreement are as follows:

1. Extension of product patent particularly , in the field of pharmaceuticals, drugs becoming expensive and beyond the reach of the common man due to heavy royalties being charged by the patent holder of such drugs, raising the drug prices[14].
2. In the agriculture sector the farmers would be loaded with the burden of paying royalties to the supplier of the improved variety of seeds who would be the patent owners for such seed.
3. The Government will be handicapped in granting of compulsory license on the ground of non-availability of the patented invention.
4. The provisions of "Licence of Right" outlined in section 89 will have to be re-examined in the light of the TRIPS Agreement.
5. The TRIPS Agreement will have adverse impact on domestic Reasearch and Development once the patent law includes product patent in pharmaceutical industry. Indian drug companies may not be able to face global competition due to the lack of sufficient financial resources and technology.
6. The traditional knowledge of medicine in India i.e. Unani and Ayurvedic are also threatened by the system of product patent.

Obligation under TRIPS

Under the TRIPS Agreement it is the obligation of the member countries where their patent laws are not consistent with the TRIPS provisions of the agreement, to take steps to modify their legislations to make them consistent. The TRIPS provisions of the agreement provide a period of 5 years from 1-1-95 for developing countries for implementation of all provisions of TRIPS. Further, it also provides for an additional period of 5 years to developing countries like India to comply with the TRIPS Agreement. India being a member of WTO has to implement the TRIPS into to. If the TRIPS Agreement is not implemented in its letter and spirit, the WTO may take retaliatory action against such country.

Therefore, the Patent Act of 1970 has been amended thrice in 1999, 2002 and 2005 in tune with the TRIPS.

The third Amendment Patent Act and its Controversies

A great acrimony was created when the Government of India proposed to introduce a third set of amendments to the Patent Act. The Government of India, however issued ordinance on 26th December 2005 which was subsequently replaced by the Patent(Amendment) Act 2005. The Amendment to the Patent Act 1970 was inevitable as India had to comply with the international obligation under the TRIPS within its deadline 1st January 2005. India being a founder member of the GATT 1948 cannot avoid its obligation nor procrastinate to change the law beyond the moratorium.

With the effect of the Patent (amendment) Act 2005 India recognizes the extention of the scope of patent from the process to the product patent. As a result, India has to relax the definition of the invention and grant product patent in all fields of science and technology especially in food drugs and medicine. The Controller is no longer an authority to grant compulsory license to any person interested on the ground of non-availability of the patented article. The term of protection extends to 20 years. In addition to this, India will have to provide protection for micro-organisms and new plant varieties.

Here, the controversy crops up. Firstly *medicine beyond reach:* Patents and medicine are inextricably inter-linked. Patent is a monopoly right. Drug companies possess separate monopolies over many life-saving and other drugs, including those that treat HIV-AIDS. As monopolists, these companies have no compunctions about fixing high prices for essential drugs. High prices create a clear divide between the rich who can afford the medicine and the poor who cannot[15]. India is turning its own international law upside down by rushing to comply with the TRIPS deadline. India has given greater credence to WTO deadlines than democracy jeopardizing its sovereignty. The WTO is not the only treaty that India has to comply with. It is also a signatory to the Universal Declaration of Human Rights 1948, the Civil and Political and Economical and Social Rights covenants 1996 . The Supreme personal liberty provisions of Art.21, including the right to health in its interpretations. The WTO cannot override these obligations[16].

Secondly, *Threat to domestic industry: The Indian pharmaceutical Alliance* says that the new Patent Amendment Act will seriously compromise the ability of domestic industry to achieve its ambitious target of Rs. 90,000 crores by 2010 as many patents would have expired in the U.S but Indian companies will be bound to patents in this country, Therfore delay the entry of generics such as patents for polymorphs, hydrates, isomers, metbolites, substantially pure, particle size and blood levels must not be permitted[17]. India not only has to provide patent protection for medicines developed after January 1, 2005, it also has to consider the applications filed during 1995-

2005 under the mailbox provision[18]. There are 7000 applications in the mailbox filed since 1995. If these applications are considered, surely it will have serious ramifications and dimensions on the Indian industry. Out of 7000 applications, only 250 application relate to chemical entities and associated new drugs that were developed outside India and remaining 6750 applications relate to minor thing such as inventions with little change in the structure of existing drugs.

Applications in the mail box are seeking patents protection for drugs which are already being marketed by domestic companies. Unless these applications are regulated nearly 3000 crores of the drugs market will be captured by the foreign patents and as result, Indian companies will be forced to withdraw patents from the market. India is the 4th largest country in producing drugs and medicines and a leading country in supplying medicine or pharmaceutical products to the least developed countries at a affordable price. India may not be able to export the drugs to its dependant countries like African countries.

Another apprehension is that new IPR regime will have adverse impact on domestic R & D in the pharmaceutical sector. Indian industry is unable to engage in the development of new molecules due to the lack of sufficient financial resources and in case of any litigation over the patent, Indian industry cannot fight the major multinational pharmaceutical companies.

Thirdly & Lastly- *likely impact of monopolies:* Health activists allege that primary purpose of the present amended Patent Act is to introduce product patent, as required by TRIPS particularly in the pharmaceutical sector. The earlier Act provided patent protection for process only. The implication of this is that by giving to the owner exclusive right over manufacturing process, any person can make and sell a particular product as long as he uses a different process to produce it. On the other hand, a product patent prevents others from manufacturing, selling, distributing or importing the patented product even if the product is produced through different process. India is only country in the world which supplies drugs at lower price. With the introduction of product patent regime, patent owners will be able to monopolise the market for 20 years and fix exorbitant prices on the essential medicines and thereby keeping the majority of Indians (poor patients) out of the reach of drugs.

The present Act of 2005 does not strengthen the state power to issue compulsory licence in the public interest. The introducing of a product patent would not promote the public health.

Strategies to meet Challenges Under New IPR Regime

According to the Commerce Minister the above raised objections are based on misconceptions. While acknowledging the fact that the present patent (Amendment) Act 2005 being passed in line with global norms, Commerce Minister asserts that amendment to Patents Act does not affect the IPR protection, rather it enhances the country's credibility in the field of drug discovery and intellectual property[19]. As India is emerging as a low cost center for medical research , more research has to take place and enable us to use the large pool of technical and scientific talent in country. The Patent (Amendment) Act provides cost benefit pharma companies, it is also a huge opportunity for small international companies which do not have well developed drugs discovery programmes[20]. In, other words there is an enormous scope for investment of capital by both indigenous and foreign market forces for manufacturing of drugs in India. India's vast scientific man power can be harnessed to make industry an innovator of new drugs at lower cost. This will help the Indian drug industry take advantage of product patents, instead of making it dependant on the development of drug abroad for producing copies[21]. It was observed that new patents regime would not affect domestic price as 97% of drugs were already off patented.

The patents Amendment Act has introduced a provision for enabling grant of compulsory license for export of medicines to the countries, which are known for manufacture to meet emergent public requirement, a clause availed under the Doha Declaration on TRIPS and Public Health. In addition, it has incorporated provisions relating to opposition-procedure covering both pre-grant and post-grant opposition in the patent office. It also strengthen the provisions relating to national security to guard against patenting abroad of dual use of technologies. It also provides provision relating to Intellectual Property Appellate Board to extend its jurisdiction to revocation of patents under certain cases. Necessary safeguards have been built in the legislation to protect the interest of the Indian pharmaceutical industry and prevent an inordinate rise of prices. On the issue of 'evergreening' where the discovery of new properties for the existing drugs is concerned, new patents will not be allowed. On 23rd March 2005, the Union Commerce Minister declared " the new regime will not result in shooting up of prices of drugs as it is entirely up to the Government to declare a drug as essential and bring it in the drug prices control order."

Conclusions and Suggestions

In the above discussion, one can assess the pros and cons of the product patent under the new IPR regime. Admittedly, India was a reluctant state in introducing changes to the Patent Act 1970 in tune with international obligation under the TRIPS Agreement. However, it was international mandate to comply with TRIPS. The present Indian Patents Act was passed in 1972 when there was incessant development of science and technology especially in the pharmaceutical, food and industry. Had the Indian Patent Act been changed from time to time during the development stage of chemical industry and provisions were modified in the light of international development, industry would have acquired the expertise to develop product patent as well. India never allowed product patent in the field of food drugs and agriculture. If product patent were allowed India would have been in a position to manufacture drugs and supply not only to the domestic needs but also to the needs of least developed countries like Kenya, Tanzania, Ethiopia and so on. For India, drug is not a matter of trade but concern with life and death of the people attacked by the severe disease like HIV-AIDS , cancer, epilepsy, tuberculosis, pneumonia. For instance a patient suffering from Chronic Mycloid Leukaemia (CML), the generic version of the drug costs Rs. 9000 to 12000 p.m. the Government has now granted EMR to Novartis AG for their version of the drug, Gleevec. It is needless to say the said drug is a life saving medicine. Now, patients suffering from CML will have to pay price about 1,20,000 p.m. Similarly a typical anti-psychotic drug is a drug for the treatment of life long mental illness-schizophrenia. There is price difference between the locally manufactured and those of MNC's. As such, hospitals prescribe the latter. At present, 14 million people die each year from infectious diseases in developing countries from Africa, Asia and South American regions, jointly constituting 115 of world population. HIV-AIDS alone have caused death of about 3 million people including 60,000 children. Around 95% of AIDS victims are people living in developing countries. Only 3 lacs out of 60 lacs patients of HIV-AIDS have access to life saving drugs (The ICFAI Journal of IPR Vol III 2004). With reference to Karnataka state alone, the report of the HIV Sentinel surveillance reveals that HIV+AIDS is spreading fast. Belgaum top the list for HIV positive case with 27% followed by Gulbarga (17.2%), Dharwad (16%), Bangalore (10.4%), Bellary (10%), and Mysore (9.3%)[23]. Most affected victims of HIV/AIDS are women and truck drivers who are living below the poverty line. About 5 lakh people in the state are HIV infected in such being the case, prices of drugs will go up substantially once the product patent is allowed under the present IPR regime. It has been suggested by the health activists that India has to make use of flexibilities in the TRIPS Agreement. TRIPS provided following flexibilities in favour of developing countries.

(a) It allows for parallel imports under the doctrine of "Exhaustion of Patent rights" (Art.6 of the TRIPS agreement).

(b) The agreement shall be conducive to social and economic welfare and contribute to a balance of rights and obligation (Art.7).

(c) Government can take measures necessary for protection of public health and nutrition and to promote the public interest in sectors of vital interest. Compulsory Licence and Licence of rights are such instruments (Art. 8).

(d) It allows national legislation to give government the right to grant compulsory licence to third parties to manufacture a generic version of a product without authorization of patent holder (Art. 31).

In order to take advantage of flexibilities available in the TRIPS Agreement, the following suggestion can be considered:

(a) As there is no mechanism to deal with 'Mailbox' application for patent filed during the transitional period of 1995 and 2005, the patent regime should be made applicable from the prospective date and not the retrospective effect.

(b) As per the art. 27 of TRIPS, the criteria for patentability are 'novelty', "inventive step" or "non-obviousness" and "capability of industrial application". India should adhere to the strict requirements of patentability under

TRIPS and insist on clinical demonstration to show therapeutic improvement over previously patented form of the medicine.

(c) Rate of royalty to the inventors should be fixed and regulate the price control system.

Constitutionality

At this stage, one may raise a question that what is the rationality behind the above suggestions. Can India go for suitable legislation? If so, how is it justifiable under the National law and International conventions/treaty? Under the Universal Declaration of Human Rights 1968 and the Civil and Political and Economic and Social Covenants 1966, right to health is a basic human right which requires the state to manufacture and supply life saving drugs to the people at affordable price. Article 21 of the Constitution casts the obligation on the state to preserve life. In Paramananda katara Vs Union of India[24], Supreme Court has held that it is the obligation of those who are in charge of the health of the community to preserve life so that innocent may be protected. In P.B.K. Mazdoor Samiti Vs State of West Bengal[25] the Supreme Court has further observed that the denial of the medical aid by the hospitals to an injured person on the ground of non-availability of beds amounted to violation of right to life U/A 21 of the Constitution. In Consumer Education and Research Centre Vs Union of India[26] it was held that the right to health and medical care is fundamental right U/A 21 as it is essential for making the life of the person meaningful and purposeful with human dignity. In Welfare State providing medical facility for the people is an essential obligation of the Government. The expression 'right to life' has included 'right to health'. Therefore, the State should step in to ensure that the price of the drugs will be regulated by certain mechanisms and no pharmaceutical industry will be allowed to monopolize the market.

NOTES AND REFERENCES

1. Hand Book of Indian Patent Law and Practice by N.R. Subharam.
2. Patents, Trade Marks, Copy right, Design and Geographical Indication by B.R. Wadehra.
3. Section 2 (1) (j) of the Patent Act 1970.
4. Sections 3,4 and 5 (Ibid).
5. Taxmann's Indian Patents Law.
6. Supra 1.
7. Supra.
8. Intellectual Property Rights and Law by Dr. G.B. Reddy.
9. Section 3(i) of the Patent Act 1970.
10. Section 3 (h) (Ibid).
11. Ibid Section 53 (a) and (b).
12. Ibid Section 84.
13. Ibid Section 86.
14. Law relating to Patents, Trademarks (Supra 2.).
15. The Hindu of 10-12-04.
16. Supra 15.
17. The Hindu of 28-11-04.
18. Art 70 & 80 of TRIPS.
19. The Deccan Herald at 29-1-05.
20. Supra
21. The Hindu of 9-12-04.
22. The New Indian Express of -03-05.
23. The Hindu of 22-5-05.
24. 1989 SC 2039.
25. 1996 (4) SCC 34.
26. 1995 (3) SCC 42.

12 PROTECTION OF INDUSTRIAL DESIGNS– A CRITICAL ANALYSIS

*N. Vani Shree**

Introduction

Industrial design as a form of endeavor, and as part and parcel of the business of manufacture, is something which has existed ever since the production of useful article engaged the attention of man from the days of the ancient civilizations, through the middle ages, the eighteenth century and the Victorian era, down to the present day thought and effort have continually been devoted to the outline and the ornamentation of the article produced sometimes more consciously, at times less consciously the designer, who in earlier days was often the craftsmen himself, has sought to blend the efficiency of the article for its purpose with the appeal which is the finished product must make to the eye of its observer.

If good design is to be encouraged, those for producing designs; must be protected against the promiscuous taking by others of the fruits of their labour. To this end, industrial designs have been safeguarded by legislation for a great many years. The method chosen has been to confer copyright in their work upon the owner of such designs.

* Faculty, JSS Law College, Mysore.

The law of designs in India is controlled by Designs Act, 1911 and the Rules made there under in Design Rules and now by Designs Act 2000. The copyright in Industrial Design is an Industrial Property. This paper discusses about the protection of industrial Designs. It also discusses in brief about industrial designs under TRIPS agreement and Paris Convention.

Definition

Section 2 (4) of, Designs Act 1911 defines Industrial design as follows:

"Means the exclusive right to apply a design to any article in any class in; which, the design is registered".

As regards the term "Design' Sec 2 (5) of the Act defines it as follows:

It means only the features of shape, configuration, pattern ornament applied to any article by any, Industrial process or means whether manual, mechanical or chemical, separate or combined, which in the finished article appeal to and judged solely by the eye; but does not include any mode or principle of construction or anything which is in substance a mere mechanical device, and does not include and trade mark defined in clause (V) of Sub. Sec (1) of the sec (2) of the trade, and Merchandise Marks Act, 1958 or property mark as defined in sec. 479 of the Indian Penal Code.

From the definition it is clear that the definition is exclusive and only those which have the following characteristics can be brought under the purview of design namely.

1. There should be a definite shape, configuration, pattern or ornament.
2. Such shape, configuration, pattern or ornament should be applied to any article..
3. Such application to be any Industrial process or means whether manual, mechanical or, chemical, separate or combined.

4. And more important such application gives a finished article that, appeals to and judged solely by the eye. And Design does not include.
   (a) Any mode or principle of construction or
   (b) Mere mechanical designs and
   (c) Not a Trademark defined under Sec 2 (1) (V) of the Trade and Merchandise Marks Act 1958 or property mark under Sec. 479 of the Indian Penal Code.

'Design' means only the features of shape, configuration, pattern or ornament applied to any article by any industrial process, or means, which in the finished article appeal to and are judged solely by the eye and which is not a mere mechanical device. A design in order to be registerable must be new or original not previously published in India. A design may be, incorporated in the article itself as in the case of a shape or configuration which is three dimensional in nature, or it may be represented two dimensional in nature or it may be represented two dimensionally on a piece of paper in such a way that the article to which it is applied could be visualized, shape and configuration which is three dimensional in nature, or it may be represented two dimensionally on a piece of paper in such a way that the article to which it is applied could be visualized, shape and configuration are three dimensional, eg., The shape of a bottle, vase and so on; while patterns or ornament are two dimensional as in the case of patterns for textiles, wallpaper etc., which serves the purpose of decoration. A design may be the shape of a wash basin, a motorcar, a locomotive engine or any material object, it may be the shape embodied in a sculptured or a plastic figure, which is to model for commercial production, or it may be a drawing in the flat or a complex pattern to be used for the manufacture of things such as linoleum or wallpaper. A design must have individuality of appearance, which makes it not merely visible but noticed although it need not possess any artistic merit.

Meaning

Industrial Design

Industrial designs can be both aesthetic and functional. Industrial design laws generally protect designs that are ornamental or aesthetic, and are applied on industrial products. Such designs are usually non–functional and merely enhance the aesthetic appeal of industrial products, although purely artistic designs that cannot be applied to any utilitarian objects are excluded. Similarly, purely functional designs are also generally excluded i.e, designs that are dictated solely by the function which the articles, to which these are applied, are to perform.[1] Typically products on which industrial designs are applied include furniture, packaging, watches, textiles and handicrafts. Such designs, while being creative do not usually take up huge investments. Their economic value lies in enhancing the aesthetic appeal of industrial products to consumers.

Industrial designs can also be protected under copyright law, thus obtaining simultaneous and concurrent protection. This means that even designs that fail to obtain industrial design protection can be covered by copyright. Copyright protection is automatically available, without formalities, upon the creation of a design in the form of a drawing, a photograph, data or a 3-dimensional shape. However, even while copyright gives a longer term of protection, unlike industrial design rights, copy-right protects only against direct reproduction and not against independent development of a similar design. Some copyright laws also specifically deny protection to making of articles based on copyrighted industrial designs. In some jurisdictions trademark laws also protect 3-dimensional marks, including trade dress, if these are distinctive signs capable of deceiving consumers with respect to the origin of the goods.[2] Laws of unfair competition, including the common law of passing off, would also apply to designs.[3]

Perhaps, the protection of industrial designs is the only area of intellectual property under TRIPS where no new ground has been broken in terms of substantive improvements over the pre-existing national laws. This subject matter was not on the agenda of the US at the initial stage of the TRIPS negotiations. The subject was introduced into the negotiations at the initiative of the EC and Switzerland. On account of the differences in the legislation on industrial designs in the US and Europe, there could be an agreement on only a basic framework in spite of ambitious proposals made, especially on the protection of textile designs.

Nevertheless, it is the first time that substantive obligations on the protection of industrial designs have been agreed to in a major multilateral treaty.

Functional Design

Designs which are functional are not registrable under the Designs Act, thus if a designer makes an article in a certain shape not in order to make it appeal to the eye of a customer but solely to make the article work o to perform functional requirements, no registrable design exists. The drawings or diagram on the basis of which the articles are made artistic works within the definition of the articles being three-dimensional representations of the drawing are reproductions in a material form of the drawings. Thus such drawings and the articles made there from enjoy copyright protection for the lifetime of the author plus sixty years.

Subject Matter and Procedure

Design Must be Applied to Articles

A Design is something which is applied to an article and is not the article itself. A piece of paper on which a pattern is drawn cannot be a subject matter for registration of design. But a paper on which is drawn a three dimensional object with the pattern shown on it may be registered as design because here the design is a representation of the article, on which the pattern is applied. Similarly if the drawing is that of an article is a bottle, vase, chair, table, a motor body it would be registerable as a design if it is novel. Here what may be registered is the shape of an article and the drawing on the paper is only a convenient representation of the shape of the article.

An article to which the design is to be applied must be something which is to be delivered to the purchaser as a finished article. Thus in general buildings and structures like a petrol filling station cannot be considered as article within the definition of design. But portable structures which are sold as finished articles may be subject matter for registration of design.

The design of a part of an article is not registrable as a design unless the part is sold separately as an article.

There are four features relevant to an industrial design. They are shape, configuration, pattern and ornament. The term shape and configuration refer to the form of an article and is usually three dimensional in nature. Pattern and ornament are decorative features ordinarily applied to the surface of the articles in the case of wallpaper, textile and playing cards. It is two dimensional in nature Pictures or devises printed on package are also considered industrial design.

Appeal to the Eye

The definition, of design refers to features of shape, etc., which in the finished article appeal to and are judged solely by the eye. This shows that not all shapes or configurations or patterns are registrable designs. The feature should appeal to the eye and should be judged solely by the eye and not by any functional considerations. The eye must be the eye of the customer on a visual test.

There must be a special peculiar, distinctive, significant or striking appearance. Something which catches the eye and in this sense appeal to the eye. The customer must be

Influenced only by the eye and not by the suitability of the article for any particular purpose. It is not necessary that all the features of the design should be visible at the time of purchase; but they should be visible when it is actually used for the purpose for which the article was brought, e.g., an egg shaped chocolate with exterior and interior having different colours.

Novelty and Originality

A design in order to be registrable must be both new and original not previously published in India. Natural objects applied as designs may be, novel or original example the representation of a tree or a building on a spoon may be considered new or original. Here the novelty consists in the application of a drawing or design taken from material source to an article. The words new or original involve the idea of novelty either in the pattern, shape ornament itself or in the way in which an old pattern shape of an animal may be new and original. In order to be registrable the design should be substantially different from pre existing designs applied to the class of article.

The novelty and originality of a particular part of the article may be sufficient to import the character of novelty and originality to the whole. A combination of known designs may be considered novel if the appearance of the combination as a whole is new.

Colour may form an element in a design, but colour or colouring as such does not constitute a design, unless the change of colour create a new pattern or ornament.

No Prior Publication

The design must not be previously published in India though the word publication has not been defined by the Design Act 1911. To constitute publication, a design must be available to the public or it has been shown or disclosed to some person who is not bound to keep it secret. For eg:- the display of a design on a skirt of a model in a fashion show constitutes publication of the design. In the case of *Wimco Ltd., Bombay V/s Meena match Industries*, the court held that publication means the opposite of being kept secret. It is considered published if a design is no longer a secret. There is publication if the design has been disclosed to the public or the public is put in possession of the design. The disclosure even to one person is sufficient to constitute publication.

Who is entitled to file an Application or Registration of a Design?

The proprietor can apply section 48 (1) lays down that any one person who claims to be the proprietor of any new original design which is not previously published in India can apply for the registration of the design.

Section 2 (14) defines who a proprietor of a new or original design is:

(a) Where the author of the design, for good consideration executes the work for some other person, proprietor means the person for whom the design is so executed, and

(b) Where any person acquires the design or the right to apply the design to any article either exclusively of any other person or otherwise means in the respect and to the extent in and to which the design or right has been so acquired, the person by whom the design or right is so acquired, and

(c) In any other case means the author of the design.

And where the property in or the right to apply has devolved from the original proprietor upon any other person includes that other person. In the case Viredenburg's Registered Design, it was held that if there are two persons each of whom has produced a similar design and communicated the fact of such authorship to the other, neither of them alone is the proprietor of the new, or original design. There is joint authorship, of the design.

Foreigner can Apply for Registration of Design

There is no express provisions in the Design Act which bars foreigners from applying for registration. However the convention followed is that if a country does not offer the identical registration right to Indian citizens for their designs in their country, its citizens would be eligible to apply for registration, of design in India.

Registration of Design

Registration designs is done by the patent office at Calcutta. The procedure for registration is contained in sections 43–45 of the Designs Act and Rules 34-43 of the Design Rules.

Briefly, the procedure consists of the following steps:

1. Submission of Application.
2. Acceptance/Objections/Refusal.
3. Removal of objections/appeal to central government
4. Decision of Central Government.
5. Registration of the Design.

Submission of Application

The proprietor of the design has to file application for registration of the design. 'According to section 43 (1), the controller may on application made by any person claiming to be the proprietor of any new or original design previously published in India, register the design. The application is to be accompanied by the prescribed fee.

An application may endorse on the application a brief statement of the novelty the claims for his design as for example. "Novelty resides in the shape of the ash tray as illustrated".

Acceptance / Objection

On consideration of the application if the controller finds that the design fulfills all the prescribed requirements he shall register the design. If in consideration of the application any objections appear to the controller, a statement of these objections shall be sent to the applicant or his agent.

Certain emblems and seals like the emblem and seal of the United Nations Organization, of the World Health Organisation, of the Government of India or any state and the Indian National flag are not registrable as design.

Removal of objection / Appeal to the Central Government

The applicant, has to remove the objection within one month of communication of the objections to him failing which the application shall be deemed to have been withdrawn. He may also apply to the controller for being heard on the matter. When the controller refuses the application after the submission he may directly appeal to the central government whose decision is final.

The Registration of the Design

On the completion of the above procedure, the controller shall grant a certificate of registration to the proprietor of the design.

Term (Section 47)

Registration of the design in the first instance will be for a period of five years, which can be extended to another two successive "five years" term. Thus the maximum period of copyright in design is fifteen years

Rights Conferred by Registration

The registered proprietor of a design has the exclusive right to apply a design to any article in any class in which it is registered. This right is called a copyright in the design. The nature of Copyright is different from the copyright under the copyright Act. Copyright in a design can last for a maximum of fifteen years, thereafter it becomes public property and anybody can use it.

The right conferred by registration is subject to the: following conditions:

1. If exact representations or specimens of the design are not supplied to the controller, as required, the controller may erase his name from the register.
2. When the process of registration is complete then the articles of which the design is applied must carry the word "Registered" or "RD" along with the Registration number. This condition is however waived in case of textile goods or else where it is practically difficult to imprint the words.

Registration does not in fact give any exclusive right to the registered proprietor. What it gives is the right to stop others from infringing his registration by making applying the design, or importing articles bearing the design and so on.

Piracy of registered Design

Infringement of copyright in Design is termed as "piracy of a registered Design".

It is not, lawful for any person during the existence of copyright to do the following acts without the consent or license of the registered proprietor of the design. Section 58 lays down that the following acts amount to piracy:

1. To publish or to have it published or expose for sale any article of the class in question on which either the design or any fraudulent or obvious imitation has been.
2. To either apply or ply the design that is registered to any class of goods covered by the registration, the design or any limitation of it.
3. To import for purpose of sale any article belonging to the class in which the design has been registered and to which the design or a fraudulent or obvious imitation thereof has been applied.

In fact any unauthorized application of the registered design or a fraudulent or obvious imitation thereof to any article covered by the registration for trade purpose or the import of such article for sale is a piracy or infringement of the copyright in the design.

Meaning of fraudulent / Obvious Imitation

A distinction is made between fraudulent and obvious imitation the only common factor between the two is that both should be imitations, Thus even in the case of fraudulent imitation the design applied must be an imitation of the registered design, in fraud the imitation has been made with the intention to deceive another person with the knowledge that what is done is a violation of the other persons right. Where therefore, fraudulent imitation is established even if the, imitation is rather clumsy and not obvious the court will declare it as an infringement of copyright in the design. There must be exact duplication, an imitation of the registered design. Nothing less than imitation is sufficient to establish piracy.

Fraudulent imitation must mean this "if a man knowing that the, pattern is a registered design, goes and imitates it and does that, without sufficient invention on his own, part, that would be fraudulent imitation, if in fact it is an imitation (an exact copy of the registered design. Test to determine whether Infringement.

The court has to determine whether the alleged infringement has the same shape or pattern and must eliminate the claim of similarity of function, e.g. similarity of functions would result when two articles have same shape due to the inherent nature of goods, two pens will necessarily be similar in having an ink tube, a cap and a nib for writing. This element of functional similarity *is* to be eliminated. The judge has to look at the two articles and check out their similarities and differences and through the eyes of person with average intelligence see whether the defendants article *is* substantially different from that of the plaintiff. In *Western Engineering Co. V/s Paul Engineering Co.*[4]

It was held the features of shape, configuration, pattern etc., of the two designs must be same for determining whether these was infringement or not. The sameness of the features is to be determined by the eye. The designs need not be identical on all points and differ on no points.

Judicial Remedy

The judicial remedy for infringement of a registered design recommended in the Act is damages along with an injunction. Section 53 (2) stipulates remedy in the form of payment of a certain sum of money by the person who pirates a registered design. A suit in the appropriate manner for seeking the relief in the form of an injunction is also recommended.

Position under English law[5]

One could be forgiven for thinking that a design is a plan or blue-print which shows how an item is to be constructed or how the element of the item are arranged. Intellectual property law however has never accepted that simple definition. For our purpose a design, is concerned with the article itself. To complicate things further two types of designs exist in the UK: registered designs, based on the Registered Design Act 1949, as amended, and (unregistered) designs, based on the copyright, Designs and patent Act 1988.

Registered designs are aesthetic designs which are intended to appeal to the eye. On the other, hand designs may be functional in nature exhaust pipes for cars are the prime example, but there are plenty of their examples such as kitchen utensils which fall within the scope of the unregistered design right, in reality, there is a considerable overlap. Many aesthetic designs are also functional and may meet the requirements of the (unregistered) design right, while some primarily functional designs may have eye appeal as well. Designs may be functional depending on nature of the goods.

Registered Designs-An Overview

Aesthetic features applied to an, article by an Industrial process can be protected as a registered design if the design is new and appeal to the eye. The creator will normally own the design right. Designs created by employees and commissioned designs may present exceptions to this rule though. The Owner of the registered design right will be in a position to oppose infringement in relation to goods in respect of which the design has been registered. All the right granted by a design registration expires after five years, unless the term of protection is renewed for further five year period, up to a maximum of 25 years.

Designs which appeal to the eye can be of a tremendous commercial value. They do not amount to an invention and are not necessarily a trademark. Copyright does not protect the idea behind the design. So there is a very real need to register the design as a registered design. It is the only way to prevent competitors from cashing in one a good and valuable design by using a substantially identical design.

Unregistered Designs

This type of design right, was introduced by the copyright, Designs and Patent Act 1988 in an attempt to overcome various problems. Functional non aesthetic designs, such as those for exhaust pipes for, cars, did not qualify for registered design protection and here not covered either by special intellectual property right before 1988.

Action needed to be undertaken on two points. A specific intellectual property right needed to be created for functional designs. This would mean that the whole design area would be covered, by two, specific design right aesthetical designs would still be protected by the registered design right and the non aesthetical functional designs would be covered by the new design right. The second point which needed to be addressed is the overlap with copyright. A clear delimitation or both the copyright and the design, area was required. The copyright, design, and Patent Act 1988 reform attempted to reach that conclusion and created the (on registered) design right officially it is called design right, but in order to distinguish it from the registered design and as there is no registration requirement, it is described as (unregistered) design. The technical definition of a design which is given is that it is the design of any aspect of the shape or configuration (whether internal or external) of the whole or part of an article. This means that various aspects of the shape of. configuration of an article can be the subject of different design rights, and that a design does not necessarily relate to the whole article. Aspects of the internal shape or configuration of the whole or part of an article can also be taken into account. This marks a clear difference with the eye appeal requirements for registered designs (unregistered) designs are intended to offer protection for functional, designs, eye appeal is not required. A design might even exist (and be deferent and new) if the eye is not able to distinguish the shape[6] (over other designs) Larger and clearly visible, shapes are obviously also possible and remain eligible for protection.

Industrial Designs Under TRIP's Agreement

The degree of attention given to Industrial designs within the text of the TRIP's Agreement demonstrates how insignificant a feature, in striking a balance between private interest and public benefit, is the protection of Industrial design. Sec 4 of part II, of TRIP's Agreement covers industrial design. The protection covers only those design which are "new and original". Designs which are essentially "technical or functional" are specifically excluded from the section.

The agreement provides that at least 10 years protection must be given to independently created industrial design that are new original. Textile designs have a short life cycle. They have been given special life cycle. They have been given special attention; low cost registration is provided for protection. The owner of a protected design has the power to stop unauthorized third parties from making selling or importing, for commercial purpose, products which copy the design.

Article 25 of the TRIP's agreement requires World Trade Organization members to protect designs, while article 26 lays down the standard of protection required. The full text of article is as follows:

Article 25: Requirements for Protection.

1. Members shall provide for the protection of independently created industrial designs that are new or original. Members may provide that designs are not new or original if they do not significantly differ from known designs or combinations of known design features. Members may provide that such protection shall not extend to designs dictated essentially by technical or functional considerations.
2. Each member shall ensure that requirements for securing protection for textile designs, in particular in regard to any cost, examination or publication, do not unreasonably, impair the opportunity to seek and obtain such protection. Members shall be free to meet this obligation through Industrial design law or through copyright law.

Industrial Designs Under Paris Convention

Protection of Industrial Designs in the Paris Convention

WTO members have to comply with all substantive articles of the Paris Convention, viz. 1 to 12 and Article 19 (Article 2.1 of TRIPS). The Paris Convention obliges the protection of industrial designs in its Article *5quinquies*. However, there are no details on the scope or duration of such protection in this convention.

The period of priority to be accorded for the acceptance of applications for the registration of industrial designs, filed elsewhere in a convention country, is given as six months under Article 4.

Article 5B of Paris strictly prohibits the forfeiture of industrial design rights on the grounds of failure to work or for reasons of importation of articles related to the protected designs. There is a further prohibition in Article 5D of Paris against any requirement of the deposit of the industrial design upon the goods as a condition of recognition of the right of protection.

Article 11 and 12 deal with certain procedural matters such as temporary protection to industrial designs in respect of goods exhibited at fairs and exhibitions and the provision of a special industrial property service.

Within the framework of the Paris Convention, a procedural treaty to facilitate the acquisition of industrial design rights in other member countries called the Hague Agreement Concerning the International Deposit of Industrial Designs, was adopted in 1925, and last revised in 1967. There are only 29 members of this agreement, of which nine are developing countries, including Egypt and Indonesia. WIPO has recently introduced *some* amendments to this treaty so as to attract adherence of the US, Japan, UK and the Scandinavian countries[7] These changes will in no way affect the standards set under TRIPS.

Scope of Protection

Article 25.1 of TRIPS obliges the protection of 'independently created' industrial designs that are new or original. However, member could provide that designs are neither new nor original if they do no significantly differ from known designs or combinations thereof. In this area there were more intra-North differences than North–South differences. The European Community refused to accept that some members could impose the requirement of both 'novelty' and 'originality' for the protection of industrial designs[8]. The compromise language of Article 25 was meant to accommodate both points of view as it enabled members to deny protection to designs that do not significantly differ from known designs[9]. Again like in the area of patents, no definition is given of novelty. An absolute standard of worldwide novelty can be adopted or only novelty within a particular jurisdiction or time period can be considered. For purposes of administrative convenience developing countries may allow for post–grant opposition to revoke design rights wrongfully granted rather than attempt to determine by examination whether the novelty requirement has been met. To encourage and reward true creativity, a minimum requirement of originality should be applied in developing countries. A higher standard of requiring both novelty and originality, though not prohibited by TRIPS, may result in very few domestic innovative designs being protected.

In addition, countries are free to exclude the protection of designs that are dictated essentially by technical or functional considerations, a feature found in the design laws of most countries. Such designs could be subject to patent or utility model protection. Designs descriptive of the ordinary shape of an object are also usually excluded from the grant of such protection as these may not be novel or original and, even if they are, cannot be taken away from the public domain.

Term of Protection

TRIPS obliges that the duration of protection *amount to* a minimum term of protection of at least 10 years (Article 26.3). This language is looser than that used in TRIPS for the term of protection of other IPRs such as copyright, patents, trademarks or layout-designs. This language was meant to accommodate different initial terms of protection, so long as the total number of years of protection afforded does not fall below 10 years. Many national laws in the EU provide an initial term of five years, renewable for equivalent periods for a total period well beyond the 10 years required by TRIPS, up to a total of 20-5 years. Brazil, in its new industrial property law, allows registration for an initial term of 10 years renewable, upon payment of fees, for three successive periods of five years *i.e.* 25 years of total protection[10].

Exceptions to Rights Conferred

Article 26.2 provides limited exceptions that do not unreasonably conflict with the legitimate interests of the right holder, taking into account the legitimate interests of third parties. Here the term 'third parties' could mean the general public and designs that are contrary to morality or public order could be refused registration of protection.

The UK has a system of licenses of right where non-voluntary licenses can be applied for by third parties for registered industrial designs and for unregistered industrial designs after a period of five years of protection. The Patent Office has a role only to settle the terms of the licenses in case of disagreement between the parties. The UK was accused of cutting short the term of protection but it considers this provisions to be compatible *with* TRIPS as the UK Registered Designs Act, 1949, as amended in 1989, provides for a term of protection of 25 years[11].

In the European Union, design rights on automobile spare parts have proved to be the main obstacle to the finalization of Community-wide rules on industrial designs. There was a demand for a 'repairs clause' in the EC draft directive on the subject. This clause would allow repair shops to use spare parts from sources other than the design right holders. Spare parts producers would be able to resort to compulsory licensing of designs from automo-bile manufacturers upon payment of fair and reasonable remunera-tion[12]. This clause is considered by its proponents to be compatible with the requirements of Article 26.2 of TRIPS. Considering that spare parts problem was already known to EC negotiators at time of the TRIPS negotiations, it is clear that they considered this language to be adequate. However, many others see this as a gross limitation on the design rights of automobile manufacturers. Eventually, this interpretation may be decided in a WTO dispute.

Additional Requirements for Textile Designs

Industrial design protection is usually subject, in most jurisdictions, to examination and registration procedures. The Europeans were particularly interested that protection of short-lived textile designs be granted in an expeditious and timely manner.[13] The requirement that protection for textile designs should not be unduly burdened by costly, time-consuming or burdensome procedures, pressed notably by Switzerland and the EU, thus finds place in Article 25.2 of TRIPS. This obligation can, however, be met under Article 25.2 of TRIPS through either the copyright or the design law. Under copyright law, the owner of the design would get protection automatically from the date of creation, even without any formal registration.

Most WTO members, including developing country ones, already complied with the industrial design requirements of TRIPS. Some like, Hong Kong and Malaysia, are merely changing from a system of registration based on the UK system to independent registration of such rights Although India has enacted a new design law in 1999, its, 1911 design law, in conjunction with its copyright law, met TRIPS requirements. Brazil allows for the protection of industrial designs that are both new and original setting the bar higher for its own domestic designers.

Conclusions

The design right made to see that the originator of a profitable design is not deprived of his reward by others applying it to their goods. The purpose of the Industrial design as an intellectual property is to protect novel designs devised to be applied to (or in other words, to govern the shape and configuration of) particular articles to be manufactured and marketed commercially. To come under the purview of design, there should be a definite shape, configuration, pattern or ornament should be applied to any article and more important it must appeal to and judged solely by the eye. And such a design falling under these conditions is protected by the Law.

It is unlikely that the TRIPS obligations on industrial design or on layout design will be modified in any major way in negotiations in the WTO, at least in the near future. There is also no discussion in any other forum on substantive standards related to the protection on designs.

Developing countries should aim to develop design capabilities that generate designs eligible for protection. Certainly, many of even the poorest countries have a vast talent that generates original and exclusive textile and handicraft designs. In certain circumstances the protection of such industrial design export markets would enhance their value. TRIPS given these countries the opportunity to take gives these countries the opportunity to take advantage of such protection abroad, in other developed and developing countries. At the same time, given the low level of obligations agreed to under TRIPS, not many developing countries have to introduce new laws or modify existing laws on industrial designs.

NOTES

1. WIPO (1998) No. 476E, pp. 106-13 for background information on industrial designs.
2. TRIPS only requires registration of such marks on proof of

distinctive-ness. Few countries allow for registration of such marks and since trademark protection is, in effect, without time limit, courts in countries that do are careful in judging distinctiveness and public deception. See 'Protection of Three-Dimensional Trademarks Under German Trademark Law of 1995: First Cases Try to Shape the Landscape' in *World Intellectual Property Report,* Vol. 13, No.2, 15 February 1999.

3. Note, however, that courts can take the position that, in the absence of statutory protection, copying per se is not illegal, as the copied works were in public domain. See 'South African Court Rules Copying of Unregistered Design not Unfair Competition' in *World Intellectual Property Report,* Vol. 11, No. 7, July 1997. In the UK unregistered designs enjoy protection of up to 15 years but independently developed copies are not considered infringing.
4. An English case decided on infringement of design.
5. Designs may be functional depending on nature of the goods.
6. Design must appeal to the eye.
7. WIPO press Release PR/99/180 of 6 July 1999 available at *http://www.wipo.int.* Also see 'WIPO Activities: Hague Agreement: 100 Countries to be Represented at Diplomatic Conference on designs in *Worn. Intellectual Property Report,* Vol. 13, No. 7, 15 July 1999.
8. This was seen as too high a standard of protection. See Reinbothe an Howard (1991).
9. Reichman (1995), p. 376 for his view that the US Law appears to conflict with this requirement as it also requires a true non–obviousness standard.
10. Law No. 9.279 of 14 May 1996 to Regulate Rights and Obligations Relating to Industrial Property, Title II, Article 108.
11. 'UK: TRIPs Held Not to Affect UK Design Right Legislation J:. *World Intellectual Property Report,* Vol. 11, No.2, February 1997,–the *Azrak.Hamway International Inc. V Meccanno SA* of 28 October 1996.
12. 'European Union: Parliament Casts Vote Backing Industrial Design.
13. Rights Protection' in *World Intellectual Property Report,* Vol. 11, No. 12, 15 December 1997.

14. Interestingly, the first European laws of UK and France on industrial design were meant to protect textile designs. The first UK law giving protection to industrial designs was called the Designing and Printing of Linens, Cotton, Calicoes and Muslins Act, 1787. See WIPO (1998) No. 476E, pp. 106-7.

BIBLIOGRAPHY

Narayan, P. (1999), *Intellectual Property Laws,* Central Law Agency, Allahabad.

Narayan, P.S. (2000), *Intellectual Property Laws,* Allahabad Law Agency.

Russel–Clarke–On Industrial Designs, 6th Edition-1998, Sweet and Maxwell, London.

Dr. S.R. Myneni (2001), Law of intellectual Property, 1st Edition, Asia Law House, Hyderabad.

W.R. Cornish (2001), Intellectual Property (Patents, Copyrights, Trade marks and Allied Rights), 3rd Edition, Universal Law Publishing Co., Pvt., Ltd, New Delhi.

Sawel K.Roy and Chowdhary, (1999), Laws of Trade Marks, Copyright Patents and Designs, 2nd Edition, Kamal Law House, Calcutta.

13 PROTECTION OF TRADITIONAL KNOWLEDGE– A CAUSE FOR CONCERN

*Savitha S.**

Introduction

One of the notable effects of globalization on traditional knowledge has been the shift of local and traditional knowledge into global knowledge, which by itself is not a threat to the traditional and indigenous knowledge. But the claiming of monopoly rights over such knowledge by some Western countries without acknowledging the holders of traditional knowledge is a cause for concern.

Traditional knowledge is nothing but the inheritance of ideas from generation to generation. The traditional knowledge can be attributed to various fields like food, use of natural resources, medicines etc. They are in the form of a song, a story, dance, techniques, beliefs, practices, rituals, mores etc. They have also been an essence of survival for certain communities, for example Hoodia Cactus.

It is always said that the knowledge is valuable only when shared but as far as the traditional knowledge is concerned the concept of sharing caused and is causing threat to the very knowledge and the knowledge holders or

* Faculty of Law NLSIU, Bangalore.

creators. Knowledge is transmitted by various methods like traditional practices and also by oral culture. The threat is by ways of exploiting the knowledge and claiming monopoly rights over such knowledge. But in ancient days the ideas were exchanged and propagated without expecting anything in return. One generation passed them on to the next generation in the civilization in return for a pledge that they would be used for the benefit of the society and not adversely. Knowledge was free and precious in our ancient days. But that is not the case today; we have the interference from various regimes, which is trying to monopolize the traditional and the indigenous knowledge and to slay its very essence.

Why the sudden roar and reaction? Is there a giant– trying to destroy it? The sudden reaction to protect the traditional knowledge struck like a lightning because there was a global threat to such traditional and indigenous knowledge, which was for a very long time not a matter of concern at all. The adverse use of Intellectual Property right is the cause for it.

Traditional knowledge is considered as a part of IPR and there are a lot of people who are claiming the monopoly right over such knowledge ignoring the very base of such knowledge i.e., the local people with such knowledge. Forgetting that they have a right to be compensated and receive a share of the benefits that arise from the commercialization of the product developed on the basis of the traditional knowledge.

Is Traditional Knowledge and Indigenous Knowledge one and the same?

All indigenous knowledge is traditional knowledge but all-traditional knowledge is not indigenous knowledge. The definitions of Traditional Knowledge and Indigenous Knowledge would justify the above statement.

Definition

Definition of traditional knowledge:

Traditional knowledge is a cumulative body of knowledge, know-how, practices and representations[1]. They are maintained and developed by people with long histories of interaction with their natural environment. Traditional Knowledge provides the basis for local level decision-making about many fundamental aspects of day-to-day life.

Traditional knowledge (TK) refers to "the knowledge, innovations and practices of indigenous and local communities embodying traditional lifestyles" as well as "indigenous and local technologies", according to the UN Convention on Biological Diversity (CBD).

Definition of Indigenous Knowledge

'Indigenous knowledge is the local knowledge that is unique to a given culture or society. It is the basis for local-level decision-making in agriculture, health care, food preparation, education, natural resource management, and a host of other activities in rural communities.'

Another useful definition is the following:

'Indigenous knowledge is the information base for a society, which facilitates communication and decision-making. Indigenous information systems are dynamic, and are continually influenced by internal creativity and experimentation as well as by contact with external systems.'[2]

'Indigenous knowledge is the knowledge that people in a given community have developed over time, and continue to develop. It is based on experience, often tested over centuries of use, adapted to local culture and environment, dynamic and changing.' [3]

Indigenous Knowledge may be related to a common practice seen in communities that are indigenous to a specific area or the focus might be on the long history of the practice, in which case it is often called 'traditional knowledge'. The following definition is a combination of these different aspects: 'Indigenous knowledge also referred to as traditional or local knowledge refers to the large body of knowledge and skills that has been developed outside the formal educational system. Indigenous Knowledge is embedded in culture and is unique to a given location or society. It is an important part of the lives of the poor. It is the basis for decision-making of communities in food security, human and animal health, education and natural resource management.'[4] It is a term applied to knowledge held in specific societies, worldwide[5].

An analysis of the above stated definitions leads us to the following observations:

- Indigenous knowledge is merely a compartment of traditional knowledge.
- Indigenous Knowledge is used to refer not only to knowledge but also refers to the set of people who possess such knowledge.
- It is very peculiar to a society, culture or location.
- It is to some extent area or location specific.
- Informal knowledge.
- Transmitted by word of mouth and seldom documented–therefore not a formal knowledge.
- Evolved due to close interaction with the environment.

Some examples of traditional knowledge:

- Use of tulsi for cough
- Use of turmeric to heal wounds
- Use of neem as a pesticide and as a cosmetic
- Hoodia cactus eaten by the people of Kalahari Desert in Southern Africa to fend off hunger and thirst.

Significance of traditional knowledge

Traditional knowledge in today's context is a very important resource for the modern industries. They are a major asset to certain industries like the pharmaceuticals, cosmetics, agro-chemicals etc. to some extent they are the very essence of survival of indigenous people.

Need for protection of traditional knowledge

Legal protection to traditional knowledge and the local community who possess such traditional knowledge is the need of the hour, thus avoiding its exploitation. There have been attempts to bring them under the legal umbrella. The role of intellectual Property system in protecting the traditional knowledge is an idea perceived off late. Intellectual Property Rights should ensure that the rights of the holders of such knowledge are safeguarded and protected. The western world has worked and developed on the traditional knowledge and invented medicines, cosmetics and other products and economically exploited the same but they have not compensated the holders of such knowledge in any manner. Such misappropriation of knowledge is also referred to as 'Biopiracy'. It is nothing but larceny of traditional knowledge. To cite an instance of misappropriation, Turmeric[6] and Neem[7] were traditional medicines used by our ancestors, but they were exploited and patented by some transnational companies. In these cases, invalid patents were issued because the patent examiners were not aware of the relevant traditional knowledge. Fortunately India could revoke certain patents on these traditional medicinal plants due to submission of the record of prior use.

There is no fixed definition of 'Biopiracy' the Action Group on Erosion, Technology and Concentration (ETC) defines it as "the appropriation of the knowledge and genetic resources of farming and indigenous communities by individuals or institutions seeking exclusive monopoly control (usually patents and plant breeder's rights) over these resources and knowledge"[8].

National and International Initiatives

International Protection

The following are some of the important developments that occurred off late in the International level for the protection of the traditional knowledge and safeguarding the rights of the holders of such traditional knowledge:

World Trade Organization (WTO)

The World Trade Organization has taken some steps to protect the traditional knowledge at the International level. TRIPs has failed to recognize the importance of traditional knowledge. There has been a lot of demand to review of Article 27.3(b)[9], and also a review of the whole of the agreement. It has merely required their member countries to protect the plant varieties by a '*Suigeneris* System'[10]. The *Sui Generis* System would recognize the traditional knowledge relating to the genetic resources and promote access and benefit sharing. The protection under the '*suigeneris* system' is extended even if it is in the form of oral information. The '*suigeneris* system' is adopted by a number of countries as they felt that the present Intellectual Property Rights regime would do no good to traditional knowledge in terms of safeguarding and protecting them. Philippines[11], Thailand[12], Peru and Costa Rica[13] are some of them who have worked on protecting the rights of the indigenous communities and their traditional knowledge and have evolved legislation for the same.

Convention on Biological Diversity, 1992 (CBD) and Traditional Knowledge

The Convention has recognized the rights of the indigenous people over the genetic resources. Articles 1 and 8(j) of the Convention on Biological diversity, 1992 deals with equitable sharing of the benefits that arise out of the use of traditional knowledge. The local community gets the benefit when there is a development of a novel product by utilizing the traditional knowledge[14]. Article 8(j) focuses on the preservation, protection and maintenance of knowledge, innovations and practices of the indigenous and local communities who symbolize the actual lifestyle relevant for the conservation and sustainable use of biological resources and encourage their wider application with the approval and involvement of the local and indigenous communities and by mutual agreement.

Access and benefit sharing are the most important developments in the international level under the CBD. To this effect the Bonn Guidelines on access to genetic resources and the fair and equitable sharing of the benefits arising from their utilization was adopted in Conference of Parties (COP) VI of the CBD. To access the genetic resources consent of the local community needs to be sought. This would ensure that there is no exploitation of the genetic resources. The communities also have a right to equitable benefit sharing whereby they are compensated for the use of the resources. It may be monetary or non-monetary.

The *Suigeneris* system and the CBD ensure that a prior informed consent is obtained from the local community to utilize the same. But the same consent is not required if the knowledge is already in the public domain. These are some of the important developments as they aim at protecting and safeguarding the rights of the indigenous or the local community.

For instance the 'Arogyapacha' was used by the Kani Tribes for centuries to help them during physical exertion in the Western Ghats in the State of Kerala. They used to eat the seed of Arogyapacha when they were exhausted. There were a group of Scientists who knew about this practice and wanted to investigate the same. A drug called 'jeevani' based on this 'Arogyapacha' was developed in 1995 and was thrown into the market. The Pharmaceutical industry that developed the drug agreed to share 50% of gains with the Kani Tribe as a license fee and also a 2% of royalty from the sale. This is one of the important instances of benefit sharing. The Tribals here get their fair share. Thus the Access, Benefit sharing and Prior Informed consent are some of the important tools for the protection of the traditional knowledge.

World Intellectual Property Organization (WIPO)

WIPO has brought traditional knowledge and Intellectual Property rights under Intergovernmental Committee on Genetic Resources, Traditional Knowledge and Folklore constituted in 2000.

Agenda 21

Principle 22 of the main document that came out of the 1992 Earth Summit in Rio de Janeiro recognizes role of the indigenous people in environmental management and development with their traditional knowledge and practices;

International Labour Organization (ILO)

The International Labour Organization entered into a Convention on Indigenous and Tribal Peoples. It tries to protect the rights of indigenous peoples.

United Nations Draft Declaration on the Rights of the Indigenous People

The Commission on Human Rights of the United Nations has established an open-ended, inter-session working group to elaborate a draft United Nations Declaration on the Rights of Indigenous People.

United Nations Food and Agriculture Organization (FAO)

The FAO has addressed the issue of protection of traditional knowledge by constituting a commission on Genetic

Resources for Food and Agriculture, which is negotiating the revision of the international Undertaking on Plant and Genetic Resources.

The United Nations Development Programme (UNDP) and the IBRD or the World Bank

The UNDP and the IBRD have launched various programmes to promote indigenous peoples' development and also to ensure that such programmes recognize the rights of the indigenous people.

United Nations Conference on Trade and Development (UNCTAD)

There have been a lot of deliberations and discussions with respect to protection of traditional knowledge. It also deliberated on the protection of the rights of both the custodians and developers of traditional knowledge.

National Initiatives

The Biological Diversity Act, 2002 of India

The Indian Legislature keeping in mind the benefit that is due to the local community enacted the Biodiversity Act in the year 2002. An enabling provision was included in the Act for protecting the Traditional Knowledge. Section 36(5) of the Act provides for protection of knowledge of local people relating to biodiversity through measures such as registration of such knowledge, and development of a *sui generis* system.

Section 6 provides that any person seeking any kind of intellectual property rights on a research based upon biological resource or knowledge obtained from India; need to obtain prior approval of the National Biodiversity Authority (NBA). Section 19 and 21 stipulate prior approval of the NBA before their access. This provision was inserted to ensure evenhanded sharing of benefits arising from the use of biological resources and the associated knowledge. While granting approval, NBA imposes certain terms and conditions, which ensure equitable sharing of benefits.

Section 18(4) stipulates that one of the important functions of NBA is to take steps to oppose the grant of Intellectual Property Rights in any country outside India on any biological resource obtained from India or knowledge associated with such biological resources. Section 41 provides for the Biodiversity Management Committees to undertake chronicling of knowledge relating to biological diversity[15].

The Patents (Amendment) Act, 2002 of India

The Patents (Amendment) Act, 2002, contains provisions for mandatory disclosure of source and geographical origin of the biological material used in the invention of a product while applying for patents in India. If there is no disclosure or wrong disclosure of such source the patent application will be rejected and if the patent has already been granted the same will be revoked.

Digital Library

Traditional Knowledge Digital Library

There are attempts in various countries to form digital libraries on traditional knowledge. These libraries would have a database on the prevailing traditional knowledge available in the public domain. They are the systematic arrangement of information pertaining to traditional knowledge. The information is drawn from the public domain and then the database is created. As we know one of the criteria for granting of patent is 'novelty' which means new. If there is a patent claim for an invention it is easier to track the existing knowledge and reject or accept the application for patent based on the available information in the database of the libraries. This would avoid granting of unwarranted patents.

The Science and Human Rights Program of the American Association for the Advancement of Science (AAAS) has established a new international project on Traditional Knowledge. AAAS established the Traditional Ecological Knowledge Prior Art Database with the aim of 'protecting indigenous knowledge against inappropriate patents based on this knowledge. The Traditional Ecological Knowledge Prior Art Database has issued an offer to traditional knowledge holders to submit their knowledge to the database if they want them to be placed in the public domain. The US Patent Law requires its authorities to carry out a thorough examination of available prior art. Based on this information the application for patent may be rejected if already found in the public domain[16].

In India the Indian National Institute of Science Communication (NISCOM) and the Department of Indian system of medicine and homeopathy (ISM&H) joined hands to establish a Traditional Knowledge Digital Library in 1999[17]. This is one of the major sources of resource pool of traditional knowledge. Biopiracy of the traditional knowledge from India pushed the authorities to create a traditional knowledge digital library in India too. The database is computerized and therefore easily accessible from all over the world. It contains information on ayurveda, unani, siddha, naturopathy, homeopathy and folklore medicine[18]. The patent examiners world over would have ready hand information on the traditional knowledge, which would help them in examining the patent applications that come before them.

Conclusion

Protection and safeguarding of the Traditional knowledge has been the essence of this paper. Traditional knowledge is an important lead to the developed countries for their new developments and manufacture of new products. There is a need for effective and vibrant steps taken and worked for its protection. The *'Sui Generis'* system is considered to be the only course left. It has to be conceived both at the national and international levels. The *'Sui generis'* system should ensure the protection of the rights of the creators or holders of traditional knowledge and also guarantee that they get the fair share for letting others use their knowledge and develop products which would fetch such companies a lion's share. There is a ray of hope from the *'Sui Generis'* system, which we are sure will show our traditional knowledge holders the light of the day.

It is unfortunate that TRIPs has not made any attempts to protect the traditional knowledge. TRIPs need have to work for protection of such traditional knowledge and avoid illegal access and endorse benefit sharing. It has to re-look at some of its provisions[19] and make suitable amendments to protect the vulnerable from exploitation.

NOTES

1. *"Local and Indigenous Knowledge" at* www.unesco.org, visited on 28.10.05
2. Flavier etal. 1995:479, at www.worldbank.org/afr/ik/basic.htm.
3. See IIRR, Philippines, 1996. *'Recording and Using Indigenous Knowledge: A Manual'.*
4. World Bank website text. See: www.worldbank.org/afr/ik/index.htm.
5. www.wikipedia.org.
6. The Council of Scientific Industrial Research (CSIR) in India requested the U.S Patent and Trademark Office (USPTO) which granted the patent for turmeric to review or re-examine the patent and to revoke the same. The USPTO then revoked the patent on turmeric. The ground for revoking the patent was that it was not 'novel', which is one of the important conditions for granting of patents.
7. Similarly the European Patent Office also reviewed the patent granted on Neem on the grounds of it having been already known in India.
8. http://www.iprcommission.org/papers/text/finalreport/chapter4htmfinal.htm.

9. Article 27.3 (b) - Members may also exclude from patentability plants and animals other than micro-organisms, and essentially biological processes for the production of plants or animals other than non-biological and microbiological processes. However, Members shall provide for the protection of plant varieties either by patents or by an effective *sui generis* system or by any combination thereof. The provisions of this subparagraph shall be reviewed four years after the date of entry into force of the WTO Agreement.
10. Sui generis system means "of its own kind" something unique.
11. Indigenous Peoples Rights Act 1997, Traditional and Alternative Medicine Act 1997, Plant Variety Protection Act 2000 etc.
12. Thai Traditional Medicine Act, 1999, Plant Variety Protection Act, 1999 etc.
13. http://www.shr.aaas.org/tek/handbook/handbook.pdf. *"Traditional Knowledge and Intellectual Property Rights"*.
14. Article 8 (j) declares that State Parties are required to "respect, preserve and maintain knowledge, innovations and practices of indigenous and local communities embodying traditional lifestyles relevant for the conservation and sustainable use of biological diversity and promote the wider application with the approval and involvement of the holders of such knowledge, innovations and practices and encourage the equitable sharing of the benefits arising from the utilization of such knowledge, innovations and practices."
15. The Biological Diversity Act, 2002.
16. Traditional Ecological Knowledge Prior Art Database, (2002), at http://shr.aaas.org/report/XXII/tek.htm.
17. Supra No. 7.
18. http://www.infinityfoundation.com/mandala/t_es/t_es_TKDL.htm.
19. Like Article 27.3 (b) of TRIPs.

14 THE EFFICACY OF PATENTS UNDER TRADE RELATED ASPECTS OF INTELLECTUAL PROPERTY RIGHTS–AN OVERVIEW

*Yogamala H.L.**

Introduction

The agreement on Trade Related Aspects of Intellectual Property Rights (TRIPS) is the most comprehensive and effective multilateral agreement and also most controversial of WTO agreements. TRIPS agreement came into force on 1st Jan., 1995, before TRIPs the intellectual property Rights were governed by WIPO conventions.

The TRIPs agreement aims at the reduction of distortions and impediments to international trade, to promote effective and adequate protection of intellectual property rights and to ensure that measures and procedures to enforce intellectual property rights do not themselves become barriers to legitimate trade.

Article 7 of TRIPs states that, "The protection and enforcement of intellectual property rights should contribute to the promotion of technological innovation and to the transfer and dissemination of technology, to the mutual advantage of producers and users of technology and in a manner conducive to social and economic welfare and to a balance of rights and obligations".

* Guest Faculty, Department of Law, University of Mysore, Mysore.

More over the rational behind the systems of protection of IPR lies in striking a balance between producers and users of which provides incentives for the generation of new technology.

Here the crucial question is whether the TRIPs is successfully achieving these purposes?

Whether the Article 33 (which says about protected time duration) is supportive to facilitate free trade.

Whether this agreement contains any enforceable measures to prevent the abuse of intellectual property rights by the right holder or to ensure the international transfer of technology?

What is the impact of TRIPs on developing country, is the agreement advantageous for developing countries?

Historical Evolution

The TRIPs agreement was a major addition to GATT which dealt only with goods. It was added to the original Uruguay Round agenda only in the late eighties. The original Punte Del Este declaration at the beginning of the Uruguay Round in 1986 did not make any reference to TRIPs. Developing countries agreed to inclusion of TRIPs in the Uruguay round only on condition that the textile and clothing quotes under the MFA[1] would go. The compromise was hammered out by the then Director General of GATT[2], who got the developed countries to trade removed of MFA with the acceptance of TRIPs by the developing countries.

In fact, the story goes back further. Pfizer, the major pharmaceutical transnationa put its weight being the move to stop patent piracy in the third world countries by an internationally accepted legal framework with strict enforcement. The might of the US government was brought in to the TRIPs campaign. As first step, the US omnibus Act was enacted in 1989 with the sanction of special 201 & super 201 for countries who violate IPRs. Bilaterals on IPR protection who signed with practically all the main players including China who was not a member of WTO at that time.

The TRIPs was brought in to the GATT agenda in 1993. this was followed up by more arm twisting, it was pointed out to the developing countries that having signed bilaterals, they can sign the multilateral agreement as well. It is better to negotiate with the full strength of like minded developing country in a common forum. The finishing piece was the trade in the ATC for TRIPs by the developed countries.

There is talk of bringing in TRIPs and also to cover new areas like databases. Infact, the NAFTA and ASEAN trade agreements cover advanced versions of TRIPs.

The WIPO administered Paris Convention is already covering patents well. However, it lacks the authority to enforce law. In contrast, all members of WTO are subject to the common dispute settlement system. The number of cases on TRIPs before the dispute settlement body and the substitution of process patents with product patents are evidences of the success of the move to bring intellectual property under WTO.

The TRIPs consists of 7 parts ranging from Patents, Trade-marks, Copyright, Geographical indications, Industrial designs, Integrated circuits, undisclosed information.

The Dunkel Draft has also envisaged another form of intellectual property rights known as Plant breeders' rights.

Important Provisions of TRIPs related to Patents

The TRIPs agreement prescribes universal minimum standards for all aspects of patent protection as well as other intellectual properties.

Simultaniously many disadvantages are attributed to the Intellectual property right provision of WTO such as technological dependence of foreign firms, increased out flow of foreign exchange due to commitments undertaken in the field of TRIPs, increasing intrusion in domestic Sovereignty, etc...

Article 27.3. (b) of TRIPs agreement contains 3 main components i.e.,

27.3. (b) (i) a country 'MAY' exclude from patentability of plant, animals & essentially biological process for the production of plants & animals. Here the use of term 'MAY' creates confusion and gives an impression that the country may allow the patenting of plants and animals. Here we can remember the complaint from United States against Pakistan by alleging the patent protection for pharmaceutical and agricultural chemical products[3], later which was settled in a consultation by arriving at a mutually acceptable solution.

Article 27.3. (b) (ii) a country must allow the patent for micro-organisms and non-biological & micro biological process of production of plants and animals. Further this part of article 27 lacks the clarification because the micro-organisms & non-biological & micro-biological process have not been specifically defined.

Further if we take up the compulsory licensing and government use of patent without authorization of its owner but subjected to certain conditions, which made this provision more stringent & controversial. This list of conditions carries an obligation not to grant such licences unless attempts to acquire a voluntary license on reasonable terms have been unsuccessful and a requirement to pay adequate remuneration to the right holder if this licensing system is implemented without any relaxation of course it will be a bottle-neck for the developing countries to achieve their developmental objective it is required to observe that WTO TRIPS agreement particularly drug patents hit world headlines. NGOs alleged that drug companies were misusing patent protection rights flowing from stringent provisions of TRIPS agreement. A large part of the African continent is battling with killer diseases like AIDS/H.I.V malaria & tuberculosis. The prices for life saving drugs are unaffordably high for people in developed & least developing countries, the WHO projections indicate that these killer diseases can take on more dangerous proportions in coming year.

On an average, patented drugs costs AID's patient about 1000 U.S$ P/A which is largely unaffordable for poor people, and patent protection provisions under TRIPs agreement disallow Govt. any flexibility to bring down prices under exceptional circumstances. Indian companies are now making AIDs medicines available for $ 350 p/year. However a wide section of the African continent is making use of the relatively low cost medicine.

In addition, the term of the protection has been increased universally for a minimum period of 20 years. This provision depriving the developing countries from the freedom to invent new technologies in many fields and also impeding others from developing new technology by using the protected one. Further the industrial lobbies led by the U.S would play a dominant role in the establishment of a strict & extremely protective intellectual property rights system. This not only enhances their monopoly power but also prevents developing countries from catching up by "imitative industrialization". The best example is dispute between Canada & U.S where U.S successfully challenged Canada's patent protection term of 17 years from the date of grant of a patent. Canada changed the law with effect from 1st Oct 1989, to provide patent protection for a term of 20 years from the date filing of the application for a patent. Further the protection of intellectual property rights can it self be a barrier to trade.

Impact on Developing Countries

The TRIPs agreement will have serious implications for developing countries especially on the economical & social life of the people. The adverse effect of the TRIPs is mainly on the knowledge based industries of the developing countries. Further, intellectual property protection enables small groups of companies to control the world market. This monopoly market increases the price of life saving drugs and other medicines. In addition, TRIPs is a movement in the opposite direction from the draft code of conduct on the transfer of technology. Moreover, patents will also be available in the area of computer development and information technology. Patent protection in these areas would impede the independent development of functional equivalents and reverse engineering, while enhancing the market power of large firms. Further it gave room to the technological dependence.

Conclusion

The TRIPs agreement provides a strong intellectual property regime but many disadvantages are attributed to the intellectual property right provision of WTO especially to the developing countries.

Hence, to be a most acceptable and fair agreement the TRIPs should have to be undergone with some modification to certain important provisions and provide some relaxation, rather becoming more stringent & rigid. Those modifications and relaxations are , the article 27.3 (b) needs a clarification that naturally occurring plants, animals, the parts of plants and animals, including the Genesequence and essentially biological processes for the production of plants animals and their parts must not be granted patents.

In addition this article needs an interpretation and clarification of terms like micro-organisms, non-biological and micro-biological process, etc...

Further, the stringent conditions attached to the provision of compulsory licensing should be removed. In addition, the term of protection of patent which is 20 years should be lessened in order to achieve one of the basic principle of the TRIPs i.e., to facilitate free trade.

Apart from this, the TRIPs should establish a new effective machinery in order to curb the domination of developed countries on other developing and least developed countries.

NOTES

1. Multi fibre arrangement.
2. Arthur Dunkel.
3. Pakistan–Patent Protection for Pharmaceutical and agricultural chemical products, complaint by the United States (WT/DS 36)

Setting Up of Patent Protection System

In it's request for consultations dated 30 April 1996, the US claimed that the absence in Pakistan of (i) either patent protection for pharmaceutical and agricultural chemical products or a system to permit the filing of applications for patents on these products and (ii) A system to grant exclusive marketing rights in such products, violates TRIPs agreement articles 27, 65 and 70. On 4th July 1996, the United States requested the establishment of a panel. The DSB considered the request at it's meeting on 16th July 1996, but did not establish a panel due to Pakistan's objection. At the DSB meeting on 25th February 1997, both parties informed the DSB that they had reached a mutually agreed solution to the dispute and that the terms of the agreement were being drawn up, and would be communicated to the DSB once finalized. On 20th February 1997, the terms of the agreement were communicated to the secretariat.

BIBLIOGRAPHY

Law & Practice of IPR in India, Vikas Vashishth, Advocate, Supreme Court.

WTO in the New Millenium, 5th Edition, September 2001, Edited, Arun Goyal, Noor Mohammad.

Introduction to the WTO Agreements, Bhagirath Lal Das.

IPR under WTO–Tasks before India, T. Ramappa.

The new WTO Agreements, Globalizing Law through Service and Intellectual Property, Christopher Arup.

WTO–An Indian Perspective, Jayanta Bagchi, Eastern Law House.

15 THE SUBJECT MATTER OF COPY RIGHT–AN OVERVIEW

*C. Basavaraju**

Introduction

One of the important developing areas in the field of Intellectual Property Rights Law is copy Right Law. Copyright is the intellectual property of the owner who produces a work independently with his own skill, labour and capital, which is unique and novel. This intellectual property is more useful for the development of economic and cultural growth of the country. Piracy of intellectual property has become not only domestic problem but also international problem. Copy Right of the owner of a work subsists in any original work specified in the Copy Right Act, 1957, from the moment of the publication. Therefore, there is a need to protect the Copy right of the owner of a published work from infringement of the same.

According to Black's Law Dictionary, the phrase 'Copy Right' means, it is a right in literary property as recognized and sanctioned by positive law. An intangible incorporeal

---

* Reader, Department of Studies in Law, University of Mysore, Manasa Gangotri, Mysore.

The paper presented at the National Seminar on 'Intellectual Property Rights-An Awareness Programme' held on 28th & 29th August 2004 at the Department of Law, University of Mysore

right granted to the author or originator of certain literary or artistic production whereby he is invested for a specified period with the sole and exclusive privilege of multiplying copies of the same and publishing and selling them".

According to Oxford English Dictionary, the term ' Copy Right' means, it is an exclusive right given by law for a certain term of years to an author, composer etc., (or his assignee) to print, publish and sell copies of his original work.

The sole object of the copy right law is to protect, encourage and safeguard the authors, composers, and artists original work and to provide them exclusive copy right over such original work. This clearly indicates that, law will never allow any individual to appropriate himself what has been produced by the labour, skill and capital of another[1]. Copyright consists of various rights like, right to reproduction, the right of serial publication in newspapers and magazines, the right of dramatic and cinematographic versions, the right of translation, adaptation, abridgement and the right of public performance.

There are various international conventions in which the intellectual property is very well protected. For example, India is a signatory to both the Berne Convention and the Universal Copy Right Convention. Due to the advancement in technology, there is a steady growth of intellectual property. For example, protection of plant varieties, prevention of various forms of unfair competition or misappropriation of good will, reputation or trade value, unfair business practices, slavish copying of the details of products, dilution of reputed trade marks and their commercial value by using them by competitors in the fields of activity different from that of the owners are becoming more and more difficult[2]. As there is a wide spread piracy of Intellectual Property, especially the copy right, there is a need for the effective regulatory mechanism not only to protect copy right work of the owner but also to prevent any infringement or piracy of copy right.

Subject Matter of Copyright

According to section 13 of the Copy Right Act, 1957, copyright subsists only in certain classes of works. They are;

1. Original Literary, dramatic, musical and artistic works;
2. Cinematograph films and
3. Sound recordings.

Literary work consists of computer programmes, tables, and compilations including databases. Dramatic work includes any piece for recitation, choreographic work or entertainment in a dumb show, the scenic arrangement of acting form of which is fixed, in writing or otherwise, but doesn't include a cinematograph film.

An 'Artistic work' includes, painting, sculpture, drawing (including diagram map, chart of plan), engraving or a photograph, whether such work contains artistic quality or not. Architecture means any building or structure having an artistic character or design. 'Engravings' includes lithographs, word cuts, prints and other similar works.

Cinematograph film includes any work of visual recording on any medium produced through a process from which a moving image may be produced by any means and includes a sound recording accompanying such visual recording cinematography includes video films. Sound recording which includes a recording of sounds from which such sounds may be reproduced regardless of the medium on which such recording is made.

The above information clearly indicates that copyright subsists in variety of work created or produced by the author or owner. But such production of work must be original and created out of his labour, skill and capital investment.

Following are the Requirements for the Subsistence of Copyright

(a) The work is first published in India

(b) Where the work is first published outside India the

author at the date of publication must be a citizen of India. If the publication was made after the author's death the author must have, at the time of his death, been a citizen of India.

(c) In the case of unpublished work the author is on the date of making of the work, a citizen of India or domiciled in India. This however, does not apply to works of architecture.

But the above conditions or requirements do not apply to foreign works or works of international organizations. But under the Copy Right Act, the Central Government is empowered to bring any foreign works within the ambit of the Act.

Normally, the copyright subsists in the following works.

Literary Work

Whenever the original work is converted into some other work, the converted work itself has copyright, as it is also a literary work. This clearly shows that, copyright subsists only in original work. The mere coping of original work without having any novelty or originality, no copyright would subsist over such work. The degree of originality required for copy right protection is minimal, the emphasis is more on the labour, skill, judgment and capital expended in producing the work[3]. The words 'literary work' includes all works expressed in writing whether they have merit or not. The work need not be of literature but work in the form of books, foot ball coupons, a set of logarithmic tables, railway time–table, telephone directory and income tax-returns are all literary work irrespective of their aesthetic qualities. A literary work must be in some material form i.e., writing or print or symbols. But a speech or lecture even if recorded on a dictaphone, sound film, or other recording device, they are not entitled for any copyright as they are not considered as literary work. But where computer programmes, tables and compilations, computer databases or information storage device are considered as literary works possessing copyright. But under performers right, where a person delivers an extempore lecture, or tells a story or gives a musical performance, which has not been previously written down or recorded, such person is protected.

The important thing, which we have to remember, is that, it is the product made out of labour, skill and capital expended by an author on his work that is protected under the Copy Right Act and not the elements or raw material, used in such work. This shows that, the product of the author must be different from the raw materials used in such work. The special kind of knowledge, labour, judgment or skill of the author of a work makes the author to acquire copy right over it. In order to determine whether a work is entitled to copyright protection, the practical test is, what is worth copying is prima facie worth protecting'. In *Glesson V. Denne*, 1975 (RPC 471) it was observed that;

'If one works hard enough, waling down the streets, taking down the names of people who live at houses and makes a street directory as a result of that labour, this has been held to be an exercise sufficient to justify in making claims to copy right in the work which is ultimately produced'.

Adaptation of Literary Work

It means, the conversion of the literary in to a dramatic work by way of performance either in public or otherwise. According to section 2 (a) (r) of the Copy Right Act, adaptation relates to any work includes any use of such work involving the rearrangement or alteration. Supposing the owners of the original work authorizes another person to rearrangement or adopt it, the copy right in the arrangement then rests in the arranger. That is, the owner of the original work will have no copy right over the arranged work.

Abridgement of Literary work

Some times, an abridgement of a literary work is entitled to copy right provided it is novel and original in which the author has bestowed his skill, labour on it. The precise meaning of the word 'abridgement has been discussed by the High Court of Madras in *Govindan V. Gopalakrishnan*[4], 'the view expressed on abridgement was that abridgement is the reproduction of an original work in a much more precise and concise way. So a genuine abridgement of a literary work is an 'original work' and is the subject matter of copyright. All abridged literary works are not entitled for copyright, provided it is done with originality where the author has bestowed adequate skill and labour on it. The quantum of originality is not important, but the abridged work must contain originality and novel ideas.

The Privy Council in *Macmillan and Co. V.K.J. Cooper*[5] elaborated the law on the point of abridgement. In the instant case, the plaintiffs book consisted of selected passages from 'plutarch's life of Alexander the Great', joined together by few words to give a different appearance. The book also contained introduction and notes useful for education. A similar book was published on the defendants with notes. The plaintiff alleged that the defendants had infringed their copy right in the book, which was prescribed for university examinations. The original work contained 40,000 words whereas the defendants had copied 20,000 words and 7,000 words in notes. The court observed that, there was no sufficient labour, skill or knowledge bestowed on the plaintiff's book for claiming copyright. Therefore, the abridged work is not entitled for copyright.

Collective Works

Collective works also entitled for copyright provided it is made with skill, labour and knowledge. For example compilation of various articles written by different authors, which includes encyclopedias, dictionaries, year books, magazines, Journals, periodicals etc., a person who compiles different articles and brings out a book with his skill, labour is also entitled for copy right. Because the preparation of a collective work requires considerable amount of labour, skill, judgment and investment of capital. Therefore, such compilation work is also considered as literary work entitled for copyright. There are two types of copy right in collective work.

(a) Copy right in the separate parts, which is vested in the respective author of the parts. For example, an article written in a book, which is compiled one, then, the original author of the article will have the copyright.

(b) Copy Right in the collective work vests in the individual who collects the articles, arranges and edits them. This is due to the fact that, substantial amount of skill, knowledge, judgment and investment of capital and labour used for creating such collective work.

Computer Software and Programmes

Computer software and programmes are also considered as literary work. Computer programmes devised for the working of computers is generally regarded as literary work. Likewise magnetic tapes and discs including floppy discs, which contain information recorded by means of electronic impulses also, considered as databases and they are literary work. According to section 2 (ffc) computer programme is a set of instruction expressed in words, codes, schemes or any other form, including a machine-readable medium capable of causing a computer to perform a particular task or achieve a particular result. Therefore, computer programme is also considered as literary work for which copyright subsists.

A question arose before the Allahabad High Court in *Agarwala publishing House V. Board of High school and Intermediate Education, Uttar Pradesh*[6], that whether question papers set for the examination has any copy right?

The High Court of Allahabad observed that, the person who sets the question paper invests labour, skill and time on the preparation. He is the author of the question paper and therefore he has the copy right over such question paper. Subsequent to this decision, the High court of Patna also reiterated the same view in *Jagdish Prasad V. Parameshwar Prasad*[7].

The determination of the question whether copyright subsists with the author of the question paper set for Examination came up before the English Court in *University of London Press V. University Tutorials Press*[8]. In the instant case, in 1915, the University of London passed a resolution that the appointment of examiners who have the copy right over the question papers set for the examination shall be vested with the University of London. The examiners were appointed and they prepared question papers. In the meantime, the University of London entered into an agreement with the University of London Press Ltd, and agreed to assign all such copy right of the publication as the University might have in such question papers for the period of 6 years. The University of London Press Ltd. decided to publish the examination papers. But in the meantime, the defendant company, i.e., University Tutorial Press Ltd. made a publication in which it had included 16 out of 42 of 1916 examination papers. As a consequence of it, the University of London press Ltd. filed a suit against defendant company for infringement of copyright.

The court observed that, the examination papers being a literary work, the author of such question papers has copyright. According to the agreement between the examiner and the University of London, University too has copy right over it. As the University of London has agreed to assign the publication to the University London Press Ltd, the University London Press too has copy right over such examination papers. From this it is evident that, the author (examiner), the University of London and the University

London Press Ltd, all are entitled to copy right over such examination papers.

Dissertation and Research Thesis

When the Research thesis and dissertations prepared by the students putting efforts, skill and labour in synthesizing various ideas, such thesis and dissertation possess copyright. In *Fatch Singh Mehta V. Singhal*[9], the guide copied down the same information from his student's thesis for his own Ph.D. thesis. A suit was filed against such infringement of copyright. The court held that, there is a violation of copy right of the student who had produced the Dissertation out of his skill, labour and knowledge.

Dramatic Works

Any type of dramatic work is also the subject of copyright. But the copyright subsists only if the dramatic work is original or is subjected to adaptation. According to section 2 (4), a dramatic work includes any piece of recitation, choreographic work or entertainment in a dumb show, the scenic arrangement of acting from of which is fixed in writing or otherwise but doesn't include a cinematograph film.

An interesting question came up before the Bombay High Court in *Indian Express V. Jagmohan*[10] that, the defendants made a stage play and a movie based on the central theme of certain series of Articles published by the plaintiff namely purchase of a woman by the name Kanta by a Journalist to highlight the flesh trade flourishing in some parts of the country. But the film emphasis was only on human bondage particularly of Indian women. The court held that there was no infringement of the copy right of the article published by the plaintiff.

Musical Work

Musical work is also the subject of copyright Section 13 (1) (a) recognize the copyright in original musical work. The phrase 'Musical work' means a work consisting of music that includes any graphical rotation of such work but doesn't include any works or any action intended to be sung or spoken with music. Therefore to enjoy copyright, the musical work must be original made out of skill, labour and innovations[11].

So far as songs are concerned, there is no copyright in a song as such. The works of a song create a copy right in the author of the song, and music of the song is the copy right of the composer. But where a song is written and one person composes music, such person has sole copy right over such song. Remixing of songs, which involves skill, labour and capital investment, also possesses copyright, as it is considered as adaptation of a musical work. Such remixing of songs does not infringe the copy right of the original musical composition.

Artistic Works

Any artistic work that is originated from the author will have copyright. According to section 2(C) of the Act, artistic work includes;

(i) Painting, a sculpture, a drawing (including a diagram, map, chart or palm) an engraving or a photograph, whether or not such work possesses artistic quality.

(ii) A work of architecture and

(iii) Any other work of artistic crafts man ship

How to Recognize Skill and Labour in a Work Entitled for Copyright

Where there is evidence that, there exists sufficient amount of skill and labour in producing a work, such work is capable of having copyright. In order to claim copy right in a work, there must be intellectual investment input into the work, which necessarily is original or novel. The best example, which can be quoted, is *University of London Press V.*

University Tutorial Press. What is required is that the work must not be copied from another work. If the manner of expression of thought is different and original, that is enough to claim copyright. In *R.G. Anand V. Deluxe Films*[12] the Supreme Court has held that' there can be no copy right in an idea, subject matter, themes, plots or historical or legendary facts. What is required is that, there needs to be originality only in the form of expression. In the instant case, the plaintiff was a play writer and producer of some plays including the play "Hum Hindustani". The plaintiff tried to consider the possibility of filming the said play. Therefore he narrated the whole play to the defendant. The defendant made a picture 'New Delhi' out of the play narrated to him without the knowledge of the plaintiff. The plaintiff filed a suit against the defendant for the infringement of the copy right in the play "Hum Hindustani'.

Justice Fazal Ali observed that, the defendant has not infringed any copy righted work of the plaintiff. Because, the film portrays three themes:

1. Role of provincialism in regard to marriage and in regards to renting out accommodation;
2. Evils of caste–ridden society;
3. Evils of dowry.

The themes relating to evils caste- ridden society and evils of dowry did not exist in the play. Only the first theme i.e., the role of provincialism in regard to marriage and renting accommodation was in existence. As the film of the defendant contains all the three themes, which cannot be segregated, as they are integral part of the film, there is no infringement of copy right of the plaintiff's play.

The court also observed that, where the same idea is being developed in a different manner, which is originated from the author, and then it does not amount to violation of copyright. But where the defendant's work is a literal (colorable) imitation of the copy righted work with some differences here and there, it amount to violation of copyright. This shows that where the coping of the work is substantial and material one, it amounts to the violation of copyright. Where the theme is the same but the same has been presented and treated differently so that the subsequent work becomes completely a new work, there would be no violation of copyright.

Conclusion and Suggestions

Copyright being the intellectual property of the author who produces such work is required to be protected from infringement. The Copy Right Act 1957 and the amended Acts are adequate to safeguard the copy right of the authors who produce their work out of their labour, skill and capital investment. In the commercial world, often people use the works produced by others for their personal use or for commercial purpose. The original form of expression is only protected under the copyright Act and not the idea. Copyrights over literary work, artistic work, Musical works are also protected provided they are original and substantially new work of the author or producer. Even adaptation of literary work to dramatic work by way or performance is also an intellectual property of the producer over which copyright can be claimed. Where the same idea and theme of an original work is borrowed and the same is presented in a unique way, with labour, skill and capital investment of the producer or author even over such work also the producer can claim copyright.

But claiming copy right over the collective work seems to be unreasonable. Because, in the collective work, the editor only compiles all articles written by different authors as it is and brings out in the form of a book in which one cannot find any novelty, originality, skill or special knowledge in such compilation work. As such, it is unfair to claim copy right over such work by the compiler or editor. Therefore, unless the work produced by an author is original and unique based upon his skill and labour, no copyright can be claimed over such work. In the light of the changing scenario, the copyright Act is to be amended so as to keep pace with the changes taking place in the commercialized world.

NOTES AND REFERENCES

1. B.L. Wadehra, 'Law relating to Patents, Trade Marks, Copyrights, Designs and Geographical Indications', Second Ed. 2000, p. 283.
2. P. Narayanan, 'Intellectual Property Law', 2nd Ed., p. 6.
3. Ibid, p. 223.
4. AIR 1955 Mad. 391.
5. AIR 1924 PC 75.
6. AIR 1957 Allahabad 9.
7. AIR 1966 Patna 33.
8. (1916) 2 Ch 601.
9. (1990) IPR 69 Raj.
10. AIR 1985 Bom. 229.
11. Supra note 1, P. 304.
12. AIR 1978 SC 1613.

16 IMPACT OF TRIPS AGREEMENT ON INDIAN PATENT LAW

*A. David Ambrose**

Introduction

The desire for the liberalization of the multilateral trading system was not a recent 21st century phenomenon. In the post war period itself ITO-International Trade Organisation was envisaged as a third pillar along with the International Monetary Fund (IMF) and International Bank for Reconstruction and Development (IBRD) (Later World Bank). The negotiations for a multilateral trading system in the post war period even though could not pave way for an acceptable International Trade Organisation, multilateral tariff negotiations were held under the auspicious of GATT. The Uruguay Round Negotiations culminated in the establishment of World Trade Organisation (WTO). The WTO is the legal and institutional foundation of the multilateral trading system. Members of the WTO have agreed to reduce all trade tariffs and subscribe to nondiscriminatory trade thereby facilitate international trade. Thus the main object of WTO is to

* Department of Legal Studies, University of Madras, Chennai-600 005.
Paper presented in the two day National Seminar on *"Intellectual Property Rights A Public Awareness Programme"* held at University of My sore on 28-29, August 2004.

reduce trade barriers and encourage liberalization of multilateral trade.

However, of late, increased interdependence and globalization created a kind of sensitivity to foreign competition that resulted in the urge for a "protectionist regime" in many industrialized countries. Accordingly the "protectionist attitude" started reflecting in the multilateral trade negotiations too. Even though many efforts within the WTO frame work have been taken to reduce the trade tariffs the "protectionist approach" also found its place in the multilateral trade negotiations resulting in the adoption of Agreement on Trade Related Aspects of Intellectual Property Rights (TRIPS) within the WTO frame work. Therefore it should be noted that the prime objective of TRIPS Agreement is "technological protectionism".

If that is so, TRIPS Agreement, which compels all member states to provide minimum intellectual property (IP) protection within their municipal sphere, will necessarily have an impact on our Indian IP Regime, as India is a welfare state and our philosophy of IP protection varies, enormously from that of TRIPS[1]. Consequently in order to fulfill its obligations under TRIPS, India has altered or in the process of altering its IP regime. To provide the minimum IP protection as envisaged by the TRIPS, India has either amended some of the then existing laws[2] or enacted new legislations[3].

The TRIPS impact could be considerable or minimal, could be advantageous or adverse and could be felt in many fields of IP. The present paper aims at discussing the extent as well as the nature of the impact of TRIPS Agreement particularly on Indian patent regime as many of India's vital interests (pertaining to pharmaceuticals and biotechnology) are involved in patent protection. Moreover, while the laws relating to trademarks, copyrights and designs are almost in conformity with the provisions of TRIPS Agreement, the patent laws are the ones which are the cause of concern.

The first part deals with the TRIPS Agreement. The second part deals with the Indian response and-the third part contains the conclusion and the suggestions.

The TRIPs Agreement

In 1986 the Uruguay round of negotiations began under the GATT which concluded in Marrakesh on 15th April with the signing of the "Final Act". This Final Act contained 28 agreements. One of the decisions taken in Marrakesh was the formation of a World Trade Organisation. WTO agreement is a package deal. The member countries have to accept all of the agreements *in toto* and cannot opt out of anyone of the provisions without quitting WTO itself.

The WTO Regime is composed of three important fields namely goods[4], Services[5] and intellectual property rights. While various aspects of Trade in goods are governed by GATT and Trade in services are regulated by GATS. The TRIPS governs the Intellectual Property Regime.

The TRIPS Agreement which is binding on all members of the WTO has *inter alia* the following objects:

(i) To reduce distortions and impediments to international trade by taking into account the need to promote effective and adequate protection of IPR.

(ii) To provide a multilateral framework of principles, rules in respect of international trade in counterfeit goods;

(iii) To cater to the special needs of the least developed countries in respect of maximum flexibility in the domestic implementation of laws in order to enable men to create a sound and viable technological base; and

(iv) To resolve disputes on trade-related intellectual property issues through multilateral procedures.

TRIPS and Patent Protection

The TRIPS Agreement incorporates the WTO Principles of non-discrimination[6] and transparency and provides for the establishment of minimum standards of protection to creators of IP[7]. Articles 27 to 34 of the TRIPS Agreement contain provisions exclusively relating to patents. In addition to this the general provisions and basic principles of TRIPS applicable to all of IP are also relevant\applicable to patents. Article 7 of the Agreement says that the protection and enforcement of intellectual property rights (IPRs) should contribute not only to technical innovation but also to the transfer and dissemination of technical knowledge ....in a manner conducive to economic welfare, and to the balance of rights and obligation". Article 8 provides that WTO Members may.....adopt measures necessary to protect public health and nutrition, and to promote the public interest in sectors of vital importance to their socio-economic and technological development, provided that patents shall be available and patent rights enjoyable without discrimination as to the place of invention, the field of technology and whether the products are imported or locally produced.

Patents protect the patent owner of an invention with the legal means to prevent others from making, using or selling, importing or offering for sales for a period of 20 years[9] which is to run from the date of filling of the application[10].

Under Art 27(1) of TRIPS Agreement patent shall be available for any invention whether products or process provided they are new. Article 27 (2)[11] and 27(3)[12] give the option to exclude a number of well defined subject matter from patentability. It is of interest to note that in case of allegation of infringement of a process patent the burden of proof lies upon the person against whom allegation of infringement is made[13].

Article 30 provides that limited exceptions to the exclusive rights conferred on by a patent are permissible, provided that such exceptions do not unreasonably conflict with the normal exploitation of the patent and they do not unreasonably prejudice the rights of the patent holder. Article 31 deals with "other use" of the subject matter of the patent without authorization of the right holder. Article 65 of the Agreement deals with transitional arrangement for developing countries and Article 66 specifically deals with the case for least developed countries. Under these provisions, the developing countries are allowed up to January 2005 to introduce pharmaceutical product patent protection. While the least developed countries have time until 2006, with the possibility of an extension.

The Indian Response

The unaltered earlier Indian patent regime under 1970 Indian Patents Act differed in many ways from that of the TRIPS Agreement. The Patents Act drastically restricted the rights of patent holders in fields linked to basic needs. This is due to the fact that the adoption of the Patents Act 1970 was based on a lengthy legislative process and careful consideration of the socio-economic impacts of the patents in sensitive fields such as health and food. Therefore India had to considerably alter its patent law.

The Indian response to TRIPS was in two stages. That is to say first by way of 1999 Amendment followed by the 2002 Amendment.

The 1999 Amendment

It will not be an exaggeration to say that mainly in order to comply with the findings of WTO's Dispute Settlement Mechanism, India has amended The Patents Act 1970 in 1999.

It is pertinent to note that the TRIPS Agreement provides for 10 years transitional period for developing countries that have no provisions for product patent in their law, to alter their patent regime to be in conformity with the Provisions of TRIPS Agreement. Accordingly, India has to provide for product patent from 1.1.2005. However, this is subject to the grant of Exclusive Marketing Right (EMR) during the transition period[14]. As India did not provide for EMR during the transitional period, the US complained to the WTO's Dispute Settlement Body[15].

After hearing both sides the Appellate Body came to the conclusion that India had not complied with its obligations under Arts. 70 (8) and 70 (9) of TRIPS Agreement, as it had failed to establish a mechanism that adequately preserves novelty and priority regarding applications for product patents in respect of pharmaceutical and agro-chemical inventions during the transitional period to which it is entitled under Art.65 of the Agreement. India should also notify and publish adequate information regarding Mail Box System and EMR.

Therefore the 1999 Amendment Act provided for the grant of EMR[16]. In addition it had provisions for compulsory licensing[17] and mailbox facility[18] for pharmaceuticals and agro-chemicals.

The 2002 Amendment

The Patent (Second Amendment) Bill was introduced in 1999 and as a result of it the Patent (Amendment) Act, 2002 was passed by the Parliament. This is the second major effect undertaken by India to comply with TRIPS Agreement. This Act makes the Indian Patent law not only TRIPS compliance but also incorporates safeguards for protection of public interest, national security, biodiversity, traditional knowledge etc. The opportunity has also been utilized to harmonize the patent granting procedures with international practices and to make the system user friendly.

It is, therefore, pertinent to mention some of the important changes that have been made in the Amendment Act, 2002:

(a) The definition of the term "invention" has been modified in consonance with international practices and consistent with TRIPS Agreement.

(b) Inventions, which are harmful to environment, human, animal and plants, cannot be patented. The patent can be opposed on the ground of traditional knowledge according to Sec. 3.

(c) The rights of patentee have been aligned as per Article 28 of the TRIPS Agreement. (Section 104 A).

(d) A provision for reversal of burden of proof in case of infringement suit on process patent, in accordance with Article 34 of the TRIPS Agreement, has been added.

(e) Uniform term of patent protection of 20 years for all categories of invention as per Article 33 of the TRIPS Agreement has been prescribed.

(f) An application for a compulsory license can be made under Sections 84 and 92. Under Section 84, three years after the sealing of patent and under Section 92 any time after the sealing of the patent with respect to patent notified by the central government.

(g) The patent owners will have the exclusive right to prevent others who do not have their consent, not only for making, using or selling the invented product or prices in India, but also importing from other countries.

(h) To ensure smooth transition of a product from the monopoly status created by the patent to the public domain, a provision has been incorporated for obtaining marketing approval from the appropriate regulatory authorities.

(i) The provisions relating to national security has been strengthened.

(j) A provision has been incorporated for hearing of appeals which at present, lie before High court, by the Intellectual Property Appellate Board, for speedy disposal of such appeals.

(k) The central government may use an invention or acquire an invention for the purpose of non-commercial use by payment of adequate compensation according to Sections 99 to 103.

Conclusion and Suggestions

The un-amended Indian Patents Act, 1970, an outcome of lengthy discussions and based on the wise recommendations of learned committees, to a greater extent was successful in tactically balancing the individual's (inventor's) interest with that of society's interest. The 1970 Act had many provisions that envisaged social control over individual rights that is to say it had provisions for government's effective control over patent rights. The shortened period of protection for the patent in the field of food and medicine, the absence of product patents for medicine and the provisions for governmental control all cumulatively suggest this. However, to be in tune with the TRIPS Agreement several changes have been introduced in the then existing patent regime in India altering the position. It is generally feared that after the changes the present patent regime in India is infavour of protection of individual's interest. Because of the introduction of 20 years uniform patent protection period and because of product patent, a general feeling among the pharmaceutical industry is that these changes may effect the increase of the drug prices, as the Indian drug companies will be discouraged to locally manufacture same products using different processes.

Moreover, it is also feared that bio patent may lead to bio-piracy[19]. Article 27 of TRIPS Agreement *inter-alia* require that members state to grant patent in all fields of technology provided they are new, involved inventive step and are capable of industrial application. This requirement is subject to certain exclusions. However, micro-organism has been included in the subject of patent under Article 27 (3) (b). Provision regarding non-patentable inventions under Sec. 3 of Indian Patents Act has been modified to include exclusions permitted by TRIPS Agreement under Article 27.

It is of interest to note that here micro-organism is not excluded under Sec 3 (j) of Indian Patents Act there by permitting grant of patent to micro organisms[20]. Thus the exclusionary provision of Sec. 3 (j) permit grant of patent to micro-organisms. But a joint reading of Sec. 5 (b) with explanation makes it clear that only process patent in this regard will be granted. Granting patent rights to micro-organisms would, it is feared, allow just a few MNCs to exploit the situation and result in bio-piracy[21].

Then how to safeguard India's interest? It should be pointed out that though the TRIPS Agreement advocates strong patent regime, there are some provisions in the TRIPS Agreement that allow the use of patent by others without the consent of the patentee. For example, Article 31 of the TRIPS Agreement permits a WTO member to pass a national law providing use of the subject matter of the patent without authorization of the right holder under certain conditions.[22] This can be done by granting "compulsory license"[23]. That is to say that a third party is allowed to use a patented product or use a patented process without the consent of the patent holder. The newly added chapter XVI of the Indian Patent Act 1970 on "Working of Patents, Compulsory License and Revocation" deals with the compulsory license[24].

Another method available under the TRIPS Agreement for dealing with other use is "parallel importing".[25] A joint reading of Article 6[26] and Article 28[27] of the TRIPS Agreement reveals that the TRIPS Agreement recognizes the right to import as a right that the patent holder enjoys subject to the national exhaustion[28] policy that is not challengeable in a WTO dispute. It should be remembered that compulsory licensing and parallel imports are the two effective tools that can be used to implement the right to health and they allow the TRIPS Agreement to be flexible. In case of developing nations that cannot use compulsory licensing effectively, the Doha Declaration[29] in Para 6 instructed that council for TRIPS to find an expeditious solution to this problem and accordingly "Implementation of paragraph 6 of the Doha Declaration on the TRIPS Agreement and public Health" was adopted[30].

The Doha Ministerial Conference provided that for the protection of public health, compulsory licencing and parallel imports can be used. The Doha Declaration came about in the 4th Ministerial Conference of the WTO at Doha, Qatar on the 14th of November 2001. The Declaration reaffirms that 'TRIPS Agreement can and should be interpreted and implemented in a manner supportive of the WTO members' right to protect public health and promote the right to access to essential medicines. The declaration accordingly recognizes that (a) each member has right to determine what constitutes a national emergency or other such circumstances of extreme urgency; (b) each member has the right to grant compulsory licences and freedom to determine the grounds upon which each licences are granted upon. The declaration also provides for the least developed countries a longer period of time for full implementation of TRIPS Agreement i.e. up to January 1, 2016. India should take advantage of this position and see that these provisions are used effectively.

There are certain other general provisions providing for in-built flexibilities in the TRIPS Agreement that can be used for our advantage. Article 7 of the TRIPS Agreement states that 'the objective of protection and enforcement of IPRs should contribute to the transfer and dissemination of technology in a manner conducive to social and economic welfare and to a balance of rights and obligations'. Article 8 of TRIPS further states that members in amending their laws may take measure to protect public health and nutrition. These general provisions thus provide for some flexibility. Article 30[31] is another provision in the TRIPS Agreement that constitutes the flexibilities, as it provides for limited exceptions to the patent rights. Similarly Article

31, on Other Use without Authorization of Right Holder, supports the cause of public health as it categorically provides that in cases of national emergencies remedies such as compulsory licencing may be restored.

Another option available for India is the "early working" exception otherwise known as "Bolar exception". Under this exception a patented product can be legitimately manufactured by a third party little before the expiry of the patent term for release of the product immediately after the expiration of the patent. By 2005 January India has to amend its patent law to be totally in tune with the TRIPS provisions and grant product patent to drugs. It is earnestly hoped that India while going for the amendment will consider the challenges and the available options pursue a stronger and sensible national and policies and strive for greater third world cooperation in this regard to safeguard the public health of the Indian poor masses.

NOTES

1. In India where the notion knowledge is free IP is perceived as public good and should be used to promote economic development.
2. For example, after 1995 amendments have been made in the 1957 Copy Right Act and 1970 Patents Act. The earlier 1958 Trade and Merchandise Marks Act was replaced by the new 1999 Trade Mark Act.
3. New legislations like the Geographical Indications of Goods (Registration and Protection) Act, 1999 and the Designs Act, 2000 have been enacted.
4. Trade in goods of all descriptions-Agricultural industries or others, is to be governed under General Agreement on Tariffs and Trade (GATT).
5. Trade in services of all kinds for e.g. business services including professional and computer: communication: construction and engineering; distribution, educational and environmental services; financial services, banking and insurance; health services, tourism and travel services; recreational, cultural and sporting services; transport services

and consultancy is to be regulated under General Agreement on Trade in Service.

6. The Most Favoured Nation Concept and National Treatment Concept.
7. The TRIPS Agreement has enlisted in Annex 1 C as many as 8 items as the subject matter of IPRs. The items are: (i) Copyright and related other rights. (ii) Trade marks. (iii) Geographical Indication. (iv) Industrial design. (v) Patents. (vi) Layout designs (Topographies) of integrated circuits, (vii) Protection of undisclosed information and (viii) Anti-competition practice in contractual licences.
8. For the Rights of patentee see Art 28 of TRIPS Agreement.
9. Art 33 of TRIPS.
10. For the requirement of filling an application for patent is see Art 29 of TRIPS.
11. Inventions that are necessary to protect public orders or morally including protection of human, animal plant life or health or to environmental or which can be excluded from patentability under Art. 27 (2).
12. Under Art 27(3) patentability may be excluded for (a) diagnostic, therapeutic and surgical method for the treatment of humans or animals (b) plants and animals other than micro organisms and essentially biological process for the production of plants or animals other than non-biological and microbiological process. Plant varieties could be protected either by patents or by an effective *sui generis* system or by any combination these of.
13. See Art. 34 of TRIPS Agreement.
14. See Art 70 (a) of TRIPS.
15. The European Community and their member states also made a similar complaint.
16. See Chapter IV A consisting of Sections 24A to 24F.
17. See Sections 24 C and 24 D.
18. See Section 5 (2).
19. Bio-piracy can refer to unauthorised use of biological resources e.g., plants, animals, organs, microorganisms, genes and unequal share of benefits between a patent holder and a developing country whose resource has been used.
20. Sec. 3 (j) reads as follows: Plants and animals in whole or any part thereof other than micro organisms but including seeds,

varieties and species and essentially biological processes for production or propagation of plants and animals.

21. The amended Indian Patents Act in Section 10 (4) (d) (ii) (D), in order to minimize the instances of bio--piracy, requires that the source and the geographical origin of the biological material should be disclosed in the patent application if the application is concerned with a biological material.
22. For the discussion on conditions generally see Mitsuo Matsushita, Thomas J. Schoenbaum and Petros C. Mavroidis, *The World Trade Organization: Law, Practice, and Policy* (Oxford University Press, 2003) at p. 419-420.
23. The WHO defines compulsory license as follows: "When a judicial or administrative authority is allowed by law to grant license without the permission from the holder, on various grounds of general interests". See http://www.who.org.
24. The grounds for granting compulsory licenses are found primarily in Sections-84 (I) and (7) of the Act.
25. "Parallel Importing" is the term used for importing a legally produced product from a low priced distributor instead of buying directly from manufacturer.
26. Article 6 of the TRIPS Agreement states that exhaustion of intellectual property rights is matter left to members to determine.
27. Article 28 grants the right of importation to the patent holder as a part of the exclusive rights that come with patent.
28. Exhaustion means that once a patented product has been sold anywhere under the authority of the patent holder the patent holder has no right to prevent further sale or importation anywhere in the world; *supra* Note 23 at 421.
29. The Declaration on the TRIPS Agreement and Public Health, adopted on 14.11.2001.
30. The decision of the General Council of 30 August 2003 rpt. in ILM, Vol. 43 (2004) at p. 509.
31. Article 30-exceptions to rights conferred-members may provide limited exceptions to the exclusive rights conferred by a patent provided that such exceptions do not unreasonably conflict with a normal exploitation of the patent and do not unreasonably prejudice the legitimate interest of the patent owner, taking account of the legitimate interest of third parties.

17 BALANCING OF INTERESTS IN PATENT LAW

*J.S. Patil**

Introduction

Twenty-first century is described as an era of intellectual property rights due to the exponential growth of the regime of intellectual property right. It has brought about revolutionary changes in the fundamental concept of property and a variety of economic concepts. There is a shift from the collective rights of the society to that of individual's rights. In the last one decade the intellectual property regime has attracted the world attention as a very important asset for individual), corporations and nations. Opening of the doors of every national market for worldwide competition in the wake of globalisation, liberalization and privatization has added a new dimension to trade, business and commerce. The traditional GATT was only an international body regulating the tariff for international trade. After 1994, a new regime of WTO replaced the traditional GATT. This organization lays down the guidelines for the conduct of international trade in addition to regulating the tariff. Various agreements have been entered into by the international community setting out the international

* Department of Law Gulbarga University, Gulbarga.

standards for trade, business and commerce in various fields. Trade Related Intellectual Property Rights Agreement is one such important agreement. It lays down international guidelines for various regimes of intellectual property rights that were earlier left totally to freedom of the country concerned. This development has forced many countries that are parties to the new agreement to change their national laws in accordance with the international guidelines. India is also a party to the TRIPS. This has necessitated the Indian government to effect series of changes in its law and make new laws so as to conform itself to the international obligations undertaken under the TRIPS. A birds eye view of the Indian laws relating to the intellectual property lights and the changes affected recently would reveal the shift from collective rights to the protection of individual's rights which of course is a global trend.

The Concept of Property

Before going into the survey of Indian IPR, it is worthwhile to understand the jurisprudential meaning of the concept of property. The term property possesses a singular ,variety of different applications having different degrees of generality. In its widest sense, property includes all a person's legal rights, of whatever description. A man's property is all that is *his in law.* In a second and narrower sense, property includes not all a person's rights, but only his proprietary as opposed to his personal rights. The former constitutes his estate or property, while the latter constitutes his status or personal condition. In a third application, the term includes not even all proprietary rights, but only those which are both proprietary and *in rem.* Finally, in the narrowest use of the term, it includes nothing more than corporeal property, i.e. the right of ownership in a material object[1].

All property is either corporeal or incorporeal. Corporeal property is the right of ownership in material things;

incorporeal property is any other proprietary right *in rem*. Incorporeal property itself is of two kinds, namely (1) *jura in re aliena* or encumbrances such as leases, mortgages and servitudes, and (2) *jura in re propria* over immaterial things such as patents, copyrights, trade-marks, etc. This second category of incorporeal property is popularly described as the intellectual property rights[2].

The Concept of Intellectual Property

The term "intellectual property" has come to be internationally recognized as covering patents, industrial designs, copyright, trade-marks, know-how and confidential information. Geographical indications, integrated circuit, layout designs, protection of plant varieties and information technology have also been included to this list. Earlier, patents, designs and trade-marks used to be considered as different kinds of "industrial property". But when copyright, confidential information and other types of property are included, the term "intellectual property" is considered as a more appropriate description for this class of property.

The scope of intellectual property is expanding very fast and attempts are made by persons who create new creative ideas to seek protection under the umbrella of intellectual property rights. There are many similarities in the law relating to the different species of intellectual property in regard to the nature of the property, the mode of its acquisition, the nature of rights conferred, the commercial exploitation of these rights, the enforcement of these rights and the remedies available against the infringement of these rights[3].

The statute law relating to intellectual property in India is undergoing changes so as to bring them in harmony with the law in the developed countries, especially the United States. This has become necessary after India signed the GATT and TRIPs and became a member of WTO.

The Indian Patents Act, 1970

The law of patents in India is governed by the Patents Act 1970 as amended by the Patents (Amendment) Act 1999, the Patents (Second Amendment) Act 2001 and the Patents (Third Amendment) Bill 2004 passed by the Lok Saba and pending before the Rajya Saba. The amendments are effected to fall in line with the requirements of the WTO regime.

A patent is a monopoly right granted to a person who has invented a new and useful article or an improvement of an existing article or a new process of making an article. It consists of an exclusive right to manufacture the new article invented or manufacture an article according to the invented process for a limited period. After the expiry of the duration of patent, anybody can make use of the invention[4].

Grant of patents stimulates technical progress in four ways: (1) It encourages research and invention. (2) It induces an inventor to disclose his discoveries instead of keeping them as trade secret. (3) It offers a reward for the expenses of developing inventions to the stage at which they are commercially practicable. (4) It provides an Inducement to invest capital in new lines of production which might not appear profitable if many competing producers embarked on them simultaneously[5].

A patentable invention means any new and useful art, process, method or manner of manufacture; machine, apparatus or other article; substance produced by manufacture and includes any new and useful improvement of any of them; and an alleged invention; a method of testing a manufacture; and method of treating a plant[6]. The last two aspects are included by the Patents (Second Amendment) Act, 2001.

Following inventions are not patentable as per Sections 3-5 of the Patents Act 1970:

1. Frivolous inventions.
2. Inventions contrary to law, morality, or injurious to public health.

3. Invention of mere scientific principle of abstract theory.
4. Invention of new property or new use of known substance.
5. Invention of only admixtured substance.
6. Arrangement or rearrangement or duplication of features of known substance.
7. Method of agriculture or horticulture.
8. Process of treatment of human beings or animals.
9. Inventions relating to atomic energy.
10. Invention of a plant or animal as a whole or in part (other than micro-organism) including seeds, varieties and species and their production and propagation.
11. India's traditional knowledge.

The process of treatment of plants is patentable after the Patent (Second Amendment) Act is brought into force. India's traditional knowledge is also added as non-patentable by this amendment. But micro-organisms are patentable. In *Dimminaco* v *Controller of Patents* (AIPC (2002) 717) the Calcutta High Court held that "manufacture" did not exclude Jiving substances and cleared the patent in respect of a biotechnological process for producing a vaccine containing a living micro-organism.

The term of patent is raised to 20 years for all the types by amending the Patents Act. Under the Act as it stands today, term of patent for inventions relating to food, medicine and drugs is five years from the date of sealing of the patent or seven years from the date of filing the complete specification whichever is shorter and it is for the process only. In the 1999 Amendment to the Act, exclusive marketing rights were provided in these areas for those who have filed an application in a convention country before 1-1-1995 and got approval to sell or distribute them; or after 1-1-1995 they must have filed a claim for manufacturing an identical article in India and obtained patent. All these process patents are changed to 20 years product patent by the Second Amendment to the Patents Act, 1970. Expressing their concern over this development, the Pharmaceutical companies have asked the government to include some protective measures in the third amendment so that the companies manufacturing life-saving drugs need not have to withdraw hundreds of brands amounting to nearly Rs. 4,000 crores[7]. The Second Amendment is challenged in Supreme Court as violative of fundamental right to life which includes right to health and access to curative drugs[8].

A patent can be obtained by filing an application in a prescribed form along with the prescribed fee by the actual inventor or his assignee or the legal representative. It should be accompanied by a provisional specification or complete specification. A provisional specification need describe the invention only briefly and need not contain the claims. A complete specification must be filed within 12 months from the date application failing which the application will be treated as abandoned. The complete specification should fully and particularly describe the invention and the method by which it is to be carried out. It should disclose the best method of performing the invention known to the applicant and end with a claim or claims defining the scope of the invention for which protection is claimed. It will be examined by examiners as to its compliance with requirements of the Act. Examination of an application will be at the request of the applicant and not automatic. This change is effected by the Second Amendment. If there are any objections, the same will be communicated to the applicant. After the removal of objections it will be published in the Official Gazette. Publication of Patent application must be made within 18 months of filing date or priority date after the Second Amendment. This change is brought to speed up the patenting process as it is there in some of the countries like the U.S. Interested persons can oppose the application on various grounds. Patent will be granted after giving due consideration to the opposition, if any.

Following are the grounds on the basis of which a patent application can be opposed:

1. Obtaining wrongfully.
2. Prior publication.
3. Prior claim in a concurrent application.
4. Prior public use or public knowledge.
5. Obviousness and lack on inventive step.
6. Invention not patentable under the Act.
7. Failure to disclose information as to foreign application.
8. Insufficient description of the invention.
9. In the case of convention application, it is not made within the prescribed time[9].

There is a proposal in the Third Amendment to do away with the provision for pre-grant heating of opposition to patent applications by third parties, after the Controller "accepts" the patent application and comes to a positive conclusion on its eligibility to grant of a patent. Some have suggested that the Controller should have the discretion to "assess" views expressed by third parties while deciding on the grant of patent[10]. In many countries pre-grant hearing is not in existence. Doing away with this system would help the applicants in getting the patent quickly.

Abuse of patent rights can take place by way of meeting the demand for patented articles solely by importation from abroad, refusing to grant licenses to work the patent locally, imposing unreasonable terms on licensees and imposing restrictive conditions on the use of patents. To ensure the balance between the monopoly rights of the patentee with that of the society, a system of compulsory licensing is established in the Act. There are three types of compulsory licenses. First, a compulsory license to work a patent can be granted by the Controller to an interested person on the ground that the reasonable requirements of the public have not been satisfied or the patented invention is not available to the public at reasonable price. Secondly, a compulsory license may be granted in respect of a patent without the use of which another patent cannot be worked out. Lastly, the Central Government may notify in the Official Gazette that compulsory licenses should be granted in respect of certain patents or classes of patents.

Patent for inventions relating to food and medicine are endorsed with the words "licenses of right" after completion of three years so that any person may obtain license as a matter of right without having to establish a case as in a compulsory license. This is a very good example of providing preference to the collective interest of the society at large as against the individual interest of the patent holder. But this provision has been deleted along with the deletion of process patenting of these inventions by the Second Amendment.

Another provision which goes in favour of the collective rights is revocation of the patent for non-working under Section 89. If the reasonable requirements of the public are not satisfied and the patented invention is not available at a reasonable price even after all these types of licenses are granted, then the patent itself may be revoked by the Controller so as to facilitate its free use by the public.

Balance of rights is reflected in the series of provisions relating to the revocation of patent as well. Various modes of revocation of patents include: revocation in the public interest by the Central Government; revocation of patents relating to atomic energy by the Controller; revocation for non-working; revocation by the High Court on petition for failure to, comply with the requirements of the Central Government to use the invention; and revocation by the High Court on petition by a person interested on various grounds.

Grounds on the basis of which a patent can be revoked are:

1. Patentee is not entitled to the patent.
2. Patent wrongfully obtained as against the person entitled.
3. Patent obtained by false suggestion or representation.
4. Failure to disclose information regarding foreign applications.
5. Non-compliance with directions of secrecy.
6. Amendment of specification obtained by fraud.
7. Subject of a claim not an invention.
8. Subject of a claim not a patentable invention.
9. Invention claimed already the subject-matter of a prior grant.
10. Invention claimed lacks novelty having regard to prior knowledge or prior use.
11. Invention is obvious or does not involve inventive step having regard to prior knowledge or prior use.
12. Invention not useful.
13. Invention not sufficiently described, and the best method of performing is not disclosed.
14. Claims not clearly defined or not fairly based.

In spite of all such provisions which weigh in favour of the promotion of collective rights of the people at large, some of the procedural reforms proposed in the third amendment such as to curtail the timeframe, especially extensions, available to the applicant/Patent Office in various stages like filing and amendment of specifications, compliance with directives of the Controller, withdrawal of application, etc. and for the examiner to submit his report to the Controller and sealing of the patent are all aimed at easing out the bottle necks in the patenting process that go in favour of the patentee. Further, in the case of renewal patents in force, more time was proposed to be made available to the patentee to comply with requirements like payment of fee, etc.[11].

Evaluation & Conclusion

Government of India has been very cautious in protecting the national interests along with fulfilling its commitments by signing the TRIPS. Although many aspects of the amendments brought about to the Indian Patent Act, 1970 tilt the balance infavour of protecting the individual interests of the patent holders there are some protective measures that are included to protect the societal interests as well. Providing exclusive marketing rights in respect of food, medicine and drug patent applications filed in India in the First Amendment; providing for product patent to these inventions and increasing the term to 20 years; making examination of the application at the request of the applicant; keeping 18 months period for submission of the report by examiner; removal opposition system; simplification of the procedure; etc. will go in favour of the interests of the patentees. But the provision that India's traditional knowledge is not patentable is a welcome change under the Second Amendment where under a halt is brought to the indiscriminate patenting of India's treasure of traditional knowledge by outsiders. No more incidents like the patenting of basmati, turmeric, brinjol, ashwagandha, wheat, tur dal, tulsi, methi, cow urine, etc. will have to be encountered by India.

By creating a sui generic model for protection of plant varieties instead of providing patent protection and also providing series of rights to farmers and communities for their contribution in conserving and developing the plant varieties and genetic material required for inventing new varieties of plants, India has ensured the protection and conservation of its biological resources. A separate law, namely the Protection of Plant Varieties Act, 2001 has been passed for this purpose which is an example of the efforts on the part of Indian Government to balance the collective interests of the people with those of individual interests of patent holders and breeders of plant varieties.

Thus it can be concluded that Indian patent law is a well-balanced system of law that seeks to strike equilibrium between individual interests and the interests of the society even in the wake of global pressure infavour of more protection to the individual monopoly holders.

NOTES

1. Fitzgerald p. l *Salmond on Jurisprudence,* 12th Ed. 1966, 411-412.
2. Ibid. 418.
3. Narayanan P., Intellectual Property Law, 3rd Ed. 2001, 1.
4. Ibid. 11.
5. Ibid 12.
6. Section 2 (1) (j) of Patents Act 1970.
7. IPR IEWS, Journal of Intellectual Property Rights, (2) 2004, 180-181.
8. *The Hindu,* July 27, 2004.
9. For details see Narayana P. *op. cit.* 38-46.
10. Patent Law: Procedural Reforms on the Hindu, 12.2.2002.
11. The Hindu, August 6, 2003.

18 THE NEW IPR STATUTES AND THE TRENDS OF DEVELOPMENTS

*G.B. Reddy**

"For more than a century, the world's wealthiest human being has been associated with oil. Now he is a knowledge worker."

Lester C. Thurow[1]

Introduction

This statement sums up the importance of the knowledge in a rapidly changing society, the world over. In the good old days, the popular adage was that 'knowledge is power' but in modem times, knowledge has been recognized not only as a source of power but also as the primary source of property. It is this recognition that justifies the protection of intellectual property (IP) created either by individuals or by communities. Bill Gates' is the embodiment of the new centrality of intellectual property. As the above statement rightly says that for more than a century the world's wealthiest persons were associated with oil starting from John D. Rockfeller in late 19th century and ending with Sultan of Brunei in the late 20th century. But today for the

* Assistant Professor, University College of Law, Osmania University, Hyderabad - 500 007.

first time in the history, the world's wealthiest person is a knowledge worker. One of the wealthiest persons in India is Azim Premji of WIPRO and he owes all his wealth to the knowledge. The World's major growth industries today such as Microelectronics, Biotechnology, Designer made materials, Pharmaceutical Industries and Telecommunications, all are brainpower industries. This brings us to the meaning and evolution of intellectual property.

Property in the legal sense is something, which can be owned, possessed, enjoyed and disposed of. It is a legal institution, an economic institution and also a social institution. The traditional classification of property can be made into (i) Corporeal (Physical) and incorporeal (invisible) property. In so far as the corporeal property is concerned it can be classified into movable as well as immovable property. The incorporeal property primarily consists of reputation of individual, securities and intellectual property rights. Therefore IPRs are the rights in respect of the property created by human intelligence and which manifests in the form of literary property, industrial property and other kinds of property.

As a result of industrial revolution and rapid developments made in the fields of science, technology and culture, new kinds of property apart from the aforementioned traditional forms came into existence. This property is known as IP, which can be defined as that property which is created by human intelligence, or mental labour and it is mostly in intangible form even though it can be reproduced in tangible form. In the broadest sense, all rights resulting from Intellectual activity in the industrial, scientific, or artistic fields become part of the IP It is so called because the objects of IP are the creations of the human mind, the human intellect. As mentioned above, the major classification of IP has been into (1) Industrial Property; and (2) Literary Property. In the category of Industrial property fall the *patents, trademarks, industrial designs,* and *layout designs.* The literary property includes primarily *copyright* and *neighboring rights,* which include performers' rights. Apart from the above two broad classes, there are also found certain other forms of IP like the *plant varieties, plant breeders rights, traditional knowledge, geographical indications* and *micro-organisms.* Many of these new forms are related to Information Technology (IT), Chemical Technology (CT) and Bio-Technology (BT).

Characteristics of IP: The IPRs have the following characteristics[2]:

(i) Intellectual property is a concept comparatively new to the modem jurisprudence;

(ii) IP is predominantly recognized in the commercial world to protect the interests of mercantile community;

(iii) IP is specially created and recognized in law inspite of its monopolistic nature, for a definite period or for an unlimited period based on the nature of creation;

(iv) It is value added system in view of the special intellectual contribution clearly identifiable whether registered or not;

(v) IPRs create monopolies and vest the same in the inventors and owners who can use the economics of scale to maximize their returns;

(vi) IP is transnational in nature as its use can not be confined to any boundary or territory;

(vii) Like the other forms of property the IP is also not absolute in nature and it is subject to certain exceptions, restrictions and limitations that can be imposed by the State in the larger interest of the public; and

(viii) IP is mostly intangible like the copyright and patents but it manifests ultimately in the form of tangible property.

Theories of Protection of IPRs

The protection IPRs is based on three theories viz.,

1. *The Natural Rights Theory*–which recognizes that one who creates something has a right to own it.
2. *The Economic Incentive Theory*–which provides that creator of a particular thing has a right to exploit it commercially in order to get economic returns in the form of returns; and
3. *The Public Trust Theory*–which envisages that any monopoly right conferred on an individual by the state is subject to the power of the state to act as a public trustee.

The first two theories stated above are capitalistic in nature and the third one is socialistic in its content.

One unique development that has taken place after the industrial revolution is that the IP has become the subject matter of commercial exploitation, which was not the case before. Whereas the creators in the past had concentrated mostly on the protection of their moral rights i.e., the right to be recognized as the author/creator of the work and the right to protect the integrity of the work created, the economic and commercial rights have taken center stage after the-industrial revolution.

Different Kinds of IP

Before discussing about the Indian legal regime to protect the IPRs it would be essential to explain the meaning of various kinds of Intellectual property.

1. *Copyright:* It is an exclusive right of the creators of original, literary, artistic, musical and dramatic works etc. which are created with the creation of the work, to certain things like reproduction, public performance, translation, adaptation and broadcasting. This right is in fact a bundle of rights, which are negative as well as

positive. In India the term of copyright is generally lifetime of the author plus 60 years.

2. *Patent:* It is an exclusive right awarded to an inventor to prevent others from making, selling, distributing, importing or using his invention without license or authorization for a fixed period of time. The invention must be novel, industrially applicable and non-obvious for being protected as a patent. The Government confers this limited monopoly right for a period of 20 years.

3. *Trademark:* It is an exclusive right to use distinctive signs such as symbols, colours, letters, shapes, or names to identify the producer of a product, and protect its associated reputation. It includes trade names also. The subject matter of Trademark protection may be either goods or services in respect of which trade takes place. In India, a Trademark may be registered initially for a period of 10 years but can be renewed indefinitely.

4. *Designs:* It means only the features of shape, configuration, and pattern, ornament applied to any article by any industrial process or means, which in the finished goods apply only to the eye and are judged solely by the eye. In other words they protect the decorative or ornamental value of an article. The term of their protection is 10 years and it can be extended by another 5 years.

5. *Lay-out Design:* It means a lay-out of transistors, and other circuitry elements including any lead wires connecting such elements in a semi-conductor integrated circuit. They are also known as topographies. The term of their protection is 10 years and it can be extended by another 5 years.

6. *Geographical Indications:* These are the names that identify the specific geographical origin of a product when, certain qualities, reputation or other characteristics of the products can be associated with

that origin. For example, food products sometimes have qualities that derive from their place of production and local environmental factors. The Geographical Indication prevents unauthorized parties from using a protected Geographical Indication for products not from that region or from misleading the public as to the true origin of the product. A GI may be either an appellation or origin or indication of source e.g. *Paris Perfume, Darjeeling Tea, Scotch Whisky, Champagne,* and *Basmati Rice* etc.

7. *Traditional Knowledge:* There appears to be no definition of Traditional Knowledge (TK) universally accepted. Different persons define them differently depending on their intellectual persuasion and professional interest. Many of them use the concept of TK interchangeably with that of indigenous knowledge (IK).

Traditional Knowledge is a knowledge, which is held by members of a distinct culture and/or sometimes acquired "by means of inquiry peculiar to that culture, and concerning the culture itself or the local environment in which it exists."[3]

On the other hand Indigencous knowledge is that knowledge that is held and used by people who identify themselves as indigenous of a place based on a combination of cultural distinctiveness and prior territorial occupancy relative to more recently arrived population with its own distinct and subsequently dominant culture.[4] IK fits neatly in the category of TK but TK need not fit in the category of IK. In other words, all IK is TK but all TK is not necessarily IK. TK is therefore the totality of all knowledge and practices whether explicit or implicit, used in the management of socio-economic and ecological facets of life. It is based on past experiences and observations and is usually a collective property of a society. This knowledge-is transmitted from one generation to other generation.[5] Examples of Traditional Knowledge include knowledge about the use of specific plants and/or parts thereof, identification of medicinal properties in plants and harvesting practices. In India the TK includes the usage of *Neem, Turmeric* and *Tamarind* etc., for medicinal and other purposes and *Ayurveda* system of medicine. It is also related to traditional designs, songs dailces that have been used by the fashion and entertainment industries to create works which are protected by the IP. In other words they include the traditional folklore.[6]

The unique nature of TK is that the common property resources are not controlled by a single entity. Access to these resources is limited to members of an identifiable community. Each user has a separate entitlement to the common property and no single user has the right to abuse or dispose of it. More often, users of common property are subject to rules and restrictions embedded in cultural or religious customs. The net result of such customs and practices is that the users perceive themselves mainly as possessors of their habitat but not as resource owners. In other words, the members of the community have only community rights.[7]

The third world countries mostly in the continents of Africa and Asia have accumulated a broad technological base conserve and sustainably use plant genetic resources. The local people embodying traditional lifestyles and knowledge have devised and deployed various technologies to conserve the environment in general and bio--diversity in particular. For instance local communities and households in different parts of Africa have accumulated a broad technological knowledge base to conserve and use plants and their genetic component. These systems include *home gardens, seed banks* and *sacred grooves.* In Ethiopia, for example the Tigray Communities' efforts specifically address the problems of home gardens and seed banking like the loss of traditional seeds (genetic resources) and TK for selection and conservation.

In India the TK is mostly used in textile designs, making medicinal preparations, folklore and cultivating certain agricultural products.

The IPR Regime in India

There are number of statutes concerned with the protection of other forms of IP like patents, copyright, designs and trademarks. The specific laws can be listed under:

1. The Designs Act, 2000.
2. The Trademarks Act, 1999.
3. The Patents Act, 1970.
4. The Copyright Act, 1957.
5. The Geographical Indications of Goods (Registration and Protection) Act, 1999.
6. The Biological Diversity Act, 2002; and
7. The Plant Varieties Protection & Farmers Rights Act, 2001 etc.

These laws protect different kinds of IP for limited periods, provided the stipulated conditions are satisfied. However, there is no special law in India that deals with the protection of traditional knowledge.

NOTES

1. Thurow, Lester, *Needed: A New System of Intellectual Property Rights,* Harvard Business Review, Sept.-Oct. 1997, pp.95-103.
2. See Reddy, G.B, Intellectual Property Rights And the Law, 4th Edition, 2004, Gogia Law Agency, Hyderabad, pp. 38-39.
3. UNEP/CBD/COP/3/Inf. 33, Annex ii.
4. Supra note 1.
5. See generally Dr. John Mugabe, Intellectual Property Protection and Traditional Knowledge-An Exploration in International Policy Discourse, Paper presented for the World Intellectual Property Organization (WIPO), Geneva, December, 1998.
6. See, Footnote 1, Supra.

7. See Patricia Kameri-Mbote, Community, Farmers' and Breeders' Rights in Africa: Towards a Legal Framework for Sui Generis Legislation, ICFAI Journal of Intellectual Property Rights, Vol. II No. 4, November 2003 pp. 57-78.

19 EVOLUTIONS AND DEVELOPMENT OF COPYRIGHT LAW

*E. Vijaya Kumar**

Evolution and Development of Copyright Law

The history of copyright Law in India is a history of series of legislative enactments both in British regime as well as Independent India. The importance of copyright protection was recognized since ancient times but particularly after invention of the printing press during the 15th century[1], which enable reproduction of required number of books for circulation in the entire world.

Pre-Independence Legislations

Indian Copyright Act, 1847

The first statute law in British India on copyright was applied during the East India Company's regime with the title "The Indian Copyright Act, 1847"[2]. It was passed by the Governor General of India in Council on 15th December, 1847. This legislation was in operation during the period 1847-1911.

Copyright Act. 1911

The law of copyright was codified in England for the first time in 1911 as Copyright Act and this was the law in force

* Professor & Dean, Faculty of Law, S.K. University, Anantapur-515 003 (AP).

in India and similarly applied to all the countries under the British Dominion.

The Indian Copyright Act, 1914

The Dominion legislation was empowered to modify or alter the provisions of Copyright Act, 1911 to suit for the natives and as a result the Governor General of India enacted the Indian Copyright Act, 1914.

Incorporation of British Copyright Act, 1911 to Act 1914

For the Copyright Act of 1914, the copyright Act of 1911 of England was added as its First Schedule.

Salient Features of Indian Copyright Act of 1914

The Indian Copyright Act of 1914 and the British Copyright Act of 1911 constituted the copyright Law in India.

This Act consist of 15 Sections. The infringement of Copyright was not considered as a criminal offence under this Act. It authorized the owner of copyright destruction of the infringing copies of their delivery. It was also laid down that non registration of a book for copyright protection was not a bar to file a civil suit or start a civil proceedings against any one who infringed copyright. The following were some of the important provisions laid in the legislation;

(i) The registration of the authors work not necessary.

(ii) The author's rights came into existence as soon as the work was created.

(iii) Protection was afforded not to the idea but the material form in which the work was expressed.

(iv) Only original work attracted the protection of copyright law.

(v) The term of copyright protection was fixed as the lifetime of the author and 25 years after the death.

(b) Providing adequate protection of authors rights and

(c) Removing administrative drawbacks and other lacunae experienced in administration of copyright Act of 1957.

To give effect to the above purposes, the proposed 1983 Amendment bill brought the following corresponding changes:

(i) To provide for compulsory licencing for translation of a foreign work after expiry of 3 years from the publication of the work and if the translation of the work is in a language not in use in any developed country, after the expiry of 1 year from such publication if such work is for the purposes of teaching, Scholarship or Research.

(ii) To provide for compulsory licencing of the reproduction of any edition of a foreign literacy, scientific, or artistic work for the purposes of systematic instructional activities.

(iii) It also provided that in case of unpublished works where the author is dead or unknown or owner of copyright cannot be traced, may advertise his proposal and apply to the copyright Board for permission which would grant such permission and fix an appropriate royalty. The royalty could be deposited in public account of India for a specific period so that in the event of the owner of the copyright becoming unknown he could claim it.

(iv) To provide for the manner of assignment of copyright from authors to publishers and to empower the copyright Board to decide disputes arising out of such assignment.

(v) Broadcasting authorities are permitted to translate foreign works for broadcasting for the purpose of systematic instructional activities.

(vi) To provide for copyright in lectures, addresses etc., delivered in public and for the publication of the entries made in copyright register.

1984 Amendment-to the Copyright Act, 1957

The main object of this Amendment is to curb piracy which has become a global problem due to advancement in technology. This has become a challenge in the contemporary world. There are 3 types of piracy viz.,

(i) Piracy of the printed word.

(ii) Piracy of sound recordings and

(iii) Piracy of cinimatograph films.

In all the above cases the pirates made quick money and avoid payments of legitimate royalties and taxes. The emergence of new techniques relating to recording, fixation and reproduction of audio performances combined with the advent of video technology have helped the pirates to resort to commit this crime. The evasion of tax resulted in loss of crores of rupees to the Government also. It was also found that many uncertified video films are being exhibited on a large scale. In view of all these evils it was proposed to amend the copyright Act, 1957 to combat effectively the piracy which was rampant in the country.

Consequently, this Amendment, 1984 provided the following changes.

(i) To increase punishment provided for infringements of copyright for 3 years with a minimum imprisonment of 6 months and a fine upto Rs. 2 lakhs with a minimum of Rs. 50,000/-.

(ii) To provide for enhanced punishment in case of continuing convictions.

(iii) To provide for declaration of the offence of infringement of copyright as an Economic offence so that the period of limitation as in Cr. P.C. will not be applicable to these offences.

(iv) To specifically make provisions of this Act applicable to video films and computer programmes.

(v) To require the producers of records and video films to display certain information in the record, video films and containers there of.

Soon after coming into force of the 1984 Amendment on 8-10-1984, several writ petitions seeking a stay of the amending law were filed in number of High Courts and the Supreme Court of India.

By and large the Courts were reluctant to accept as a principle that a beneficiary of a statute is entitled to be heard in addition to the state or union Govt. as the case may be in support of a statutory enactment.

Anyhow the anti-piracy provisions incorporated in the 1984 Amendment would not work effectively because of some lacunas. A working group was setup in 1987 by the Govt. to study the provisions and recommend suitable amendments taking into consideration the advancement in communication technology such as video, satellite and other means of simultaneous communications and to full-fil. India's role and obligation as a signatory to:

(i) the erne Convention and

(ii) the Universal Copyright convention.

1994 Amendment to the Copyright Act. 1957

The statement of objects and reasons of the bill of the proposed 1994 Amendment clearly reads as follows:

"Effective copyright protection promotes and rewards human creativity and in modern society, an indispensable support for intellectual, cultural and economic activity. Copyright law promotes the creation of literary, artistic, dramatic and musical works, cinematography of films and sound recordings by providing certain exclusive rights to their authors and creators. The law relating to copyright and related rights have been under comprehensive review of the Government for some time, taking into the difficulties expressed by different groups of copyright owners and others, the experience gained from the administration of the existing law and the situation created by various technological developments that have taken place".

A joint committee of both Houses of Parliament consisting of 45 members, examined the bill taking into consideration the representations received from various organizations and individuals, the memoranda received from the general public and organizations concerned with copyright. The committee recommended several changes in the bill which was accepted and passed by the Parliament in May, 1994.

Important Features of the 1994 Amendment

This Amendment provides for:

(i) Performers' rights protection covering any visual or artistic presentations made live by one or more performers.

(ii) Copyright societies seeking to promote collective administration of the rights of the authors, composers and other creative artists.

(iii) Assignment of copyright by an author or artist to protect the interest of both the assignor and assignee and;

(iv) Computer programme, cinematography of films and sound recordings; protection.

The other provisions in the amending legislation are usual and self-explanatory in nature.

1999 Amendment of the Copyright Act, 1957

Recently the Copyright Act, 1957 was again amended in the year 1999 and amendments were made to the following interalia:

(i) Definition of literary work

(ii) Meaning of copyright in respect of computer programme

(iii) Increase of the term of copyright of performers from 25 to 50 years.

(iv) Insertion of certain in new provisions pertaining to power of the central Govt. to apply the provisions relating to broadcasting organizations and performers to broadcasting organizations and performers in certain other countries and

(v) Power to restrict rights of foreign broadcasting organizations and performers.

International Instruments

Instruments relating to Copyright and Neighbouring Rights

The term "Neighbouring rights" in broad terms cover all other rights similar to copyrights such as the protection of photographs etc., where as the term in the narrow sense covers those rights granted to protect performers, producers of phonograms and broadcasting organizations in the performance of their work.

Following are the important conventions evolved at the Global level concerning the protection of the literary and artistic works:

Berne Convention for the Protection of Literary and Artistic Work

The object of the convention is mainly to protect the literary and artistic works. It was established in 1886 in Berne, Switzerland. It came into force on 5th December, 1987. It has been revised several times and it was administered by world Intellectual Property Organisations-WIPO.

The Convention provides for protection for a period of life and 50 years or an alternative of 50 years from publications for anonymous and pseudonymous works.

Universal Copyright Convention

The Universal copyrights convention was signed and came into force on September, 1952 and it was revised in 1971 at Paris.

Eventhough the Berne convention has been the mainstay of *International Copyright*, certain major states viz., USA, Soviet Union and China did not join it. Hence UCC was developed as alternative to Berne Convention and to allow these countries into agreement. The Convention gives protection to published and unpublished works. The member countries must grant a minimum copyright term of 25 years from date of publication or the life of the author and 25 years.

The foreign authors of the other countries must be granted exclusive rights for at least 7 years.

International Convention for the Protection of Performers Producers of Phonograms and Broadcasting Organizations (Rome Convention)

The Convention came into force on may 18, 1964 and intends to protect the neighbouring rights.

Phonogram means a sound recording. The convention grants protection to performers of phonograms. The convention also protects Broadcast.

WIPO Copyright Treaty

This treaty was adopted by the Diplomatic Conference at Geneva on December 20, 1996. This treaty is in response to the new conditions brought about by the digital technology and internet.

WIPO Performances and Phonograms Treaty

It was also adopted at Geneva on December 20, 1996 to meet the challenges of digital technology particularly the internet.

Other Treaties/Conventions Relating to Copyright Protection

In addition to the above international instruments, there are some other treaties and conventions intended for protection of producers, phonograms against the unauthorized duplication of phonograms, distribution of programmes-carrying signals transmitted by satellite and audio-video works etc. They are, as follows:

(i) The Convention for the Protection of Producers of Phonograms Against Unauthorised Duplication of Their Phonograms (Geneva Convention).

(ii) Convention Relating to the Distribution of Programme-carrying Signals Transmitted by Satellite (Brussel Convention).

(iii) The Treaty on International Registration of Audio-Visual Works (Geneva) and

(iv) The Treaty on Intellectual Property in Respect of Integrated Circuits:

This treaty aims at protection of integrated circuits and lay out designs (topographics). An IC is a product in its final form or an intermediate form and some or all of the interconnections are integrally formed and is intended to perform an electronic function.

20 PROTECTION OF CULTURAL INDUSTRIES AND NEIGHBOURING RIGHTS WITH REFERENCE TO PERFORMER'S RIGHTS

*K. Rajani Kumari**

Introduction

The term "Intellectual Property" relates to the legal rights that result mainly from intellectual activity in the industrial, scientific, literary and artistic fields which will contribute a lot for the economic and social development of a nation. Intellectual property law provides a protection to the owners or producers under different categories and names like patents, Industrial designs, copyrights, Trademarks etc.

Performer's rights arises from copyright law. Copyright is one category of intellectual property and generally intellectual property rights exclude third parties from exploiting the protected subject matter with out express authorization of the right holder for a prescribed period of time, thereby enabling IPR owners to use or disclose their creation without fear of loss of control over their use[1].

Under the Berne Convention[2] and now under the TRIPs regime copyright law is intended to provide protection to the rights of intellectual creators with respect to their original literary and artistic works. Copyright protection is

* Lecturer, V S R Law College, Bellary.

no more confined to books, music, paintings or films, but now extends, interalia, to computer software and compilations of data[3].

Copyright consists not merely of the right to reproduction. It also consists of the right to works derived from the original works; rights like the right of public performance, the recording right and the broadcasting right which are as important or even more than the right of reproduction. These are called related rights or neighbouring rights. These rights protect persons, other than the creators of original works, who are involved in the dissemination of copyright works. The term neighbouring rights includes the following categories;

1. Performer's
2. Producers of phonograms
3. Producers of cinematographic films and broadcasting organizations.

A work protected by copyright may be communicated to people at large without being copied or reproduced. A lecture can be delivered without giving copies similarly a drama or a musical work can be performed without distribution of any copies. A story written originally in a particular way in order to be read at home may be transformed into a drama designed to be performed on the stage for public[4].

Definition and Rights of Performer

The performer stands in a way between the author of the creative work and the person who records the performance and presents it to the public through film or broadcasting. Whether the performer can be given the same right as the author of the creative work. It may be said the performer does not create anything but merely presents. So that he may not be entitled to the rights similar to that of the author. On the other hand, it may also be said that where the performer goes beyond performing and creates a new work, he will be regarded as an author. But the debate concern the general situation, where the as something different from that of the author and entitled to a lesser degree of presentation[5]. This may be to distress of performer's and their representatives. Generally, performer's have no rights in their performances except to the extent that those performances constituted copyrightable works authorized by the perfoffi1er's[6].

As per sec. 2 (qq) "performer" includes an actor, singer, musicians, dancer, acrobat, Juggler, conjurer, snake charmer, a person delivering a lecture or any other person who makes a perfonnance[7].

Performance of Work

Sec 2 (q)-defines "performance" in relation to performer's right, means any visual or acoustic presentation made live by one or more performer's[8].

To perform a work mean to recite, render play dance or act it either directly or by means of any device or process or in the case of a motion picture or other audio-visual work, to show its images in any sequences or to make the sounds accompanying it audible.

The Oxford English Dictionary describes performance as follows:

(a) the action of performing a ceremony play, piece of music etc.,

(b) formal or set execution

(c) the performing of a play of music of gymnastic or conjuring feats or the like, as a definite art or services of acts done at an appointed public place and time: a public exhibition or entertainment.

Performance of Work in Public

Sec 2 (ft)-defines "communication to the public" means making any work available for being seen or heard or otherwise enjoyed by the public directly or by any means of display or diffusion other than by issuing copies of such work regardless of whether any member of the public actually sees, hears or otherwise, enjoys the work so made available.

For the purposes of this clause, communication through satellite or cable or any other means of simultaneous communication to more than one household or place of residence including residential rooms of any hotel or hostel shall be deemed to be communication to the public.

'To perform' a work publicly means:

1. To perform........It at place open to the public or at any place where a substantial number of persons outside of a normal circle of a family and its social acquaintances is gathered; or
2. To transmit or otherwise communicate a performance .... of the work a place specified by clause 1) or to the public, by means of any device or process, whether the members of the public capable of receiving the performance.......Receive it in the same place or in separate places and at the same time or at different times[9].

The author's right to authorise performance of his work in the presence of the public has long been recognised in national and international law. With the advent of films and sound recordings at the end of the 19th century, questions arose as to whether the author of the work reproduced in the recordings could control the use of such recordings *in* the presence of the public, through cinema.

The most basic right conferred by copyright is the right to exclude unauthorized reproduction of the copyright work. In addition, certain acts such as performing the work in public, making a sound or audiovisual recording of the work, making a motion picture of the work, broadcasting or publicly communicating the work, and translations or adaptations of the work, have also come within the ambit of copyright protection. In addition to these bundles of economic rights, and other rights, which normally include the right to claim authorship and to prevent the work from mutilation or distortion have come to be recognised[10].

Before the amendment of the copyright Act in 1994, there was no protection of the rights of performer like actors, dancers, musicians, Jugglers, acrobats. In 1994, the amendment introduced the recognition of the rights of the performer under sec. 38.

The performer's right shall subsist until fifty years (as amended in 1999) from the beginning of the calendar year next following the year in which the performance is made[11].

Acts Constituting Infringement of Performer's Rights

Sec (38) provides that if any person during the subsistence of a performer's right, without the consent of the performer, does any of the following acts in respect of the performance or any substantial part thereof, he will be deemed to have been infringed the perfomer's rights[12]:

(a) Makes a sound recording or visual recording of the performance; or

(b) Reproduces a sound recording or visual recording of the performance, which was;

  (i) made without the performer's consent; or

  (ii) made for purposes different from those for which the performer gave his consent; or

  (iii) made for purposes different from those referred to in Sec. 39 from a sound recording or visual recording which was made in accordance with Sec. 39; or

(c) Broadcasts the performance except where the broadcast is made from a sound recording or visual recording other than one made in accordance with Sec. 39; or is re-broadcast by the same broadcasting organization of an earlier broadcast which did not infringe the performer's right; or

(d) Communicates the performance to the public otherwise than by broadcast, except where such communication to the public is made from a sound recording or a visual recording or a broadcasting.

When a performer has consented to the incorporation of his performance in a cinematograph film the performer loses the right to complain of infringement of that performance which means he assigned his entire rights on that performance to the producer of the cinematograph film.

Acts Not Constituting Infringement of Performer's Rights

AS per Sec. 39, the following acts do not constitute infringement of a performer's right in his performance[13]:

(a) The making of any sound recording of or visual recording for private use of the person making such recording or society for the purpose of *bona fide* teaching or research; or

(b) Fair dealing of excerpts of a performance in the reporting of current events or for *bona fide* review, teaching or research; or

(c) Other acts with any necessary adaptations and modifications which do not constitute infringement of copyright under see 52. These acts are:

   (i) Reproduction for the use of judicial proceedings–sec 2(1) (c).

   (ii) Reproduction for the use of members of a legislature–sec 52(1) (d).

   (iii) The use in a certified copy in accordance with any law in force–sec 52 (1) (e).

   (iv) Use of sound recording or visual recording of the performance in the course of the activities of an educational institution if the audience are limited to the students, parents and guardians of the students and person directly connected with the activities of the institution-sec 52 (1) (1).

The aforesaid acts can be done only with the sound recording or visual recording of the performance. Accordingly, the making of a sound recording or visual recording for the aforesaid purposes cannot also be an infringement.

Where copyright or performer's right subsists in respect of any work or performance that has been broadcast, a license to reproduce such broadcast will require the consent of the owner of rights or performer, as the case may be, or both of them.

Sec.39A-other provisions applying to broadcast, reproduction, right and performer's right[14]-sec. 18, 19, 30, 53, 55, 58, 64, 65 and 66 shall, with any necessary adaptations and modifications apply in relation to the broadcast reproduction right in any broadcast and the performer's right in any performance as they apply in relation to copyright in a work.

There are some limitations to the scope of performer's right. As already said, sec. 38 contemplates performance to be any visual or acoustic presentations made live by one or more performer's and 'performer' includes an actor, singer, musician, dancer and acrobat, juggler, conjurer, snake charmer, a person delivering a lecture or any other person who makes a performance. This definition includes only those persons who actually perform and it fails to include those who get the performance done by others. For example, directors, choreographers, composers are vital in performance but they do not perform live in a performance. In fact, it is their intellectual skill and labour when invested, moulds into a performance. It is directors, who plan, direct the movements, actions, dialogues etc., of the performer's. The copy rights in a cinematograph film vests with the producer of the film except where the director and the producer is one and the same person. Under these circumstances it would be injustice as the monetary benefits would be more in favour of the producers only.

Similarly, according to Sec. 38(4) "once a performer has consented to the incorporation of his performance in a cinematograph film, the provision of sub-sections (1), (2) and (3) shall have no further application to such performance". A cinematograph film is defined to mean any work of visual recording on any medium produced through a process from which a moving image may be produced by any means and includes a sound recording accompanying such visual recording and "cinematograph" shall be construed as including any work produced by any process analogous to cinematography including video films[15]. Perhaps, the reason for denying performer's rights to cine artists are that since cine artists in a film are numerous, recognition of such rights will create complexity in licenses and that their interests are protected through collective bargaining or better bargaining power of famous individual artists.

Contribution of Judiciary in Protection of Performer's Rights

It is actually the reasoning in Dev Anand's case[16], regarding extending protection to performer brought to light the rights of performer's. People from different walks of life as well as film artists and film producers became alert to the dispute. Prior to this case the performer was treated as a commissioned agent paying him no extra attention for his original talents in taking the concepts finally to the audience. The observation made by justice Desai in this case as against the observation made by justice Krishna Iyer in Indian performing Society Ltd., case[17], have gone a long way in raising many questions in the minds of all those who are concerned and also paying the way for bringing in an Amendment to the Copyright Law (1994) for the Protection of Performer's Right.

In Dev Ananda's case the court ruled that a 'cine artists' performance will not fall within the ambit of 'work' provided under the Copyright Act 1957.

Under Sec. 2 (Y) of the Copyright Act 'work' means the following:

1. a literary, dramatic, musical or artistic work;
2. a cinematograph film
3. a record

Dev Ananda's case unfolds an interesting development in the history of Performer's right in India. Mr. Dev Anand contracted for a leading male role in the film 'Darling, Darling'. Clause-6 of the agreement provides "that in consideration of your (Dev Anand's) all services to us (producer) for the said picture you will be paid remuneration as under". The agreement gave full particulars of the seven territories where the picture was to be released and the consideration was in the forms of suitable annuity policies of LIC worth of Rs. 7,00,000/ (Rupees Seven Lakhs only). Till the producer paid the amount the copyright in the motion picture would vest with the cine artiste Dev Anand and on payment the right would automatically vest with the producers. Violating the term of the agreement the film 'Darling, Darling' was released in Eastern Punjab without the knowledge of the artist, Dev Anand and the dispute came up before the court. The contents of the letter written by the producer to the artist was under:

"That your work in our above picture on completion will belong to you absolutely and the copyright therein shall vest in you on delivery of the annuity policies as per Clause–6 ...... your copyright will automatically vest in us...." Regarding the question whether the performer has a copyright Justice Desai said, "... In the view that we have taken of the definition of artistic work, dramatic work and cinematograph film it would appear that the Copyright Act 1957 does not recognize the performance of an actor as 'work'. The above argument was further substantiated when it said that the definition under section 2 (y) of the Copyright Act only protects films as well as the sound track which is married to the film proper (i.e. visual sequence). The Copyright in the entire film may cover portions in the film; but this idea or concept cannot be extended to encompass an idea that there would be one owner of the cinematograph film and different owners thereof in the sense of performer's who have collectively played roles in the motion picture. ......"

A ray of hope for the protection of performer's rights was observed by the Supreme Court in *Indian Performing Right Society Vs Easten India Motion Picture Association 18,* by Justice Krishna Iyer as follows:

"A cinematograph as a felicitous blend, a beautiful totality, a constellation of stars, if I may use the rule against mixed metaphor. Cinema is more long strips of celluloid, more than miracles in photography, more than song, dance, dialogue and indeed more than dramatic story, existing plot, gripping situation and marvelous acting. But, it is that ensemble which is the finished product of *orchestrated performance* by each of the several participants although the component may sometimes, themselves be elegant entitles. Copyright in a cinema exists in law. But Sec 13 (4) of the Act preserves the separate survival, in its individuality of a copyright enjoyed by any 'work' not withstanding its confluence in the film. This persistence of the aesthetic 'personality' of the intellectual property cannot cut down the copy right of the film"[19].

Further, after examining the copyright in musical work, the learned judge, opined, that the composer alone has copyright in a musical work but not the singer. This disentitles the musicians or or musical artists to have copyright. Because the major contribution to a musical performance is not the music maker but the Singer. Perhaps, both deserve to be recognised by the copyright law. I make this observation only because art in one sense depends on the ethos and the aesthetic best of a people, and while universal protection of intellectual and aesthetic property of creators of 'work' is and international obligation, each country in its law must protect such rights wherever originality is contributed. So viewed, a part from the music composer, the singer must be conferred a right. Of course, law -making is the province of Parliament, but the court must communicate to the law-maker such infirmities as exist in the law extent[20]".

The view expressed by the Supreme Court adds some more strength and vitality to the demand for protection of performer's rights in arts. It cannot be denied that there is intellectual labour or creation in the performance of artists and it is also true that, that intellectual labour alone is not capable of producing the work of art. Realising the need for protecting the performer's right, the 1994 Amendment Act has included a new head of right called performer's right. It recognizes the right of the performer to make sound recording or visual recording of the performance, also the reproduction right as well as broadcasting rights of the performer[21].

NOTES AND REFERENCES

1. Jayashree Watal, *Intellectual Property Rights in the WTO and Developing Countries* 1 (Oxford, 2001).
2. The Berne Convention for the Protection of Literary and Artstic works, as revised in 1971, provided for International Copyright Protection.
3. See, Art. 10 of the TRIPS.
4. Background Reading Material on *"Intellectual Property"* (revised), edited by Arpad Bogsch, WIPO, Geneva, 1995.
5. JAL Sterling, *"World Copyright Law"*, London; Sweet and Max Well, 1998, p. 63.
6. Davind Lange, Mary Law France, Gary Myers, *"Intellectual Property Cases and Materials* ", West Publishing Co., 1998, p. 889.

7. Sec. 2 (qq) of The Copyright Act, 1957.
8. Sec. 2 (q) of The Copyright Act, 1957.
9. Sheldon W. Halpern, David E. Shipley, Howard B. Abraham, "*Copyright Cases and Materials*", West Publishing Co., 1992, p. 238.
10. Art. 9 (1) g TRIPs; Art. 6 *bis* of the Berne Convention.
11. Sec. 38 (2) of The Copyright Act of 1957.
12. Id Sec. 38.
13. Id Sec. 39.
14. Id Sec. 39A.
15. Id Sec. 2 (1).
16. *Fortune Film* Vs. *Dev Anand,* AIR 1979 Born, p. 17.
17. *Indian performing Rights Society Ltd.* Vs *Eastern Indian Motion Pictures Association,* AIR 1977, S.C. 1443.
18. AIR 1977 S.C. 1443.
19. Ibid p. 1453.
20. Ibid pp. 1453-1454.
21. Sec. 38 of The Copyright Act, 1957.

INDEX